Isma'ili Modern

The University of North Carolina Press   Chapel Hill

Islamic Civilization and Muslim Networks
CARL W. ERNST AND BRUCE B. LAWRENCE, editors

A complete list of titles published in this series appears at the end of the book.

Isma'ili Modern

Globalization and Identity in a Muslim Community

JONAH STEINBERG

© 2011 The University of North Carolina Press. All rights reserved. Manufactured in the United States of America. Designed by Courtney Leigh Baker and set in Arno Pro and Gotham by Tseng Information Systems, Inc. The paper in this book meets the guidelines for permanence and durability of the Committee on Production Guidelines for Book Longevity of the Council on Library Resources. The University of North Carolina Press has been a member of the Green Press Initiative since 2003.

Library of Congress Cataloging-in-Publication Data
Steinberg, Jonah.
Isma'ili modern : globalization and identity in a Muslim community / Jonah Steinberg.
p. cm. — (Islamic civilization and Muslim networks)
Includes bibliographical references and index.
ISBN 978-0-8078-3407-7 (cloth : alk. paper)
ISBN 978-0-8078-7165-2 (pbk : alk. paper)
1. Ismailites — History. 2. Shi'ah. I. Title.
BP195.I8S735 2010
297.8'2209 — dc22   2010029267

cloth   15 14 13 12 11   5 4 3 2 1
paper   15 14 13 12 11   5 4 3 2 1

For Emily and Zaki

Contents

Illustrations

Acknowledgments

The list of people who were essential in bringing this book to life is too long to enumerate; any attempt to acknowledge all who helped me will necessarily fall short. I owe a great deal to Greg Urban, Asif Agha, Brian Spooner, Bruce Grant, and Stephen Hopkins, as well as to countless colleagues at the University of Vermont. The members of my writing group — Danilyn Rutherford, Vicki Brennan, Andrea Voyer, Jennifer Dickinson, Kabir Tambar, and Kelda Jamison — were particularly helpful in transforming aspects of the book in its late stages. Pablo Bose has also provided indispensable perspective in formulating the book's basic questions.

My debt of gratitude to Isma'ilis around the world is great. Innumerable individuals involved in the Aga Khan Foundation, the Institute for Isma'ili Studies, and the Isma'ili Secretariat have been of assistance. Of particular note in this regard are Rafique Keshavjee, Aleem Walji, Azim Nanji, Anise Waljee, and Tom Kessinger. In Gorno-Badakhshan, no individual was more important for my work than Shodmon Hojibekov. Without him this book could not exist. Essential help was provided by Harpreet Singh and Salima Samji. Sarfaroz Niyozov, Olimsho Vatanshoev, Dagi Dagiev, Sharofat Mamadambarova, Nasir and Roza Virani, and Sultonbek Aksakolov were all also particularly helpful for my work in Tajikistan. I am grateful to the entire staff of the Aga Khan Humanities Project in Dushanbe. Khaleel Tetlay was important for my research in both Tajikistan and Pakistan.

I received crucial assistance for my research in Pakistan from my adoptive families in Altit and Yasin Center, who teach me more about Isma'ilism every time we speak, and also from Muzaffaruddin, Mushtaq Ahmed Rahi, Annie Harper, Khurram Khan, Tabinda Malik, and many others. The staff of the Aga Khan Rural Support Programme in Gilgit and Islamabad, who graciously accommodated me during four separate periods of fieldwork, deserve special mention. Villagers of the Karakoram and Hindu Kush ranges from Phander to Thui, from Darkot to Gupis, were unbelievably hospitable.

They gave generously and selflessly of their modest resources, always offering me food and a place to stay.

My son, Zaki, has kept a smile on my face and helped me to take everything in stride as I brought this book to completion. More thanks are due to my wonderful wife, Emily, than to anyone else. She has made this idea a reality. I owe her my deepest love and gratitude.

Abbreviations

AKDN	Aga Khan Development Network
AKES	Aga Khan Education Services
AKF	Aga Khan Foundation
AKFED	Aga Khan Fund for Economic Development
AKHS	Aga Khan Health Services
AKRSP	Aga Khan Rural Support Programme
AKTC	Aga Khan Trust for Culture
IIS	Institute for Ismaʿili Studies
ITREB	Ismaʿili Tariqah Religious Education Board
ITREC	Ismaʿili Tariqah Religious Education Committee
MSDSP	Mountain Societies Development and Support Programme
UCA	University of Central Asia
VO	Village Organization
WO	Women's Organization

Isma'ili Modern

Beyond Territoriality

The organizational dynamics of the Isma'ili Muslim community raise important questions about the nature of citizenship and political identity at this moment in history. They present a basic challenge to theoretical and popular understandings of the state, of globalization, and of Islam. They point to a transformation in the relationship between territory and allegiance, a fundamental shift in the possibilities for sociopolitical organization. The Isma'ilis are widely scattered across the planet, but their community's institutional infrastructure is highly centralized and provides for subjects a vast array of services, symbols, and social spaces. Isma'ili institutions penetrate deeply into participants' lives; they suffuse the fabric of their daily activities. In this way, the complex of Isma'ili forms, processes, and structures seems to represent a new possibility for transnational social organization, for sociopolitical participation beyond the nation-state, for citizenship without territory.

The Isma'ili community is neither national nor ethnic; it is bound neither to a territorial unit nor to a government; it is politically anomalous while it enjoys, in many contexts, legal recognition and autonomy; at its foundation is religion, and yet it provides for its members a staggering set of secular structures. While in some cases these services are provided in addition to those provided by the state, in others, where the state is either unwilling or unable, they are provided in the place of state infrastructure. Thus in some settings Isma'ilis live and move within a centralized, nonnational, nonterritorial polity from which they derive the central emblems of their identity. They enjoy both material and symbolic benefits from their membership in this transnational network.

This book is an exploration of the complex and intricate details of global Isma'ilism. But it is also a meditation on the nature of sovereignty and political subjectivity and on their historical transformations. Through an examination of the implications of the Isma'ili transnational complex, I seek to raise questions about certain aspects of human sociopolitical organization, to examine the *longue durée* of identity and territoriality through the example of a community in which long-distance consolidation of its membership has been central for over a thousand years. The time-depth of Isma'ili organization presents exceptional possibilities for the examination of the effects of empire, capital, and the nation-state on the construction of community across (rather than within) territory. My interest here, however, goes beyond political forms alone; the scale of the inquiry is at once more intimate and less quantifiable. I also seek through the lens of the Isma'ili community to explore the role of the personal, the subjective, the phenomenological in transnationality and human organization. Thus this book is also an excavation of shifts in identity, citizenship, and affiliation in the context of rapidly changing social worlds.

Locating the Subject: Isma'ili Lives and Selves

It is individual lives, in my view, that most clearly demonstrate the meaning of historical conditions and social change. For that reason there might be no better place to begin the intellectual exploration of Isma'ili globalization, and Isma'ilis' engagement with globalization, than in the home of my oldest Isma'ili friends, Sher Ali Khan and Sultan Ali Khan, in the Hunza valley of Pakistan's Northern Areas.

When I read the news on September 23, 2008, that the Islamabad Marriott had been destroyed, I feared the worst. For several years Sher Ali had been working as an assistant and bellhop in the front office of the hotel. Almost every time he called me it was from work. So as I looked at images of the building in flames, I was unable to suppress a growing feeling of certainty that he had burned in that inferno. I tried to reach Sher Ali immediately.

Unable to track him down, I tried throughout the day, without success, to find his older brother, Sultan Ali. And finally, at the end of the day, I got through to Sultan's cell phone: Sher Ali was on his way home from work when the blast happened and escaped unharmed. I could not bear to imagine the alternative. Shortly thereafter, the boys' mother, deeply unsettled, asked them to travel the long distance back to the village. Within days, they had returned to their settlement, where they remained for a time, in the company of Isma'ili family and friends.

It had been a long time since I first met the two brothers, and they had come a long way from their homes. Sher Ali was about eleven and Sultan

Ali about sixteen when I first met them and their family, fifteen years earlier, in a small hamlet adjoining the village of Altit in the Hunza valley. Altit is itself adjacent to Baltit, now also called Karimabad, the traditional capital of Hunza (though no longer its administrative center). Hunza is in the heart of the Karakoram Range of the Pakistan Himalaya, an area of high, glaciated mountains. Most of its residents speak Burushaski, a language unrelated to any other on earth. And almost all of them are Isma'ili.

Through numerous periods of ethnographic fieldwork during the course of those fifteen years, I learned that the social fabric of daily life in the village in which Sher Ali and Sultan Ali grew up, along with all of the villages surrounding it, is pervaded with the structures, discourses, and institutions of global Isma'ilism. Nothing competes with it. And it penetrates the most basic details of space, place, language, and life course. Karimabad itself, for instance, was renamed for the current imam, Prince Karim Aga Khan. His visits have taken on the stature of myth in the narratives of the villagers' lives: every detail—where he stood, where they stood, where his helicopter landed—is cherished, told, and retold. Every week the villagers of Karimabad and Altit listen in their *jama'at khanas* (houses of worship) to the *farmans* (edicts or dicta) of the Aga Khan; these edicts govern the moral blueprints by which they live their lives. Sultan Ali and Sher Ali, who used to volunteer most days as "scouts" in the *jama'at khana*, even claim to have received their names at birth from the Aga Khan, in his distant home in France. Sher Ali, Sultan Ali, and all adult Isma'ilis in the village pay to the Aga Khan a tithe of 12.5 percent, a long-standing and time-worn Isma'ili custom.[1] Their lives are governed, in addition to the law of Pakistan, by the law of a global Isma'ili constitution.

The brothers and their family have long participated in a rural development program in which the men join a "Village Organization" and the women join a "Women's Organization." These structures, as we will see below, provide a forum for local participation in a global network and socialize the villagers to basic ideological tenets of liberal modernity, entrepreneurial capital, rational humanism, and civil society. All villagers donate part of their earnings to the organization, which provides for them a wide variety of services. The development organization, the Aga Khan Rural Support Programme of the Aga Khan Foundation (AKF), in turn is a subsidiary of the Aga Khan Development Network, or AKDN. On its encouragement, hillsides are greened with new trees, fields are irrigated, small businesses established, hotels built, roads constructed, bridges completed, livestock vaccinated. In these villages, the Aga Khan's network has also built schools

Altit, Hunza, Pakistan, from the path to Melishkar-Duikar, the settlement's high pastures.

of remarkably high quality that have attracted international teachers, fostered scholarships for international study, and funneled talented students into universities created by the Aga Khan. When Sultan Ali's mother fell ill, which has happened often, or when his wife needed treatment for diabetes, they sought assistance at the excellent Aga Khan Health Services hospitals and clinics in the immediate area. When the traditional fortresses of Altit and Baltit fell into disrepair, the Aga Khan Foundation funded massive renovations.

Growing up, Sher Ali and Sultan Ali, along with their many siblings, had daily contact with Isma'ilis from North America, Africa, and Europe as well as other parts of Pakistan, who were working as staff members for the Aga Khan Foundation. Their presence, much more than the presence of global tourists, engendered and reinforced in the whole village an awareness of the simultaneous existence of Isma'ilis elsewhere, of a transnational community with which the villagers believe themselves to share something fundamental. Their contacts with the global network are diverse, constant, and immediate. Sher Ali and Sultan Ali's immersion in global Isma'ilism has also indirectly opened up the possibility for them to be global in other ways as well and exposed them to new potential modalities for the accumulation of wealth. Two of their older brothers, Dildar Khan and Nuruddin Khan, work in tourism, and Sultan Ali is working on creating a simple hotel in one of his village's traditional pastures. Sher Ali, for his part, befriended a young Afghan Isma'ili woman, who also worked at the Islamabad Marriott before the explosion and before she migrated to Québec. As these examples illustrate, the connections forged by membership in the global Isma'ili community span oceans, cross borders, enter the realm of intimacy, introduce subjects to the workings of capital, and determine livelihoods.

But global Isma'ilism, and the interaction of Sher Ali and Sultan Ali with it, is at once more complex and less utopian than the initial description suggests, and is intimately tied up with empire and the expansion of markets. It was the channels opened up by European imperialism that created the opportunity for the construction of a more broadly global Isma'ili ecumene; the British in particular played a key role in fostering the formation of a diaspora around the rim of the Indian Ocean. Out of that diasporic population emerged the Khoja elite, who form the imam's inner circle of advisers and direct the development projects in Altit, Baltit, and elsewhere. The British Empire also enabled the construction of a strong connection between the Aga Khan, then based in Bombay, and the northern limits of the raj, in places like Hunza. And it was, as we will see below, the British Empire that bestowed upon the figure of the Aga Khan his particular role in the community of Ismaʿilis and that in part produced the notion of a single Ismaʿili community.

The Ismaʿili institutional forms and initiatives that so suffuse the social fabric in Altit, Baltit, and all of the surrounding communities operate under the banners of "development" and "progress." These structures, comprising the building blocks of an expansive, transnational assemblage, seek to instill in the local population at the very peripheries of Ismaʿili society the values of "participation," "democracy," and "civil society"—not to mention "prosperity." But they also serve to bring those populations into active participation in the Ismaʿili community, incorporate them into its transnational flow, and contribute to its consolidation as a single society under a single leadership. They provide a local forum for participation in a transnational network and play some role in socializing those borderland societies to values associated with capitalism, modernity, and liberal individualism. And they serve to inculcate isolated Ismaʿili societies with enthusiasm for the modern values and practices that are espoused by its central directorate.

Two of the central questions I explore in this book: What does it mean to say that Sher Ali and Sultan Ali participate more in the institutions of transnational Ismaʿilism than in any other political or social form? And does globalization produce new types of citizens?

Theorizing Ismaʿili Lives

In her recent exploration of the changing dynamics of sovereignty, Saskia Sassen (2006) asks what the emergence of global "assemblages" will mean for the territoriality of power and the future of citizenship. She speaks cautiously of "changes in the relationship between citizens and the state" (2), of "multisided, transboundary networks and formations which can include normative orders" (3), and of newly emergent "alternative notions of membership in a community" (305). At the center of her analysis is a concern with a weakening of "the exclusive authority, both objective and subjective, of national states over people, their imaginaries, and their sense of belonging," which "facilitates the entry of nonstate actors into international domains once exclusive to national states" (299). Running through this, however, is a concern with the continued primacy of the nation-state despite its profound alteration and a rejection of the triumphalist language all too often deployed to herald the end of the nation-state and usher in the era of the global (see Tsing 2000).

Sassen's use of the notion of assemblage (see also Ong and Collier 2004), her focus on the perduring role of the nation-state in global process, and her questions surrounding the relative configurations in the constellation of territory, authority, and rights serve an analysis of the complex, unruly, and polycentric nature of global Ismaʿilism very well. Ismaʿilis certainly embody the fundamental repositioning of citizenship that she observes. And Sassen's theoretical emphasis on the tenacious persistence of the state as a conduit or channel for global processes effectively illuminates the long and messy engagement between Ismaʿilism and the colonial and national states in which its followers and leaders have been situated.

The very repositioning of the relationship between subject and polity is at stake here. For Ismaʿili subjects like Sher Ali and Sultan Ali, the complex of global Ismaʿili institutions is certainly an "alternative" to the nation-state. But the state remains; it does not disappear. And all Ismaʿilis live in sovereign territorial units, just as they follow the Ismaʿili constitution, serve on Ismaʿili councils, and pay tithes to the Ismaʿili imamate. At the same time, the Ismaʿili ecumene, while functioning in part as an "alternative" or "parallel" sphere for citizenship and membership, cannot be accurately characterized as a utopian, egalitarian escape from all strictures of political power. As Sassen observes, emergent global assemblages may enact their own normative codes and disciplinary orders. Foucault's (1991) concept of "governmentality" is thus also relevant here, for transnational bodies are certainly in the business of governing, often through the very types of rationalities, practices, and disciplines Foucault described. What they govern, however, and how they do it seem to represent something new. The modalities and spatialities of the relationship between global assemblages and their subjects reveal fundamentally altered historical configurations of power and participation: a "shift from centripetal scalings framed through the master normativity of the nation-state to centrifugal cross-border assemblages of territory, authority, and rights" (Sassen 2006: 403).

The Basics

Before the histories of Ismaʿili globalities can be rendered theoretically legible, a sketch must be drafted of the basic contexts in which Ismaʿili subjects and institutions are situated. The picture, as presented here, is necessarily partial and shamelessly simplified, but it will help us build an analytic framework to apply to Isma'ili historical process. Though cursory, it is the backdrop to Sultan Ali and Sher Ali's lives, at the core of their village's life-worlds, but it did not exist in its present form at the time of their parents' birth.

The Isma'ili community formed in the eighth century in a schism over the rightful succession to the imamate, much as the Shi'a and Sunni sects had split earlier. While the formation referred to under the rubric of Isma'ilism split into a number of smaller groups during the last millennium (i.e., Druze, Da'udi Bohras, or Musta'lian Isma'ilis), the Nizari Isma'ilis who follow the Aga Khan as their imam remain the most numerous. Throughout their history the various structures named "Isma'ili" maintained with relative consistency a somewhat oppositional stance toward the established powers of the Islamic world. Beginning in the tenth century, significantly, the Isma'ilis established a territorial state, the Fatimid Empire, which included much of North Africa, southern Europe, and western Asia. They built the city of Cairo, and their religio-political network stretched from Africa to India. As the Fatimid Empire fell, another schism produced what became the Nizari state in Iran, with its network of fortresses connected by intensive communication. The radical Nizaris repeatedly launched covert attacks on the various dynasties of the era, especially the Seljuqs, for which they gained the epithet "Assassin," from which the English word derives. The Mongol invasions in the late thirteenth century destroyed the Nizari state and dispersed the Isma'ilis far and wide. As I will explain below, establishing a direct connection between these medieval roots and modern Isma'ilism is difficult; nonetheless, Isma'ili institutions work to claim continuity with them.

Isma'ilis are very widely scattered across the planet. There are Isma'ili communities in Pakistan, India, China, Tajikistan, Afghanistan, Syria, the United Arab Emirates, several East African countries (including Kenya and Tanzania), Canada, the United States, the United Kingdom, France, Switzerland, Portugal, and a number of other nation-states. There are no reliable sources on their numbers, and estimates range from 2.5 to over 12 million; the former is a conservative figure but probably closer to reality (Farhad Daftary, pers. comm.). The Khoja Isma'ilis form a prominent diasporic sector of the community that has been highly mobile in the past two centuries. Originating in India, the now wealthy Khojas migrated throughout the Indian Ocean rim to parts of Arabia and East Africa, sometimes as merchants, and from there to Europe and North America. Other Isma'ili communities are comprised of indigenous societies who converted to

Isma'ilism, particularly in the Himalayas. There is now extensive interaction between these two constituent parts of the global community, particularly through the structure of the Aga Khan Development Network. Different countries have national councils with elected leaders who are responsible for ratifying and implementing the Isma'ili constitution.

Isma'ilism is syncretic and eclectic, fusing elements from numerous religious traditions but maintaining the primacy of the Qur'an and the centrality of Islamic thought. It has incorporated, in various areas, elements of Gnostic Neoplatonism, Manicheanism, Zoroastrianism, and, in India, Hinduism. A view of time and history as cyclical is a key tenet of Isma'ili philosophy (see Corbin 1983). Also central is an emphasis on a distinction between the outward message of revelation (*zahir*) and its inner, esoteric meaning (*batin*). This distinction is connected with an emphasis on *ta'wil*, or interpretation, to reveal that meaning and with a view of certain doctrines, such as *qiyama* (resurrection), as allegorical or metaphorical, that other Islamic sects interpret literally. It is only the *ta'wil* of the imam that can reveal the true, inner meaning, the *batin*, of religion.[2] Isma'ili men and women may pray in the same space, known as a *jama'at khana*, where worship takes a quite different form from that in other Islamic communities and may involve singing and chanting. Non-Isma'ilis are not permitted to enter the *jama'at khana* during worship. Until recently, Tajikistan had no such houses of worship, and the primarily Pamiri Isma'ilis there, from the country's southern mountains, pursued their own practices in homes, shrines, and outdoors.

The Isma'ili imam, who is now known as the Aga Khan, is simultaneously a social, political, and spiritual leader to Isma'ilis, embodying in many ways the historical ideal of the Muslim imam or caliph. He is an intermediary between the divine and human realms, and only he is sanctioned to prescribe doctrine and practice. Only he can elucidate and explain the truth behind the outward messages of Islam.[3] The Aga Khan is not considered, nor does he claim to be, a divinity or deity, as a common misconception would have it, but he is nonetheless said to possess the *Nurullah*, or the light of God.[4] In other words, he and the institution of the imamate are seen as imbued with divinity and a divine mandate; furthermore, he is only one bodily manifestation of the eternal and unchanging reality of the imam.[5] While the historical record itself is a bit inconclusive on this matter (see Daftary 1990), the official Isma'ili view states that the Aga Khan, as "a direct lineal descendant of the Prophet Muhammad, through his daughter Fatima and her husband Ali bin Abu Talib, the Prophet's cousin, is the 49th hereditary Imam" (University of Central Asia 2004: 17). The current Aga Khan lives in Aiglemont, near Paris, where his secretariat is located. He was educated at Harvard, during which period his grandfather named him through *nass* (the designation utterance) the next imam.

As mentioned above, the institution of the imamate has allowed Ismaʿilis to adapt their practices to new social realities. The Aga Khan issues regular *farmans*, or decrees, prescribing appropriate conduct and belief for Ismaʿilis everywhere. Ismaʿilis in Canada and in Pakistan may hear the same *farman*. In the last century Ismaʿili religious discourse has been deeply concerned with modernity and with responding to its perceived social exigencies.[6] Ismaʿili women are not required to wear a veil, and Ismaʿilis are encouraged to participate in promoting the social welfare of their coreligionists, as well as others who are in need, particularly through the global structure of the AKDN, a secular, global organization involved in providing everything from schools, clinics, and roads to musical recordings and architectural design awards. AKDN is most active in areas where at least some Ismaʿilis live, though they also work with non-Ismaʿilis in all of their focus countries. The highest representatives of AKDN in poorer countries enjoy diplomatic status;[7] their vehicles bear diplomatic plates, and the national "resident representative" has legal ambassadorial status.

One of the most visible and important activities of AKDN is that of rural development, executed through AKF. The foundation has implemented an unusual approach within the metadiscourse of "development," creating new forms of civil society and political participation. In essence, AKF offers villagers resources and technical assistance in exchange for their forming local councils through which all subsequent aid is channeled. These "Village Organizations" and "Women's Organizations," whose dynamics in relation to localities will be discussed below, thus become the primary agents of their own "development" and the primary decision-making bodies in villages where they have been implemented.

AKDN is critical in inculcating in Ismaʿilis an awareness of their connection to a global community and its institutional network. Through interaction with its complex structure, whose activity reaches even into the local and domestic spheres, Ismaʿilis come into contact with other Ismaʿilis from both their own and other regions and become conscious of their membership in a larger global society and polity. Individuals from disparate localities come to see themselves and each other as parts of a unitary and cohesive whole through the dynamic and ceaseless flow of communications between various nodes of the transnational network. Learning through multiple media of communication of the existence of other Isma'ilis elsewhere whom they have neither seen nor met creates a strong sense of connection to a deterritorialized community and suggests the development of a new type of global "imagined community" (Anderson 1991): one in which subjects' knowledge of distant localities (through novel forms of mobility and media) participating in similar processes across the planet facilitates integration into a single transnational ecumene that is nonetheless not a state. Thus it is through the common experience in different localities of globally connected institutions, in the flow of Isma'ilis to areas where culturally different Isma'ilis live, and in shared rituals of inculcation that a cohesive Isma'ili community begins to emerge.

This, then, is the assemblage in which transnational Isma'ili participation becomes possible. These building blocks, however, do not explain its emergence. Making sense of Isma'ili globality requires finer analytic tools and an appreciation of historical processes at once messier and more complex. It would be easy to take for granted, for example, that the Isma'ili transnational structure is a single, seamless system. But such a presupposition might overlook the possibility that the Isma'ili assemblage is *not* so unitary as it appears to be, even if it appears otherwise. It is possible that there are multiple modes, spaces, and channels of globality here that only appear or are *made* to appear unified. It is possible that Isma'ilis participate in multiple, overlapping Isma'ili spaces, some global, some regional, and some local; that the system is fragmentary and complex, or even constituted of multiple systems; that it is not a single thing, neither entirely global nor entirely local. It is probable that global Isma'ilism means and constitutes something different for different people and different classes. And it is certain that they are fighting over what "it" *should* constitute.

Historicizing Isma'ili Globality

Isma'ilism came in a different form centuries ago to the Himalayan regions of present-day Pakistan, Afghanistan, China, and Tajikistan. But Isma'ili institutions working to consolidate scattered and pelagic populations into a single "community" came only very recently. Primarily over the course of the last century, Himalayan Isma'ilis have been incorporated into an intensive project of modernization, institutionalization, and centralization. How this happened and why are key questions I attempt to answer in this book. As we will see, the story of Isma'ili globalization cannot be separated from histories of empire and the spread of capital. It was the geographies of power instituted by colonial states and the expansion of markets that opened the channels of movement and interaction required for Isma'ili globalization to unfold as it has.

Whether or not global Isma'ilism is indeed a unitary assemblage, it is not without a history (or multiple, convergent histories). To avoid giving a decontextualized representation of Isma'ili globality, one of the central goals of this book will be to historicize the phenomenon, to problematize the scattered polity in the context of its own pasts, on the one hand, and in the context of the history of human political organization, on the other. Too much of the scholarship on globalization presents a utopian, futurist triumphalism (see Tsing 2000), a static, synchronic account of the excitement of syncretism and the adventure of cosmopolitanism whose analytic explanation, grounded in the observation of surface features, ignores the historical conditions that produced those features. Globalization's epiphenomena should not be mistaken for the thing itself.

I thus seek in this book to construct a loose periodization of Isma'ili globalization (though not of Isma'ili *history* more broadly defined), a genealogy of the community's emergent transnationality. If we are to come to conclusions about what kind of thing Isma'ili globalization really is, a story of some temporal depth must be told. To avoid essentialist assumptions, wherein Isma'ili globalization might be explained by virtue of some internal feature of Isma'ilism, I delve into the agents, engines, and antecedents of the profuse institutional structures we see now. I follow in part the multisited, hybrid approach of Engseng Ho's (2006) sweeping analysis of Hadhramawti Sayyid diasporas in interrogating the historical antecedents of emergent Isma'ili configurations and structures, in striving to "treat the present as a historical moment" (Appadurai 1996: 64). In my examination of the meaning of transnationality in the *longue durée* and globalization in historical context, I look carefully at the role of capital and empire in the transformation of human communities into diasporas and other forms. The discussion is further informed, at some level, by the writings of Braudel (1979), Frank (1998), and Chaudhuri (1991).

This book examines specifics of the long engagement between Isma'ilism and multiple modernities, rooted in colonial states, national states, and markets, among other forms. These include the intimate relationship between Isma'ili diasporas in the Indian Ocean and the British circulation of laborers, managers, and merchants; the special role of wealth accumulated in and tithe paid from those diasporic contexts; a decision by the Bombay High Court to legally designate Aga Khan I, the forty-sixth Isma'ili imam, supreme leader of all Isma'ilis; and the later infusion of modern ideologies of liberal humanism and rational individualism into the agendas of contemporary Isma'ili institutions of social service.

Among the broader historical concerns to be addressed is whether contemporary Isma'ili modes of global organization represent something truly new or not. In light of almost a thousand years of intricate, translocal Isma'ili polities, a question may be raised about the degree to which the structure under current observation embodies something substantively different and worthy of analytic attention. My position on this is that the continuity between those earlier forms and the currently active one is unclear. "Isma'ilism" does not necessarily represent a temporally stable and unitary "community" or "polity" throughout the entire millennium, despite official depictions of its uninterrupted evolution. Even if it did, however, I believe that current Isma'ili modalities of political organization and long-distance communication emerge out of historical conditions firmly rooted in modernity. I also seek to isolate the analytically relevant variables here. A second theoretical question informed by historical concerns is thus the question of whether or not, taking into account only the present moment, the dynamics of the Isma'ili community constitute something unique and distinct, or whether they are a token of a type. For that reason, I seek to understand how much of what we see now is due to widely shared historical conditions rooted in globalization, and how much of it is due to the special features of the Isma'ili community and its religious foundations. If the former, extrinsic factors were to be the more important, we could expect to see the contemporaneous emergence of other structures analogous to transnational Isma'ilism. And yet I am not sure that there is anything else like it. If not, then the interest of this case lies in the dynamics it reveals about the way profound and massive social change transforms extant human communities.

In this book I attempt to explore the degree to which Isma'ili globalization is imbricated with a project of modernization, with the politics of empire, and with the mobility of capital, to excavate the story of how Isma'ilism went institutional and global. At what point, I ask, did the enterprise become one of centrally directed transnational community-building? What were the intentions and historical conditions behind it? How far back do we have to look to locate the beginnings of the system that to Sher Ali and Sultan Ali is the very order of things? Perhaps not very far.

Elites and Peripheries: Borderlands into the Fold

A consideration of the process by which an increasingly centralized, self-consciously transnational Isma'ili assemblage has been built from a more fragmentary configuration forms perhaps the most basic concern of this book. I seek to examine both how the Isma'ili imamate itself constructed a global community and how exogenous historical processes constructed a global community *for* the Isma'ili imamate. My focus here is on an intensive process of consolidation by which populations once only loosely connected to each other and to the imamate have been progressively bound into a highly centralized, nonterritorial transnational structure (whose operation bears much resemblance to the government of a polity). It is clear that the Isma'ili leadership has worked very hard to enact enthusiastic global participation and to encourage the incorporation of far-flung communities into the sphere of global Isma'ilism. What is less clear, however, as we begin a close read of the events of the past few centuries, is how intentional this process has been.

Of particular interest here is the intensive and continual process of incorporating disparate and scattered communities into the Isma'ili complex, of bringing them into the fold of the imamate. In my interpretation, this involves, first, an effort to teach the far-flung communities *that they are Isma'ili* and to present them with a standardized version of what that means (in part through the narrative vehicle of an official history). Second, it is tied up with an attempt to teach them the details of *how* to be Isma'ili. And third, it functions (and, I believe, it is intended to function) to socialize them to *modern* ideals and ideologies through the *medium* of Isma'ilism. Through an inspection of this process of consolidation and centralization, I will endeavor to illuminate the processes that crystallize, reinforce, and maintain the operation of the Isma'ili complex as a unitary system (which its participants crucially *see* as unitary).

An examination of the role of modernity and capitalism in the Isma'ili assemblage requires careful scrutiny of the intimate and sometimes fraught relationship between diasporic (and usually affluent) Khoja Isma'ili elites and the scattered and isolated communities with whom they interact, largely through the medium of global Isma'ili institutions.[8] Those institutions, religious and secular alike, are largely led by Khojas, and there is thus an imbalance of power, prestige, and wealth between the two sectors. There are, moreover, other forms of "ethnic" tension: Khojas, as they introduce their view and version of Isma'ilism to the Himalayan borderlands, engender a degree of resentment among communities who have long practiced their own, "non-standard" forms of religious practice. Particularly in Tajikistan, local Isma'ilis express resentment at the infringement on their lifeways and autonomy—and sometimes they resist or reject it.

In some sense, then, it could be said that there are two globalizations here, their encounter mediated by an array of institutional channels and spaces that privilege a metropolitan diasporic elite. For this reason, Isma'ili globality cannot be characterized solely as emerging from diaspora; rather it is an *interaction* between a diaspora and less-mobile autochthonous communities whose ties to the places they inhabit are very old indeed. The formation of the diasporic Khoja Isma'ili community cannot be separated from the historic movement of capital around the Indian Ocean rim. The community's later expansion to "global cities" is bound to more recent processes of urbanization and postcolonial migration. For these reasons, among others, the emphasis on inculcating "borderland Isma'ilis" with norms associated with modernity and the market is of great interest, as is the dissemination into those communities of the language of liberal humanism couched in the lexicon of Isma'ilism.

I would like to stress, here, the agentivity of Isma'ilis in all contexts: Isma'ili subjects and communities are not just pawns following the directives of the Aga Khan's institutions. They actively interpret and mold Isma'ilism and Isma'ili institutions to their own goals and articulate their own set of meanings. They make Isma'ilism their own in a process of active interpretation, contestation, and semiotic production. And the institutional globalization of Isma'ilism, led by the Aga Khan and the Khoja elite at the top of his structures, is also intentional, although less transparently so. The individuals that occupy and navigate the institutional structure *also* exercise agency over the same system that circumscribes their activity. Thus the individual and the local figure prominently in transnational Isma'ili process.

Isma'ili globalization can, in sum, be seen as a process in which scattered marginal populations are socialized to the values of modernity, capitalism, rational individualism, and modern discourses of rights and membership. This book tracks the story of the gradual incorporation of those remote communities into the global polity, their consolidation into a single global structure, and their inculcation with enthusiasm for prescribed Isma'ili ideals.

But to say that there is a single history to be told here would be misleading; the history is contested and contextually contingent. A discrepancy emerges in the spaces between, on the one hand, the official, institutional versions of the story of Ismaʿili history, which emphasize (or even construct) connections between the present moment and the distant past, and on the other hand, unofficial, unwritten versions. Boivin (2003) illuminates the conscious mobilization under Aga Khan III, an intensive modernizer, of the Fatimid past as an effective political symbol and a core paradigm for the Ismaʿili community.[9] The modern is represented as causally linked to earlier Ismaʿili structures. Under this paradigm communities that have always been "Ismaʿili" are simply brought into the fold. In nondominant, "subaltern" versions of Ismaʿili history, a different type of story is suggested; here it emerges that communities with indeterminate historical connections to structures loosely related to current Ismaʿilism are taught that they are Ismaʿili and recruited into its global structures—a process perhaps not unlike the inculcation among scattered populations of Jews (e.g., Yemeni, Kurdish, Bukharan, Cochin, Ethiopian) with a belief in an autochthonous, primordial, empirical, and historically objective connection to Israel, and an invitation to "return." Perhaps the story of modern Ismaʿili community-building might be seen as a different sort of invitation to return.

Nation-States and Transnational Formations

I have already pointed to critical parallels between the Ismaʿili "polity" and the processes characterizing nation-states. Another theme for discussion here is that of the complex relationship between the Ismaʿili transnational structure and the nation-state. I refer to "relationship" here in both its formal and material senses: the Ismaʿili global assemblage has real-time, historical relationships with individual states, but as a sociopolitical structure (idealized and abstracted) it also demonstrates a morphological relationship to (though certainly not an identity with) the generalized form of the nation-state. I also aim to explore the larger implications of formations like that of global Ismaʿilism for the future of the system of national states. Sassen (2006) observes that the global is deeply imbricated with the national and rejects their representation as mutually exclusive sites of identification and organization. I hope to avoid the implication that I believe Ismaʿili transnationality is a "wave of the future" that signals any kind of end of the era of "nation-states." It certainly suggests a transformation in the role of the nation-state, but not its replacement. The territorial state is clearly here for the long haul. Nonetheless, with increasing frequency it will have to reckon with the expansion of alternative, nonnational, nonterritorial sites of social organization and personal identification with which it will co-exist.

The notion of the emergence of a new type of transnational structure can stir in enthusiastic observers a sense of anticipatory excitement, hopes for grand (and revolutionary) things to come, a world in flux. It seems to occasion comments of new utopias and democratic worlds defined by syncretic cosmopolitanism, radical equality, and polyvocality. Perhaps some of this is indeed true. Perhaps parallel and empowering spaces in the seams between culture and the state *are* emerging, and perhaps they will allow some relief from domination and subordination. But global Isma'ilism also produces its own governmentalities (and other, similar formations will likely produce similar dynamics). Even as it presents a site for resistance, it also produces new spaces for the exercise of power, new forms of subjectification and subjugation, and new configurations of normativity. Isma'ili institutions govern, sanction, and provide disciplinary order. Polycentric systems of global organization, despite their scattered modes of organization and possibilities for cosmopolitan egalitarianism, may thus also be sites of governmentality and subjectification.

All that said, something compelling — and compellingly new — is happening here. Surely a "sea change" is occurring, and Isma'ili globalization may well reveal something about it. But just what it reveals is not yet clear and will require careful scrutiny. In diverse contexts across the planet, individuals *are* certainly increasingly able to affiliate themselves not only with the nation-states in which they live, but also with transnational, nonterritorial sociopolitical formations. Sassen (2006) observes:

> If important features of the territorial and institutional organization of the political power and authority of the state have changed, then we must consider that key features of the institution of citizenship — its formal rights, its practices, its subjective dimension — have also been transformed even when it remains centered on the national state. This territorial and institutional transformation of state power and authority has allowed operational, conceptual, and rhetorical openings for nation-based subjects other than the national state to emerge as legitimate actors in international global arenas that used to be confined to the state. (306)

The Isma'ili Muslim community provides us with an opportunity to examine the possibility for emergent global modes of human organization rooted in local contexts. It is an ideal subject for the examination of whether transnational, nonterritorial formations can act, at this moment in history, as primary sites of identification, allegiance, and membership. The Isma'ilis are widely scattered across the planet, but their community forms a highly organized, centralized, integrated network with constant contact between all of its component parts. And, as mentioned, the institutions of the Isma'ili structure, beyond their religious role, provide for their subjects many secular services and symbols conventionally provided by nation-states, and yet they have no territorial base.

I attempt cautiously to explore in this book how it is possible that individuals and localities become more closely affiliated with a transnational, nonterritorial organization than with the territorial nation-state of which they are citizens or administrative units. The question of how subjects come to feel themselves part of a nation-state has been asked and explored exhaustively (Anderson 1991; Kertzer 1988; Gellner 1983). But the question of how citizenship and membership has shifted as the status of the nation-state has changed has been investigated less thoroughly. I believe that it is true that notions of citizenship have been unhitched, at least to a degree, from the need to be cast in terms of either nation-state or place. Does this really mean that a parallel system of transnational formations is now emerging alongside the system of nation-states? The study of the globalization of identity and deterritorialization of political allegiance, because of its prevalence, is increasingly becoming an imperative for anthropological inquiry.

In this analysis I will explore what has made possible transnational affiliation and organization on such a scale, whether it is unique to this case, and, if not, what it means for the people and places that experience it. Most important, the Isma'ili case, I believe, raises questions about the spatiality of power and membership and about the changing nature of cultural selfhood under emergent historical conditions. I aim to explore the sociohistorical preconditions underlying the possibility for the globalization of human communities, the mechanisms through which such globalization occurs, and the phenomenology of their experience. In the face of processes of globalization, the fixity of the system of nation-states does emerge clearly transformed. The trend toward identification with nonterritorial, translocal, global polities portends diminished borders and decentralized authority. In Pakistan, Tajikistan, and elsewhere, new alignments of identity indicate the simultaneous existence of parallel political systems, despite the recognition of only one form being vested with legitimate power. Such unruly and scattered formations as global Isma'ilism are not locatable on a map, not classifiable on a grid; they escape the fixity of the nation-state's enumerative and totalizing epistemologies and must be taken as signs of major transformations in global cultural configurations. The pervasive emergence, entrenchment, and legitimization of transnational discourses of identity in local contexts can only indicate that the social and political realities of the world may indeed be very different from those indicated by the atlas and the identity card.

All this raises again the question of citizenship. If Isma'ilis favor the imamate's transnational religious structure as their primary site of allegiance, does that make them citizens of something besides (or in addition to) a state? Does it make them postnational citizens (see Hedetoft and Hjort 2002; Cheah and Robbins 1998)? A claim that they are citizens of an Isma'ili assemblage could be said to ignore the possibility that the adoption of Isma'ili transnational identity might have primarily *local* relevance, as an element of regional identity politics. Whether or not participation in Isma'ili institutional structures in Hunza, for instance, or Badakhshan, constitutes transnational or postnational citizenship is unclear. Certainly, Isma'ili subjects in such remote regions participate more in Isma'ili structures than in those of the states they inhabit. From the Isma'ili complex they derive rights, but within it they also are bound by obligations and rules that regulate their behavior and have sanctioning power. But the exclusive force of global Isma'ili institutions over the political identity of members is highly variable, and thus it is difficult to make universal claims and authoritative conclusions about the implications of Isma'ilism for understanding transnational citizenship on the basis of the specific cases under consideration. In my examination of Isma'ili lives in local context, I seek to pay special attention to the ways Isma'ili transnational structures have altered and reconfigured subjective framings of the self.

Muslim Modernities: Global Isma'ilism as Global Islam

In this book I attempt to shed light on some aspects of the contemporary life of a little-studied form of global Islam. It bears virtually no resemblance to the varieties of "global Islam" so frequently depicted in the media. It defies the widely circulating popular imaginaries of that object of public obsession. And yet, it is of interest in part precisely for this reason. Not all transnational Muslim networks are militant. Not all are radical, revivalist, and literalist. This one, in fact, defines itself, in some ways, as the very antithesis of militant radicalism and Qur'anic orthodoxy. Its constituents and leaders imagine it as modern, progressive, cutting-edge, and liberal, an Islam able to adapt to changing times. And their imaginings are, more or less, true. As described above, the Qur'an and Islamic ritual practice are, to Isma'ilis, fluid and flexible, their inner truth to be revealed (and altered) from lifetime to lifetime by the succession of imams.

That the "global Islam" of the Isma'ilis defies *expectations* about Islam is, however, only a starting point. We are dealing here with a Muslim transnational structure, but it is one that self-consciously rejects the tenets and the tone of most Sunni global networks. It appears that the politics of the post-9/11 era have played a role in engendering a new sense of Isma'ili identity, one in which its embrace of liberal modernism is thrown into sharp relief by the galvanization of radical Sunni Islam. The conditions of the moment have made it possible for Isma'ilism to cast itself and emphasize its role as the counterfundamentalist form of Islam, to present itself as an alternative to the dominant impressions set by some Sunni factions. These political conditions have also changed the *actual* interaction between transnational Muslim communities and politicized the differences between them. The nature of Isma'ili–Sunni interaction is profoundly altered in the process. The "War on Terror" not only made Islamic formations the target of the United States and its allies; it made the definition and practice of Islam itself a charged site of local and regional contestation.

Another objective of this book, then, is to explore the suggestions of this case for understanding global Islam and to interrogate the role of the specifically Islamic aspects of global Isma'ilism. The Isma'ili self-representation as the "Modern Muslims," has the potential to disturb and destabilize popular (mis)representations of just what Islam *is* and to complicate and problematize uncritical constructions of a homogenous, univocal "Islamic World." In fact, Isma'ilis and other global Muslim organizations and communities occupy a polyvalent space, with communities constructing their identities in relation to each other and to non-Muslims, in a sort of multivariate dialectic. Moreover, in media, in popular writing, and even in scholarship Islamic societies are often imagined and represented ahistorically, with little attempt to anchor claims in contexts. In this book I work hard to avoid that by means of a careful examination of the ways that capitalism and empire interact with an Islamic community.

Isolation, Globalization, and Allegiance

A central concern of this book is the relationship between isolation and globalization. As I have suggested, in the Isma'ili Himalaya, the transnational structure of Isma'ilism becomes a part of local social relationships. Most important, here and perhaps in other, similar contexts, it seems that the transnational formation under discussion is perceived as an opportunity for advancement by traditionally disadvantaged groups and individuals. Thus transnationality plays heavily into marginality on the local level. A central assumption of my hypothesis is thus that transnationality resonates in local contexts among people who have been marginalized in the nation-states where they live. It is this marginality that encourages them to look for some other, nonnational locus of identification and organization, to be receptive to some *alternative* to the state that has alienated them. The arrival of the Isma'ili transnational complex gives the Isma'ilis of the Himalayan areas under discussion the opportunity to be one-up on their neighbors for the first time in history. Sassen (2006) observes that "as the unitary character of the nation-state disaggregates, even if only partially, sovereign authority is itself subject to partial disaggregations. . . . As this centripetal dynamic of the nation-state becomes less significant, we also see exit options for the disadvantaged" (423). But all of this happens within the framework of the state. The transnational structure neither supplants nor obviates the state. It is not in any way *post*-national, nor are it and the state mutually exclusive bodies. Transnational communities thus may develop out of a set of processes firmly rooted in the cultural politics of nation-states.

The Isma'ilis of Pakistan and of Tajikistan's Gorno-Badakhshan have both suffered violence and persecution. In both Tajikistan, with its civil war, and northern Pakistan, with its sectarian violence, Isma'ilis have had few advantages in local and regional social relationships. Thus it makes sense that the transnational structure would appeal to them, for it offers them strategic, symbolic, and material benefits in relation to other groups. It gives them, perhaps for the first time in history, the opportunity to gain a comparative advantage in local interactions. While local groups have had some hand in persecuting Isma'ilis, it is more often the agents of the nation-state (and their collaborators) who have been responsible for their marginalization. The local success of transnational formations in various areas thus seems to depend on the actions of the nation-state, and without it this necessary sense of marginality would not exist. Without the nation-state there is no such marginality, and it is a necessary condition of the transnational structure. Thus the transnational structure is *not* truly an alternative to the nation-state — it is a different kind of functional organization and alliance of people who are made residual in the nation-state. And this residuality, and the consciousness thereof, becomes one of the criteria for the development of their sense of commonality across territory.

The ethnographic focus area of this book is a highly isolated one, situated

in some of the highest areas in the Himalayan ranges. The location is interesting in part because it gives us the opportunity to examine the process of
globalization in one of the remotest parts of the world. It is even more interesting because the region has been significantly bisected by the boundaries
of nation-states, and this process of political division has been powerful
enough to have caused the local cultures of the region to diverge from each
other. For the past century, the Isma'ilis of western China, southern Tajikistan, eastern Afghanistan, and northern Pakistan have had very little contact
with each other. Previously, as we will see, they had a great deal of contact.
Thus the cultural divergence in the region is a good testing ground for the
real significance and success of the arrival of a possible unifying force, that
of transnational Isma'ilism. In other words, the power and resonance of the
Isma'ili assemblage can be assessed, in part, by the degree to which it is able
to serve as a unifying factor across international boundaries that have created fundamental differences in the region.

Methodological Concerns

I first came into contact with the Isma'ili community on a trip to Hunza in
1993, at the age of eighteen. I was welcomed into the home of Sher Ali and
Sultan Ali in a hamlet adjoining Altit village, where I would stay repeatedly
over the course of numerous trips to Pakistan from 1993 to 2001. From that
point on I maintained close contacts in Hunza and Gilgit, regions in Pakistan's far north. I stayed with other Isma'ili families throughout Pakistan's
northern mountains during these visits, when I sometimes worked as a re-
searcher for the Aga Khan Rural Support Programme (AKRSP) based in
Gilgit. AKRSP was an ideal site from which to observe global processes at
work. The office itself was a forum where Isma'ilis from all over the world
came together and discovered their common identity. And AKRSP's activity
in the villages provided fascinating examples of the operation of a global set
of institutions in remote rural localities and of the participation of villagers
in a transnational sphere mediated by those institutions. It was during these
periods that I made my initial observations about Isma'ili organization and
interaction on the local and global levels.

Later, in 2003, I went to conduct further research in the nearby region
of Gorno-Badakhshan, in Tajikistan, which is predominantly Isma'ili, and
also in the Tajik capital of Dushanbe, where the majority of Isma'ili global
institutions in Tajikistan are based. In both Tajikistan and northern Pakistan I explored and documented the points of contact between rural Isma'ili

localities and the Isma'ili global network, trying to compose an inventory of all of the transnational connections experienced by Isma'ili subjects in these areas. I also looked at broader elements of the social context that may play some role in making the globalization of social organization possible. In 2003 I also visited the Institute for Isma'ili Studies in London, a forum for transnational contact and the development of global programs. Finally, in 2004, I completed my research with a further visit to London and to the Isma'ili institutions in Paris and Geneva, where the headquarters of the Aga Khan Development Network is based and where I was able to look from the other side at the interaction of Isma'ili metropolitan institutions with the remote and scattered localities they administer. In all of this I followed a formal ethnographic method, living among Isma'ili students and functionaries as they participated in the life of official Isma'ili institutions in Europe. I stayed in their residences, carried out interviews with them, recorded their seminars and meetings, and went to their workplaces daily. I also met with the leaders and elites of these institutions, including Tom Kessinger, general manager of the Aga Khan Development Network, and Azim Nanji, director of the Institute for Isma'ili Studies. This component of my research could be characterized as institutional ethnography—I immersed myself in the contexts created by the institutions and documented patterns in individual interaction with those institutions.

In the course of my research in the Isma'ili region of the Pakistan Himalaya, I carried out research in the following settlements, among others: Gilgit; Gahkuch, Gupis, Phander, Shamran, and Teru in Ghizar; Yasin, Hundur, and Darkot in the Yasin valley, along with Harf in the tributary Thui valley; Karimabad-Baltit, Altit, Mominabad, Aliabad, Murtazabad, Sost, Chapursan (particularly Shutmerg), Misgar, Kermin, Zoodkhun, Morkhun, Khunjerab, Dainyore and Sultanabad in the Hunza-Gojal area; Chitral town; Zhitor, Izh, Munoor, Kiyar, Hart, Begusht, and many other villages of the Lutkho-Garm Chashma tributary system in Chitral; and the cities of Rawalpindi-Islamabad, Peshawar, and Lahore. I stayed in village households in Gahkuch, Yasin, Shamran, Altit, Sikanderabad, and Sultanabad. In Tajikistan, besides the capital, Dushanbe, I lived in the town of Khorog, the capital of Gorno-Badakhshan; I visited the Pamiri villages of Porshnev, Saroi Bahor, Khuf, Rushan, Yemz, Baghow, Ishkashim, Upper Ryn and Lower Ryn, Garm Chashma, Murch, and Jelandy, among others. Over the course of this period, I had contact with the following Isma'ili institutions: the Aga Khan Rural Support Programme (Pakistan), the Mountain Societies Development and Support Programme (Tajikistan), the Aga Khan Development Network, the Aga Khan Foundation, the Aga Khan Health Services, the Aga Khan Education Services, the University of Central Asia, the Aga Khan Health Education Initiative (Tajikistan), the Aga Khan Humanities Project, the Aga Khan Trust for Culture and Award for Architecture, Focus Humanitarian Assistance, the Aga Khan Fund for Economic Development, the Serena Hotel Chain, the Isma'ili Secretariat (Paris), the Institute for Isma'ili Studies and the Isma'ili Center (London), and the Isma'ili Tariqah Religious Education Board (worldwide) and Committee (Tajikistan), among others. For most of these organizations I visited multiple sites. I have also had contact with members of the Isma'ili National Councils in various countries.

Most of my research in Pakistan was carried out in Urdu, a well-established *lingua franca* of the region that I speak fluently. In Tajikistan, I spoke to subjects in Tajik, a regional dialect of Persian, and in Russian, and sometimes, in remote villages, I had help with translation and logistics from Safdar Alibekovitch, a highly educated resident of Porshnev village fluent in English and a number of Pamiri languages.[10] In all settings I used a combination of traditional immersion and participant observation, semiformal interviews, and documentation of spontaneous discourse.

The global fervor surrounding Islam was present even during the development phase of this project. The research was carried out in situations where Islam was a central factor in social life and sometimes a sensitive topic of discussion. This was salient both in northern Pakistan, where the religious community has been the focus of a good deal of violent conflict and open discussion of sects is sensitive, and in Tajikistan, where religion was a key element in the civil war and was intensely regulated until very recently. The dynamics of Islam pose unique challenges and opportunities for ethnographic researchers, particularly in the present context. Events surrounding September 11, 2001, and its aftermath had a direct effect on my research. Precarious conditions in Pakistan motivated me to work in Tajikistan in 2003 rather than return to Gilgit and Hunza. Moreover, the realities of the "War on Terror" and post-9/11 events have changed the very social environments that are at the center of this analysis.

This project also raises important questions about the change in ethnographic method produced by globalization. Changing historical conditions necessitate new research methods and questions and new ways of thinking about social units and field contexts. An important consideration in this undertaking was the degree to which Isma'ilis could be considered a single group, which raises the question of whether ethnography needs to focus on a single space. Ethnographic technique focused on the complexities of globalization as a historical condition has yet to be standardized and fully formulated, but it is being negotiated and interrogated in the literature of the moment.

George Marcus (1995) has provided an influential commentary on the concept of multisited ethnography in a "world system," an ethnography that "moves from its conventional single-site location, contextualized by macro-constructions of a larger social order, such as the capitalist world system, to multiple sites of observation and participation that cross-cut dichotomies like 'the local' and the 'global,' the 'lifeworld,' and the 'system'" (95). The ethnographer of multiple sites follows "connections, associations, and putative relationships" (97). Appadurai (1996) also provides insight into the implications of globalization for ethnography, pointing out that "ethnographers can no longer simply be content with the thickness they bring to the local and the particular" (54).

Multisited ethnographies of global formations also provide their share of challenges, including confusion about when one is in and when one is outside of one's "sites." Moreover, multisited ethnography can make methodological rigor difficult to maintain and can make it easy to lose track of the central question or process one is studying. But a "deterritorialized" community (see Appadurai 1996); necessitates a deterritorialized ethnographic practice. The Isma'ilis are an ideal multisited subject for a global ethnography. Few communities are simultaneously as widely dispersed and, at the same time, as intensively centralized. The many *types* of Isma'ili subjects, from wealthy members of the Indo-African Nizari Khoja diaspora living in Canada, to Himalayan villagers living in mud houses in Afghanistan, also necessitate a multisited approach. Any other method would be fatally partial.

More recent work shows well the direction ethnography has taken in its approach to questions of globalization and transterritorial connectedness. Of note for its innovative exploration of connections and linkages across territory is Adriana Petryna's *Life Exposed: Biological Citizens after Chernobyl* (2002). Anna Tsing's (2004) ethnography of Kalimantan forests, which she describes as "an ethnography of global connection," is also an important contribution and demonstrates well the new ethnographic connections in the face of conditions of globalization. "Global connections are everywhere," she writes. "So how does one study the global?" (1). Tsing, whose earlier work focused on marginalized and remote Malaysian localities, explains her new method: "Following global connections out of Kalimantan, I found myself exploring other sites, including powerful centers of finance, science, and policy. But these, too, produce only fragments" (271). Aihwa Ong, in her important book *Flexible Citizenship: The Cultural Logics of Transnationality* (1999), explores diverse forms of transpacific connection between North America and East Asia. In ethnographies like these, the influence of the global on the patterns of social life and its consequent influence on the field of anthropology are clear. A new direction emerges wherein the unit of analysis is not necessarily tied to a locality but is defined by social connection. In my research on Isma'ilism, I have worked to trace and locate the linkages that form Isma'ili community across territory and at the same time discern the ways in which they remain stably situated in localities and lives despite their flexibility and fluidity.

Plan of the Book

In this book, I seek most fundamentally to explore through the lens of Isma'ilism how emergent historical conditions engender new modes of subjectivity and new framings of self. I approach this in part through an exploration of the interstitial points of interaction between Isma'ili individuals and localities, on the one hand, and Isma'ili institutions, on the other. Much of the material I present deals with how (and whether) Isma'ilis come to feel themselves part of a collectivity, and how social solidarity is developed transnationally (see Durkheim 1933; Cheah and Robbins 1998; Anderson 1991). How do people come to feel that they are part of the transnational community of Isma'ilism? How do they gain a sense of belonging to it, and even of belonging to it more than to anything else?

Such a process requires a ritual apparatus. Kertzer (1988) writes of the rituals that polities effect to inculcate loyalty and allegiance in their subjects. What I strive to locate are the corresponding semiotic mechanisms for transnational polity-building. The institutions, rituals, and interactions I describe are on some level the global network's mechanisms for incorporating subjects, the ritual apparatus for imbuing subjects with loyalty and encouraging participation. My concern is ultimately with transnationality as *local* experience. How do people experience the apparatus? And what are the mechanisms through which that experience is made possible? Consider the following statement by an Isma'ili from Tajikistan's Gorno-Badakhshan region:

J: Do you feel that you're part of a global Isma'ili community and what things make you feel that way if you do? What things make you aware of that?

S: First of all, the entire population close to Khorog feel that they are part of this community. ITREC and other organizations have showed us that there is someone who is devoted to the Isma'ilis of Badakhshan, who are accepted as a part of this global community of Isma'ilis. These kinds of things make us sense that we are part of it. Also . . . Khoja Isma'ilis, from other places, are also working at that institute [ITREC] and they [Pamiri Isma'ilis] are accepted. . . . They are interested in Badakhshan. All these things show that we are also a part of it.

My examination of the ethnographic material here is geared toward asking *how* the institutions and structures of the Isma'ili assemblage make subjects aware of their connection to the larger system. How do subjects experience that connection?

Part of that awareness is a reflexive one. I will reference throughout the text the critical awareness Isma'ilis express of their position in a global formation. I see institutional and individual subjects' explicit discourse of participation in a transnational sphere as a crucial element of cultural globalization in general and Isma'ili globalization in particular. As is evidenced by many Isma'ili practices and activities, Isma'ilis not only participate and move through globalized institutional spaces but also know it and talk about it. I believe that to be an important part in the construction and synthesis of a global community, helping motivate a desire to keep it unified and cohesive. A transnational group's *idea* that they are connected in a globalized community, the consciousness of it, can become key in the formulation of their self-image. This consciousness may inculcate a sense of simultaneity and transregional commonality in members (Anderson 1991); it comprises the formation of a "metaculture of globalization" (Urban 2001).

In Chapter 1, I detail the historical development of a uniquely Isma'ili modernity. I cover the medieval period, whose connection to contemporary Isma'ilism is loose at best, only inasmuch as it forms the necessary background and demonstrates the precursors to the contemporary Isma'ili moment.[11] My substantive engagement with Isma'ili history begins with the relocation of the first Aga Khan to India, the formation of an Isma'ili diaspora, and the first attempts to construct a broader Isma'ili sphere. Key to this moment is the story of a Bombay High Court case, already mentioned, which decreed the Aga Khan the supreme leader of the Isma'ilis and dictated that his followers be called Isma'ilis. I move from here to a succinct discussion of the modernization policies of Aga Khan II and especially Aga Khan III, whose work began the proliferation of global institutions that was continued by his grandson, Aga Khan IV. My objective here is to outline specifically the institutional history of modern Isma'ilism to underscore the variables contributing to its emergence.

In Chapters 2 and 3 I map the vast and nebulous Isma'ili institutional structure, exploring its many nodes and circuitous tributaries, its multiple centers and its shifting spaces. I include in this discussion (in Chapter 2) AKF's "development" institutions, including, significantly, those working at the local level to construct "Village Organizations," which I interpret, in part, as local conduits for political participation in a global Isma'ili sphere. These sprawling development institutions, under the umbrella of AKDN, are generally referred to as *imamati* organizations, issuing directly from the imamate. I also provide here an exploration of the informal social configurations generated by the institutions' formal structures, their ethnographic by-products.

In Chapter 3 I deal with the so-called *jama'ati* institutions, those considered under the control of the "community." These include the important Institute for Isma'ili Studies (IIS) in London and the Isma'ili Tariqah Religious Education Boards in various countries. The London institute is responsible for the creation of a field of "Isma'ili Studies," and therefore in part for writing the Isma'ilis' history. The review boards are charged in part with standardizing and regulating Isma'ili practice and theology. Villagers visit to ask questions on such matters as proper funeral or marriage ritual, and the boards dispense advice. Both sets of institutions, it should be noted, are generally under the leadership, directly or indirectly, of Khoja elites. In my view, these *jama'ati* institutions are essential for the inculcation of local populations with enthusiasm for participation in a centralized Isma'ilism, because the spaces they provide are critical in the formation of a transnational sense of solidarity and shared experience. The historical development and lived experience of these institutions, secular and nonsectarian, are unusual in the Islamic world and warrant special attention. Chapter 3 ends with a consideration of some noninstitutional structures and processes essential in engendering a transcultural sense of shared experience.

The conceptual map of the Isma'ili structure is essential. But a top-down, institutional perspective only goes so far; it is insufficient to represent the real complexity and diversity of Isma'ili people. In Chapters 4 and 5, then, I focus on more in-depth ethnographic descriptions of the local iterations of these institutions in the Himalaya. In Chapter 4, I account for the ethnographic settings and contexts of Isma'ili institutional activity in the region. I provide a deeper background here on the primary area of research, the Pamir ranges of southern Tajikistan, and the adjacent Karakoram Himalaya of Pakistan. I look carefully at what the entry of Isma'ili institutions has meant for the region's isolated localities, how they figure into its conflicts and the ethnic politics of identity with its variable meanings for individuals in different situations. I also consider in this chapter the exogenous transformations wrought on these lives and localities by national borders, new roads, and global markets. All this sets the sociohistorical stage for the next chapter.

In Chapter 5, I consider the ethnographic realities behind the structures described. I look at the ethnographic moments (like conferences), structures (like AKF's Village Organizations), and spaces (like the IIS-sponsored Khorog English Program). These disconnected ethnographic elements reveal the role of the global institutions in local context. Chapters 4 and 5 shift the axis of my study away from an institution-internal perspective and onto Isma'ili people and places, at once messier and more illuminating. From there I move to propose, in a final chapter, some tentative conclusions.

The process by which emergent forms of Isma'ili identity are born, and the transformations of personal experience that this entails, form the big questions here. The core problematic rests in the realm of the subject. But it is not an ahistorical subject. I try here in particular to excavate the role of capital in the formation of a religiously defined global assemblage with social attributes. The focus on capital, empire, and modernity, however, should not be so heavily privileged as to obscure the important antecedents, even modernity. Capital, empire, and modernity are not the whole picture. But in those moments of contact where distant communities are intensively incorporated into the Isma'ili assemblage, they figure prominently.

Much has been written on Isma'ili history, particularly on its medieval Fatimid and Nizari phases. The syncretic doctrines of Isma'ilism, particularly those centered on cyclic views of time and history, have received a great deal of attention. Gossip-laden, sensationalist, and unscholarly tracts on the lives and times of the Aga Khans are commonplace. But the number of works on modern Isma'ilism is scant indeed. Even more scarce are books focusing on Ismaʿili people and their cultural contexts. Given the compellingly interesting dynamics of the community, this paucity is unwarranted. I offer here something, however limited, to fill that lacuna in the scholarship. I hope that my findings will be illuminated and substantiated by Ismaʿili voices and yet-unwritten histories.

CHAPTER ONE

Antecedents and Precursors

The Historical Contexts of Ismaʿili Globalization

Who Are the Ismaʿilis? A Simplified Sketch

The role of leadership, succession, and schism in the history of Islam war-rants careful (albeit brief) consideration here.[1] It is only through an under-standing of these processes that the story of Ismaʿilism can be fully ex-plained. At almost every historical moment, how the Ismaʿili community defined and redefined itself revolved around questions of succession and rightful authority. This was always an issue in Shiʿism in general, since legiti-mate authority was the domain of the *Ahl al-Bayt*, the "people of the house" of the Prophet Muhammad, especially through the line of his nephew and son-in-law ʿAli. The Shiʿa opposed the Sunni notion of rule by consensus (*ijmaʿ*) of the community, because they believed that leadership should only be in the hands of the qualified, especially since leadership involved elucidation of the underlying truth of the religion. The criteria among the Shiʿa for the selection of qualified leaders were lineal; only the descendants of ʿAli were seen to be qualified to lead Islamic society. The question, then, revolved around *who* was in fact the rightful heir in the line of ʿAli.

Since the inception of the religion, and especially after the death of the Prophet, Islamic societies and polities have devoted a great deal of atten-tion to these questions. After all, the Islamic leader, or caliph, was charged with prescribing both religious and worldly conduct. Leadership has re-mained more of a concern for Ismaʿilism than for most other branches of Islam; Sunni populations no longer have a centralized caliph, nor do the Ithnaʿashari Shiʿa, who believe in the messianic return of the twelfth imam as *Mahdi*. Ismaʿilis, however, retain a leader whom they believe to be a direct descendant of ʿAli and thus uniquely qualified to explain and interpret the meaning of their religion.

In sum: after Muhammad's death, questions of succession caused a rift between those who favored ʿAli as the leader of the Muslim community, and those who favored Abu Bakr, Muhammad's successor. Those loyal to ʿAli and his cause would become known as the *Shiʿa*, the "party" of ʿAli; those who favored the caliphs beginning with Abu Bakr would later be referred to as *Sunni*. The Shiʿa felt that ʿAli had been wronged and cheated of his rights. Each group slowly developed its own distinctive religious orientation. The Shiʿa too split into many sects, often over questions of succession. The Shiʿi Ismaʿilis were born in one such dispute: The major branch of Shiʿa and the proto-Ismaʿilis shared all the same imams through Jaʿfar al-Sadiq, the sixth imam by current Nizari Ismaʿili reckoning (and the fifth in other reckonings). When Jaʿfar's son and heir-apparent, Ismaʿil, died before his father, a dispute arose over who was the rightful successor. Those who believed that it was Ismaʿil would become the Ismaʿiliyya (Daftary 1990: 1).

The various formations referred to as the "Ismaʿiliyya" have been commonly perceived as taking a somewhat radical and oppositional stance in the Islamic world; this reputation has been at the center of the attributes bestowed upon them by other groups. They have gone through cycles of great prominence and complete obscurity over the course of their history and have been divided by schism a number of times. Beginning in the tenth century, significantly, the Ismaʿilis established a territorial state, the Fatimid Empire, which included much of North Africa and western Asia. The Fatimids built the city of Cairo (including the famous Al-Azhar mosque and university), which quickly became a cosmopolitan center; their territory incorporated Morocco and Mecca, Jerusalem and Sicily, and their religio-political network stretched from Africa to India (Daftary 1990: 2; Robinson 1996). These facts would become ethnographically important later for the influence they had on Ismaʿilis' views of themselves, but their actual relationship to contemporary Ismaʿilism is difficult to discern. In fact, despite Ismaʿili institutions' insistence on their historical salience for modern Ismaʿilism, their real shared continuity is rooted more in interpretation than historical fact.

As the Fatimid Empire began to fall apart, another major schism over succession to the Ismaʿili imamate divided the sect into branches that became the Mustaʿlawiyya (or Mustaʿlian Ismaʿilism, out of which emerged the Tayyibis and the Bohras of Yemen and India), and the Nizariyya, the branch that is our primary concern here, whose early post-Fatimid history was primarily in Iran, and out of which eventually came the line of the Aga Khans. The Nizariyya too had a "territorially scattered state" (Daftary 1990:

2) in Iran, with a center in the Elbrus Mountains above the Caspian Sea, and a vassal state in Syria with its own complex and significant history. It consisted of widely distributed fortresses that maintained intensive communication between them. While the Nizari state was not on the same scale as the Fatimid state, in the eyes of the key powers of the Islamic world, particularly the Seljuqs, it was a real threat and figures prominently in Islamic histories of the period; almost all the dynasties feared the rebellious Ismaʿilis of the time. The Mongol invasions, however, especially the campaigns led specifically against the Nizaris by Hülegü, proved to be disastrous for the sect, and as the invaders swept across Iran on horseback, the Ismaʿili community seemed to fade into obscurity; it became, for a time, little more than a conglomeration of scattered populations, with the central leadership presenting itself as a Sufi order. Only in the past century, with the explosion of global processes, has the Ismaʿili community come back into the consciousness of the non-Ismaʿili world. It should be noted that, while over the course of Ismaʿili history there have been a number of schisms producing new branches of the sect (e.g., the Druze, the Mustaʿlawiyya-Tayyibi-Bohra, the Hafiziyya, the Muhammad-Shahis, etc.), my focus here will be on the Nizaris (or Nizariyya), and more specifically on the Qasim-Shahi Nizaris, the followers of the fourth Aga Khan (His Highness Prince Karim Aga Khan al-Husayni, the forty-ninth imam of the Ismaʿilis) who remain the most numerous, the most widely distributed, and the most publicly visible.

Estimates of the world population of contemporary Qasim-Shahi Nizari Ismaʿilis vary widely and may at times be inflated; they run as high as 15 million. A conservative estimate by one expert on Ismaʿilism is 2.5 million (Farhad Daftary, pers. comm.). The most numerically significant portion of the population consists of the Khoja Ismaʿilis, who, as we have seen above, form the Ismaʿili diaspora that has become the wealthy and influential elite of the global community. This means that there is often an interethnic element to (and conflict within) interactions between local people and diasporic Ismaʿilis; these interactions are often mediated by the institutions of AKDN, many of whose administrators are Khojas. Khojas also act as important missionaries and religious emissaries of the Aga Khan.[2]

Khoja Ismaʿilis of Indian descent live in limited numbers in their ancestral region of Gujarat (including Kachchh and Kathiawar); cities of the subcontinent including Bombay, Karachi, and Lahore; East Africa (including Kenya and Tanzania); European cities including London, Paris, and Lisbon (where they came after social upheavals in Mozambique); North American cities including Houston, Chicago, New York, Toronto, Vancouver, and Calgary; and in smaller numbers in the Arab Gulf states (including the UAE), Singapore, and Australia. There also seem to be remnants of the very old communities of Multan and Sind living in parts of the plains of Pakistan (see Nanji 1978). The second major concentrated Isma'ili population spans the western Himalaya (including the Pamir, Karakoram, Great Himalaya, Hindu Raj, and Hindu Kush ranges) in Tajikistan, Afghanistan, Pakistan, and far western China. There are distant communities in the Guma and Pishan oases of the Khotan region in the Taklimakan basin of Chinese Turkestan. I will deal with the Himalayan communities that are the focus of this book in more detail below.

An outlying but large Isma'ili community in Afghanistan can be found among the Mongol-descended Hazara of the central Hindu Kush (Orywal 1986). Even more obscure, perhaps, is the small Pashai-speaking Isma'ili community in eastern Afghanistan pointed out by Emadi (2000). The Pashai are speakers of an Indic language of the "Dardic" subgroup, which is related to Kashmiri, Shina, and Khowar. They inhabit the tributaries of the Kunar River north and west of Kabul and south of Kohistan. It is unusual to find an Isma'ili community in this strongly Sunni southern area, and there is little discussion of this enclave in the literature. There are also unverified rumors, reinforced by local scholars, of a small, isolated community of Yaghnobi-speaking villagers with some Isma'ili heritage in the upper Zerafshan watershed of the Turkestan mountains in northern Tajikistan.[3] The Yaghnobis form a very remote community of Eastern Iranian-speakers whose language may be related to the Sogdian subfamily.

Numerous Isma'ilis still live in Syria, in and around Aleppo and elsewhere (Mirza 1997), and in Iran, especially in Tehran, Mashhad, and surrounding regions of Khurasan. Other schismatic groups who separated from mainstream Isma'ilism over the course of the past twelve hundred years include the Druze (largely of Lebanon), the Musta'lian-Tayyibi-Bohra community of the Da'udi (Bohra) line, who live largely in India, and of the Sulaymani line, who live mostly in Yemen. It appears that there is no substantive institutional communication between the Qasim-Shahi Nizari Isma'ilis and these various Isma'ili offshoots.

At the Dawn of Empire

From the historical vantage point, it is the Isma'ili engagement with modernity (through capital, empire, and the historical moment now called globalization) that I am most substantively concerned with. I ask here two Braudelian questions: What did the Isma'ili community look like just before the advent of empire, in the moments before modernity, as the world waited for the transformations of capital and commerce? What can be said of Isma'ili life as the world saw its first hints of the massive rupture to come? My discussion here is inflected with a consideration of the historical development of *long-distance communication* between the Isma'ili imamate and the sect's many scattered communities. In order to work toward an answer to the basic questions here, we need to understand the fundamentals of both the past and present of Isma'ili translocal organization. My focus here is on those processes that bind together a community across territory. What do we know about the history of Isma'ili translocal process? How similar is it to contemporary Isma'ili organization? Would people in the past have lived the same connection to each other and to their network as they do in the current moment? I provide a basic background on the medieval period here only to highlight and illustrate elements of continuity and difference in the past and present modes of Isma'ili transterritoriality and to underscore the historical background of Isma'ili presence in the Himalayas and the Indian Ocean rim.

As early as 875 the Isma'ili movement had sent missionaries across much of Asia and had set up tributary outposts in what was called at the time the *da'wa*, the mission. But such long-distance community-building was not supported by a state infrastructure for some time. Translocal interaction and long-distance communication in the Fatimid polity, based in Cairo, was characterized by an elaborate, hierarchical, and clandestine network of emissaries and missionaries deployed from North Africa to India. The *da'i* missionaries were now charged with carrying Fatimid propaganda beyond the borders of the empire, whose outposts went as far as the banks of the Indus; the Fatimids established a tributary state in Multan and had followers as far away as Bukhara (Hodgson 1977; Daftary 1990: 155). A strong connection was maintained between the hierarchy of *da'is* in a given region and the Fatimid capital, and between those in the regional capitals and their traveling teams in the hinterlands (Daftary 1990: 231). One of the most important *da'is* was the famous Nasir-i-Khusraw, who traveled throughout the Fatimid realm and brought Isma'ilism to the Himalayan ranges of contemporary Pakistan, Afghanistan, China, and Tajikistan.

Under the Imam al-Mustansir (the eighteenth Isma'ili imam), Yemeni *da'is* first brought the creed to the coastal region of Gujarat; after that, maintenance of the Fatimid connection with India was the domain of the Sulayhid Isma'ilis, with approval from the caliph in Cairo who may have been interested in the sea trade with India, in which Cambay was a crucial node. Thus the translocal network was both a product and a producer of independent translocal economic systems. The connection between these two regions continued into the modern era (Daftary 1990: 208–11; Dresch 1989), though only in the Tayyibi-Musta'lian-Bohra Isma'ili schism; the Nizari community in India did not maintain a link with Yemen.

The Nizari state that emerged in Iran and Syria in the wake of the Fatimids was made up of widely separated fortresses (in the Zagros and Alburz ranges) and settlements, held together by secretive organized networks of missionaries and other representatives (Hodgson 1955, 1968). But the character of the polity was significantly different now. There was no stable empire and no fixed territory. It was here that the possibility of an Isma'ili polity with little territorial contiguity began to emerge. Farhad Daftary (1990) writes that "the Nizari territories were separated from one another by long distances, and yet the Nizari state maintained a remarkable cohesion and sense of unity both internally and against the outside world" (381).

The invasion of the Mongols dealt the Isma'ili translocal network of *da'is*, *fida'is* (martyrs, mercenaries, "those who sacrifice themselves"), and *khalifas* (caliphs; "community leaders") an irreversible and catastrophic blow. Their interactive systems, which spanned much of North Africa and Asia, were utterly destroyed, and for perhaps two hundred years there was almost no recorded contact between the imam and his subjects. In both the Nizari and Fatimid polities, individuals generally remained closely tied to particular localities with which they were affiliated. The patterns of circulation never approached the complexity we see in the contemporary deterritorialized system (Daftary 1990; Hodgson 1955, 1968; Lewis 1967; Stern 1983; Ivanow 1952, Halm 1997; Brett 2001). During this period the various Isma'ili regions became more isolated; communication between followers and the imam was mediated only by the highly autonomous *da'i*, *pir* (hereditary religious leaders), or *shaikh* (religious leaders).

In the writings of an Isma'ili author by the name of Khayrkhwah, who wrote in the first half of the 1500s, we find a good deal of information on the *da'wa* of the Anjudan period; these writings confirm well-established linkages between the imams and the Isma'ilis of India, Khurasan, and Afghanistan in this time period. Khayrkhwah, an Afghan from Herat, reports that missionaries regularly paid visits from India and other distant regions to the seat of the imam to carry to him the tithe paid by the community (Daftary 1990: 469–75). Already here we can see the central importance of the revenue paid to the imam by the Isma'ili community in the maintenance of translocal circulation.

Activity in India, which would come to have an immeasurable effect on later global Isma'ilism, was particularly strong during the late Anjudan era (beginning in the 1300s); it was this population that produced the Isma'ili "Khoja" diaspora and global elite and what would become the standardized worldwide version of Isma'ilism. The *da'i* Sadr al-Din extended the movement into Gujarat, which became a stronghold and the source of populations who would in a few centuries spread across India and Africa (and eventually Canada, the United Kingdom, and the United States) (Nanji 1978; Daftary 1990: 478–84).

Into the Period of Aga Khan I: Enter Modernity

It can be argued that the current shape of the global Isma'ili community is a product of empire and its legal demarcation of groups and thus, ultimately, a product of orientalist colonial discourse on community (Shodhan 2001).[4] The claim that communities or other social forms should be framed as creations of a colonial administration is certainly neither unique nor unusual; imperial states were everywhere in the business of classifying, delineating, and recording information about social groups (see Anderson 1991, Chatterjee 1986, Dirks 2001, Mamdani 1996). The interaction of colonial law and community-formation is well-attested; the communities that crystallized into "the" Isma'ilis were undeniably subject to this process. This is not to say that there was no Isma'ili society before this, nor that the British invented the Isma'ilis; the claim is rather that the British in some ways created the boundaries that delineated the Khojas as a distinct, separate, and internally cohesive "community," and that they came to see themselves as Isma'ili through the lens of the British construction of legal community.

It was the Aga Khan case in the Bombay courts, as we will see below, that in particular played a key role in institutionalizing the office of the Aga Khan for the Isma'ilis and in crystallizing the disparate elements of the group as a community. The Aga Khan's significance in the day-to-day affairs of Isma'ilis and even the unity of the meaning of "Isma'ili" only emerge after this point. But this "critical moment" was not alone, in the colonial period, in changing the course of Isma'ili history. Instead a concert of forces and moments, incorporating the empire's essential part in creating an Isma'ili diaspora around the Indian Ocean rim, profoundly altered those scattered communities by bringing them together under a single infrastructure. The colonial moment was, for individual Ismaʻili populations, both rupture and opportunity, both formative and tumultuous.

To set the stage for the imamate's entry onto the colonial stage, we need to begin a bit earlier. I have shown that the Ismaʻili leadership, after the Nizari period, entered into a long period of obscurity. We begin here at the reemergence from that period: In the mid-1700s, when Nadir Shah's Afghan dynasty had done away with the Safavids, the imam, Hasan ʻAli, moved the imamate from Kahak to Shahr-i-Babak, primarily so that the pilgrims who brought in so much revenue would find the journey less arduous.[5] The relocation to Shahr-i-Babak meant that Indian Nizaris who came by sea then had to make only a short land journey. Coinciding with the expansion of markets in India and surrounding areas, the imam's wealth began to grow exponentially; he began to live more opulently in several residences, to re-emerge in the public (and European) eye, and to develop political influence in Iran. Hasan ʻAli's successor, his son Qasim ʻAli, was in turn succeeded by Abuʾl-Hasan ʻAli Shah, who under the Zand dynasty became the governor of the province of Kirman, lived in great comfort, and commanded his own military forces. His son, who came to be known as Shah Khalil Allah III, became imam in 1792 and eventually moved the seat of the imamate to Kirman. In 1817, when he was assassinated by militant Shiʻis, his thirteen-year-old son Hasan ʻAli Shah became imam; after Khalil Allah's widow appealed to the Qajar court for some recompense for the murder of her husband, the Qajar king granted the imam new land in Qumm, made him the governor of that region, and gave him the royal title of Aga (also Agha) Khan; from this point on, the Ismaʻili imams of the Qasim-Shahi Nizari line bore this title. Aga Khan I, also called Aga Khan Mahallati, received the court's favor, a militia, and once again, for a brief period, the governorship of Kirman (which his forefathers had held) (Daftary 1990: 498–507).

Despite his success in subjugating local restive tribes, the Aga Khan was removed from the governorship in 1837 and summoned to the capital in Tehran, a summons that he rejected. Instead, he prepared to oppose the Qajar forces by first occupying the fort of Bam. He fought them for a little more than a year, until he was taken prisoner. Even as a captive, he was able to accept tributes from Khurasan, the subcontinent, and Badakhshan; finally, after almost a year in captivity, he was granted an audience with the Qajar king, who decided to forgive him, provided he lived quietly from then on in his traditional village base (Daftary 1990: 498–507; see also Tapper 1983).

In 1840, when he was once again suspected of rebellious designs, the Aga Khan requested passage to Mecca but went instead to Yazd, where he presented the governor of that region forged documents stipulating his own reappointment as governor of Kirman. He was at first welcomed, but when the forgery was discovered, a battle broke out between the Aga Khan's forces and those of the governor; the Aga Khan won and proceeded to the old Isma'ili base of Shahr-i-Babak, where the local people were trying to drive out Afghan rulers who had installed themselves there after having been driven out of their own lands by the British. After initial advances in 1841 against the Qajar government, Aga Khan I was routed and forced to flee. He moved east across the Dasht-i-Lut (the Desert of Lot) and into Afghanistan. The Isma'ili imams would never again be seated in Iran. From the border the imam now went to Qandahar, where the British had a major presence. The empire's political agent there provided the Aga Khan with financial assistance, and he was paid tribute by pilgrims from some of the borderlands I discuss below: the Pamir mountains; the Afghan capital, Kabul; the area around Bukhara; and the Sind region of the subcontinent (Daftary 1990: 506–10). The connections formed on these journeys had the effect of consolidating and recentralizing the Isma'ili community through their renewed contact with their imam.

This was the explicit beginning of intensive, intimate relations between the Aga Khan and the British Empire, which began now to determine the channels of the Aga Khan's movement. There have been suggestions, however, that cooperation between these two entities began earlier, when the British tried to use the Aga Khan in their own designs against potential Iranian influence in Afghanistan. From Qandahar, the Aga Khan notified the British of his intention of taking over and administering Herat for them. The British representatives approved the plan, but then they began to lose ground in Afghanistan to rebellious Afghan forces, including in Qandahar, and he was forced to evacuate for Sind, the site of significant Isma'ili populations. Once there, he remained a client of the British, who made use of his military force and diplomatic clout, which ultimately protected them and helped them to seize the entire region. For this service, the Aga Khan received a large yearly stipend from the British through General Charles Napier and thus further increased the size of his treasury. With the help of his brothers, he further assisted the British in their campaigns in Baluchistan. In 1844, Aga Khan I initiated a move of his base (and the imamate) from Karachi via Gujarat, where he paused for some time, to Bombay, where he arrived in 1846. The Qajars, fearful of his movements in India and his return, decreed that he be redirected to Calcutta, further from Persia, but he soon returned to and settled in Bombay. For years he attempted to negotiate his return with the Qajars, giving one of their monarchs a giraffe and an elephant and later a rhinoceros and three more elephants (Daftary 1990: 509–13).

Aga Khan I now made his home in Bombay, where he set up an opulent residence and *durkhana* (reception hall), the impressive Aga Hall (see Aga Khan III and Aziz 1998), with secondary homes in Bangalore and Pune. These public structures were some of the first modern spaces for the fertile growth of a transterritorial Isma'ili community. He held weekly *darbar* audiences for his followers.[6] The Prince of Wales, the future King Edward VII, visited him, and he continued to enjoy the favor of the British, who bestowed upon him the title "His Highness." He began to associate himself and the imamate at this time with European royalty, with European class expectations and aspirations, and with wealth and high society.

Boivin (2003) defines the first Aga Khan's move to India as a critical turning point, when the nature of Isma'ili translocal and institutional organization truly began to change (187). In Bombay he began receiving many visitors from far and wide. The nature of the interactions between the Khojas, the Imamate, and the British (in all their permutations) were transformed in the process. The Aga Khan's presence in India may also have played some role in the formation of the Indian Khoja community as the eventual globalized Isma'ili elite. During his time in India, the first Aga Khan also further structured the operation of translocal Isma'ilism: increased the prominence of the *mukhi* as treasurer and socioreligious leader, developed a role for the *kamadia* accountant, and made the *jama'at khana* into an even more central community space. This whole system was mobilized in the collection of community dues (Daftary 1990: 513–14). Beginning at this time, with increasing exposure to capitalism, the Isma'ili central leadership engaged in a progressive process of bureaucratization, a discernable transition from "traditional" forms to more "modern" ones (Weber 1978). From Bombay, the first Aga Khan also began reshaping Khoja customary law and practice, implementing new forms of religious rigor and ritual (Shodhan 2001).

Empire and Community: The Aga Khan Case

In the same period, the imamate's early entanglement with the discourses of empire began to come into resolution. The question is, to what degree were orientalist colonial discourses and institutions responsible for the *produc-*

tion and *creation* of the Isma'ili global community in its modern form? The Aga Khan's move to Bombay was a fundamental turning point; it radically altered the very nature of Isma'ilism. As Amrita Shodhan (2001) writes, "the [colonial] courts actively defined religion" (82).[7] Shodhan is concerned with the means by which the colonial courts constructed and conjured boundaries that promoted uncritical acceptance of communities as fundamentally and historically "real." She observes:

> Legal disputation during the Aga Khan case represented the Khoja polity within an episteme which we may call "community." As a "community" its true religious beliefs were represented not as based on practice, or determined by consultation between believers, but as determined at an original moment which could be discovered by the objective study of experts. Individual Khojas claimed membership in their religion—Islam—and were not subject to any confusion that they were part Hindu. This later contention was introduced by those who studied Khoja Islam and found that it did not fit the classic Arabic Islam. This discovery of Khoja religion by reference to an externally defined Islam represented them as unable to determine their own interpretation of their religion. (83)

The so-called Aga Khan case, with its beginnings around 1861, a first court hearing in 1862, and a full trial in 1866, revolved around the claims of a set of Bombay Khoja "reformers" to rights over collective property; they sought independence from the Aga Khan in order to legitimize those claims and asked that the Aga Khan distance himself from the daily affairs of the community. Both tithe funds and the use of the *jama'at khana* house of prayer were at issue. In the wake of religious reforms and changes established by the Aga Khan, they were resentful over the scale of his collection of resources from the community and questioned his status as their rightful leader. He was framed by his accusers as antimodernist and, to a degree, leading a group of followers that were something other than Muslim (Shodhan 2001).

The court decided for the Aga Khan, claiming (or rather prescribing) that all Khojas were his followers, that he was their rightful leader, and that the dissidents' claims represented a perversion of proper Isma'ilism. The colonial court thus on its own authority decided what constituted "proper Isma'ilism." The question of establishing the Isma'ilis as a socioreligious structure of a certain *type* was essential to the case; the decision finally delineated the Isma'ili Khojas as a *sect* of the Isma'ili *community*. As Justice

Arnould explained in his decision: "In order to enjoy the full privilege of membership in the Khoja community, a person must be one of that sect whose ancestors were originally Hindus, which was converted to, and has throughout abided in the faith of, the Shia Imami Ismailis, and which has always been and still is bound by ties of spiritual allegiance to the hereditary Imams of the Ismailis" (quoted in Shodhan 2001: 83). The case was profoundly important, a critical and defining moment in the community's modern history, which among other things cemented the Isma'ili relationship with the British Empire. The judgment was taken by Aga Khan III "to be the most authoritative and succinct statement available of the [first] Aga Khan's claim" (84). At the heart of the case, perhaps, was the anomalous status of Khoja doctrine and practice in the hegemonic orientalist lexicon of Islam; Khojas simply did not fit. The court case, then, could in some case be seen as crucial to the standardization and classification of Isma'ilism into a category more comfortable to the colonial administration. The decision served to judge "Khoja behaviour and practices against a master historical narrative centered on the identification of the Shiah Imami Ismaili and on the identification of the Imam of the Ismailis" (85). It revolved around questions of the ontological status of culture, around the colonial administration's perceptions and imaginings of the true, pristine, and organic *origins* of the community. Establishing the absolute, factual truth-value of the community's origins trumped consultation with the community over its current views. The community was asked to answer for its own authenticity against the standard of orientalist scholarship *on* the community.

The ultimate significance of the case, according to Shodhan, was its removal of communal decision-making power from the community and the reallocation of that power to the court (see also Boivin 2003: 187–92). The court now defined the religion; law now took the place of community norm and dictated the very configuration of the Isma'ili community.[8] The decisions made in the case about tithes provided legitimization for the collection of *zakat* from across the community. It dictated, canonized, legalized, and standardized, based on colonial scholarly "expertise," who and what counted as Isma'ili, and decreed that the Aga Khan was the community's authoritative leader: the case "established the relationship between the Khojas and the Aga Khan, and between the Aga Khan and Ismailism so firmly that neither could be questioned. Any group that broke away had to declare a change of faith" (Shodhan 2001: 111).

Up to that point, the Aga Khan had been a symbolic figure of some religious importance for the Khojas, but not their supreme and authoritative leader. The Aga Khan may have sought an alliance with the Khojas, who were then more "modernized," wealthy, and inclined toward European norms than the imam himself.[9] The agency of the Khojas, who sought to benefit from the autonomy and entitlements a communal leader would bring, cannot be overstated here. The British, for their part, saw potential benefit in consolidating the community under the leadership of a figure over whom they could exercise a degree of control. Thus the special position, sealed by the court case, of the Aga Khan in the Isma'ili community fundamentally emerges largely out of the interaction and alliance between the Khojas and the British administration. It was that colonial moment—and not some distant past or essentialized cultural characteristic—that thus crystallized the role of the Aga Khan and set the stage for the construction and consolidation of a global community centered around him.

Genealogies of Diaspora

Engseng Ho's (2006) captivating exploration of the diaspora of Hadrami Sayyids around the Indian Ocean rim elegantly illuminates the intricate and complex linkages between diasporas, empires, and national states. Closely tied to these are concerns with the ethnographic meaning of history: with narrative and the construction of place, with genealogy and text, and with all of their imbrication with structures of power. In undertaking a consideration of Isma'ili diasporic history, our approach can derive a great deal from Ho's methodological innovations and excavations of the interstices of everyday life and distant pasts. Like Hadrami Sayyids, Isma'ili narratives of genealogy and migration are mobilized in projects of place-making and in community-building enacted through the conjuring of connections with distant populations (and pasts).

But where Hadrami diaspora has had an established fixity that allowed it to invest its stories in objects of perduring materiality, the fluidity and secrecy of modern Isma'ili organization has not produced the same types of geographic epistemology and place-based narrative. It is in more elusive moments, movements, and texts that Isma'ili histories of diaspora are told. If the Hadrami *leitmotif* is the gravestone or the genealogy, then perhaps the Isma'ili root paradigm lies in the fleeting moments (but life-changing principles) of the *farman* issued by the imam or the *didar* (audience) he holds on occasion with the faithful. Or perhaps it is counted in bodies healed, subjects helped, children educated, blankets distributed. For it is in the context of diaspora that the Isma'ili notion of "welfare" and the process of connecting subjects through service reaches maturity.

In the post-Mongol period, Indian Isma'ilism began to form a diaspora of traders around the rim of the Indian Ocean, especially in East Africa. Early in the nineteenth century, with an invitation from and the favor of the Omani sultan Sayyid Sa'id, who wanted to promote commerce and who received support from the British Empire, many Isma'ilis, both Musta'lian Da'udi Bohras and Khoja Nizaris, moved to East Africa as traders in the newly formed Omani Indian Ocean state.[10] The traders were free to practice their religion and came largely from Gujarat and its subdistrict of Kachchh on the Arabian Sea coast of India, long an important center for trade, commerce, and cultural intercourse. When the sultan moved to Zanzibar from Muscat and, in an attempt to profit from global commerce, invited Indian traders to come to the island, even more Isma'ilis made the island their home. By the time of Aga Khan I, there was a *jama'at khana*, a *mukhi*, and a *kamadia* on Zanzibar, and Isma'ilis formed the majority among Indian settlers. Soon thereafter Isma'ilis began to populate the cities of East Africa, where they thrived in business and trade. With full-fledged British colonialism in the area, Isma'ili migration intensified even more (Morris 1968; Chaudhuri 1985, 1990; Daftary 1990: 314–15); thus the British Empire acted as a channel for Isma'ili globalization.

By 1870, with enhanced transportation infrastructure between the Swahili coast and the Indian subcontinent, with improved interregional connections fostered by the British, with food and water shortages in Gujarat, and with an explosion in commercial activity in the Indian Ocean, the Isma'ili (and Indian) population of the region expanded greatly. The British had also improved the transportation infrastructure *in* Africa, which allowed for the establishment of new Isma'ili communities elsewhere in East Africa; they were, by the end of the nineteenth century, very widely distributed throughout the region, numbering more than fifty thousand by the mid-twentieth century. (Daftary 1990: 523–25). These populations were of great importance in the creation of global Isma'ilism.

Boivin (2003) further highlights the role of a vicious series of Indian famines and epidemics in propelling the Khoja diaspora. But more significant, he observes, was the imamate's active role in urging Isma'ilis to settle in East Africa. Indeed, though it appears that the genesis of the migration was not imam-directed, Isma'ilis were among the most prominent industrial and commercial pioneers of the area. Significantly, Aga Khan III construed an explicit parallel between the American settlement of the West and Manifest Destiny, on the one hand, and Ismaʿili settlement of Africa, on the other. Early pioneers of African Ismaʿili settlement in this period, like Allidina Visram and Tharia Topan, also laid the groundwork for the construction of social service institutions and built schools and hospitals (Boivin 2003: 269–71).

Perhaps the most important intellectual contribution to the study of diasporic Ismaʿilism is H. S. Morris's (1968) classic, *The Indians in Uganda*. As I explore in more detail below, Morris points to the influence of the remarkably well-organized Ismaʿili society in East Africa on other communities and to its legal ramifications in British imperial contexts. Most essential to Ismaʿili organizational success in Africa, observes Morris, was their self-formation in the era of Aga Khan III as a "corporate community," which undercut efforts at the development of either a united Indian front or a united Hindu or Muslim front in Uganda, when each communal group wanted its own entitlements (34).

Modernization, the Humanist Project, and Institutional Proliferation: The Period of Aga Khan III

Aga Khan I lived until 1881, when his son Aqa ʿAli Shah, Aga Khan II, became, for a short time, imam. He married Shams al-Muluk (also known as Lady ʿAli Shah), a princess of the Iranian Qajar dynasty and mother of Aga Khan III, and died four years later. He had worked to effect the further amalgamation of Ismaʿilis from disparate areas into a single community even before his accession to the imamate and traveled around the subcontinent in particular to set up *jamaʿat khanas* and increase the centralization of the community. During his short tenure as imam, he worked to increase connections between the imamate and the many communities of Ismaʿilis around the world, including in Central Asia, the coastal regions of Africa, and Burma and began to open schools for Ismaʿilis, especially in Bombay, and to develop services for the poor (Daftary 1990: 513–18).

His son, Sultan Muhammad Shah al-Husayni, Aga Khan III, who was raised in Bombay, now became the imam. It was this imam who most enthusiastically embraced the affiliation of the imamate with European royalty (and, by association, modernity, luxury, and modern notions of social class), and eventually moved to Europe. On his first trip in 1898, he went to England and France, visiting Queen Victoria and Prince Edward; on his next trip, two years later, he met and formed alliances with the Ottoman

('Abd al-Hamid II), Qajar (Muzaffar al-Din Shah), and Prussian (Kaiser Wilhelm II) monarchs. On his third trip, two years after that, he was invited to the coronation ceremonies of Edward VII, who promoted him from knight to "Grand Knight Commander of the Indian Empire." George V later promoted him to "Knight Grand Commander of the Star of India." Lord Curzon also placed the Aga Khan on his inner Legislative Council and during World War I gave him princely status for the Bombay region despite his lack of territory. During the war, he rendered assistance from his residence in Switzerland to the British Empire in its operations against Germany (which tried to assassinate him) in Iran and elsewhere. He traveled to Europe more and more, establishing himself in aristocratic social circles where he was welcomed, and married an Italian (Daftary 1990: 517–21; Aga Khan III and Aziz 1998: 7).

Aga Khan III became an important advocate for the Muslim people of India in general and eventually a spokesman for them. Over the course of several decades, he was involved with the All-India Muslim Educational Conference, acted as a representative of Indian Muslims at a major meeting with the British viceroy, helped establish the All-India Muslim League and the university at Aligarh, led the All-India Muslim Conference (concerned with Muslim interests in the independence of India), was a representative at and president of the League of Nations (1937), and wrote widely published works on politics and society in India. In 1935, on the golden jubilee celebrations of his imamate in Nairobi and Bombay, devotees presented him his own weight in gold. In 1946, he was presented his own weight in diamonds in Dar-es-Salaam and Bombay. In 1951 he was able to visit a traditional seat of the Iranian imams in Mahallat. In 1954–55, he was presented his weight in platinum. Apart from Switzerland, Aga Khan III also had a home on France's Côte d'Azur. He was married four times, always to Europeans (Daftary 1990: 520–22; Aga Khan 1954). The value accumulated from jubilee presentations in precious materials was allocated for community development projects, including schools (i.e., "Jubilee Schools").

After some rebellious activity aimed at undercutting Aga Khan III in Iran, Ali Shah installed a loyal religious leader (holding the title mu'allim) in the area and urged the Iranian Isma'ilis to rid themselves of their Shi'i practices and bring their religious activity into conformity with a centralized norm. They now had to learn to name the Isma'ili imams and were asked not to carry out the passion plays of Ithna'ashari Shi'ism during 'Ashura' because, as they were told, their imam was alive and in this world. And he asked that instead of focusing on the externalities of religion they try to understand the inner meaning of ritual, a key doctrine in Ismaʿilism. Soon thereafter, he began to establish social welfare projects and Ismaʿili committees in Khurasan; he asked local Ismaʿilis to use their tithe to build schools and develop programs to help farmers. The committees, in Tehran and Mashhad, began to carry out the social services initiatives established everywhere in the Ismaʿili world (Daftary 1990: 533–43; Rafique Keshavjee 1981). Of interest in this episode is the mobilization of social welfare in the service of ensuring loyalty and cultivating allegiance. Social services became the vehicle of connection between the imam and his followers.

The process of community-building was further continued by visiting remote communities in East Africa and Burma. Imam Ali Shah also began to elaborate the social welfare projects of the community and encouraged assimilation of Ismaʿilis to local societies (especially where, if they remained outsiders, they might be persecuted) and to modern conditions. Like Aga Khan I, he worked worldwide for the further standardization and universalization of Ismaʿili practice (Boivin 2003). The gold, diamond, and platinum jubilee celebrations in 1935, 1946, and 1954–55 in India, Africa, Pakistan, and elsewhere in which masses of Ismaʿilis came together, alongside the Aga Khan's 1951 visit to Iran (Daftary 1990: 517–22), can be seen as important events during this period for the formation of a sense of connection between subjects from different areas.

With Aga Khan III there began to emerge more generally a new system of translocal organization, and the beginnings of what might legitimately be called a global complex, with elaborately structured national councils and constitutions, the worldwide distribution of *farman* edicts, and a postcolonial system of global communication. These councils were of particular importance because they provided a local political structure that would act as a constituent of a global system (much like the "Village Organizations," discussed below). The role of the councils was legally formalized in the constitutions of the Shia imami Ismaili Community (Daftary 1990: 522–23). The first of the constitutions, meant to prescribe rules of conduct, seems to have entered into circulation in 1905 and into print in 1922; a new constitution was released in 1926, with yet others in 1937 and 1946, and with a new African constitution in 1954 (Morris 1968: 81). It is likely that they were also meant to play a role in consolidating and unifying the community and in preventing attrition or schism. It was in part the official status of the Aga Khan and his community in the British Empire that made all this possible; here again we see the British Empire act as a medium for the construction of a global community.

Morris (1968) suggests that the ultimate power of the constitution was to institutionalize the imam's authority: "In a system of government such as this in which power is distributed so that no individual or group can act without being checked by another, the position of the imam as final authority is well guarded" (84). Competition over influence in the Isma'ili governmental hierarchy established by the constitutions, he observes, was (at least in Africa) intense, and it likely still is. It was, moreover, dependent largely upon the preferences of the imam. But the attainment of office in this system carried with it great status and influence. According to Morris, the process of bureaucratization was an element in the socialization of the community to European norms (84–87).

The many services of Aga Khan III included housing societies, health care, schools, social and sporting clubs, hospitals, pharmacies, and libraries; they were provided to his adherents in Africa and the subcontinent as well as their non-Isma'ili neighbors. The schools, argued Morris (1968), emerged in part out of Isma'ili efforts to avoid assimilation (34–35). Before 1905, the Khoja community was governed by the structures of *mukhi, kamadia,* and *jama'at khana.* With the release of the constitutions, the Aga Khan established new hierarchical titles for his regional emissaries and representatives, including *wazir, rai, alijah, amaldar, sarkar,* and *diwan,* along with *mukhi* and *kamadia.* The latter two were until very recently chosen by regional councils and were in charge of the *jama'at* of a given area. Like earlier representatives in distant areas, they administered religious practices and gathered tributes. (Daftary 1990: 526–32; Boivin 2003: 259, 274). Morris shows how the regional councils played a critical strategic role in maintaining and protecting Isma'ili legal autonomy in East Africa.

The constitution of 1926 also authorizes the creation of provincial councils and several distinct *Panjebhai* committees to care for the poor, the infirm, and widows; to provide the poor with funerals, education, and expenses for daily life; and to facilitate employment (Boivin 2003: 275). The constitution of 1937 authorizes the creation of the supreme council, to which the provincial council is subordinate, and in which Boivin sees "un instrument majeur de la centralization de la société ismaélienne" (a major instrument for the centralization of Isma'ili society) (276). Under Aga Khan III, the community was thus ultimately divided into the following tiers: local *jama'ats,* local councils (of which the *mukhi* was now head), provincial councils, supreme councils, and the imamate (257).[11] In this period, moreover, a fund was established to build schools in larger villages (280).

Now, more than ever before, the provision of social services became an element in the integration of subjects across territory into a single community.

Sultan Muhammad Shah visited Africa in 1899 in an effort to quell dissent and secession. On the eve of his arrival a group of dissidents, not entirely like those earlier ones in Bombay, occupied and laid claim to the *jama'at khana* in Zanzibar, an attempt that spurred the Aga Khan to appoint deputies to manage Isma'ili communal property, all of which he insistently held as his own. Later attempts by the imperial government in Uganda to collectivize Indian property, to lump all diasporic South Asians into one category, evoked even further resistance on the part of the Aga Khan, and by the 1920s he had installed a deputy as "His Highness the Aga Khan's Estate Agent." Such positions, along with the regional and provincial councils, were thus in part mechanisms to protect his private property and the community's autonomy (Morris 1968: 78–80).

Monies from the Aga Khan's 1935 Golden Jubilee were funneled into the effective and profitable Jubilee Insurance Company. Tributes from the next jubilee, in 1946, occasioned the creation of a financial lending corporation to benefit the Isma'ili poor, some of whom were disillusioned by disparities between themselves and the rich of their own community. The subsequent jubilee, in 1955, saw the creation of a "building society" for Isma'ili settlers. The imam

> regarded the formation of the financial companies as an essential
> part of the economic education of the members of the community,
> who until then, according to other Indians, had been even more
> handicapped by thriftlessness, lack of capital and ignorance of West-
> ern law and economic processes than most other immigrants. The
> formation of the insurance company helped educate and consolidate
> an upper class; the finance company founded in 1946 extended com-
> mercial education to the poorer classes. (Morris 1968: 80)

The imperative to socialize the community to capitalism was thus a very real force in the politics of diasporic administration. Other forms and positions emerging from the African context were the minister for education and the treasury (in Zanzibar) (Morris 1968).

Also active in the African milieu, and salient to the discussion of the development of modern Isma'ili institutions, was a broad range of associations and other forums for membership and participation. Some of these "were the routes to power for any ambitious Ismaili" (Morris 1968: 82), but the fiscal cost of participation was high. The Ismaili Red Cross and Boy Scouts and the *Mota Kamno Panjebhai* (Great Works Association) emerged as important sites for participation during this time. When I first met them, Sher Ali and Sultan Ali already had years of experience in the Isma'ili Boy Scouts in Hunza. According to Morris, "The membership of the devotional associations cut across wealth and class divisions within the sect, and united it in prayer and charitable works around the person of the imam. The associations were internally ranked by grades and initiation into each was by fee and ritual. Each initiate was given a secret prayer to meditate on and through it attain direct contact with God" (83). Ultimately and most significantly, Morris concludes that the organizational "success" of the Isma'ilis in Africa was a result of the particular nexus of the institution of the imamate and the colonial administration. Their protection of the sacrosanct status of the Aga Khan motivated a concerted campaign to maintain independence and autonomy through the establishment of communal legal safeguards (86–89). Once again we are reminded here of the primacy of colonial law in the formation of modern institutional Isma'ilism.

Beyond services, however, Aga Khan III began to develop a vision of Isma'ilism as global and modern. The notion and discourse of the Isma'ili constitutions discussed above are a cornerstone in this vision. In his memoirs, the Aga Khan III writes:

> My normal work as Imam of the Ismailis consists of a constitutional
> leadership and supervision of the various councils and institutions
> of all the numerous and far-scattered Ismaili communities, self-
> administered as they are in each region. In addition, I am in constant
> communication with thousands of individuals in the community, on
> all sorts of diverse matters about which they seek guidance, and it
> is — as I have indicated — a community spread across the globe from
> the Great Wall of China to South Africa. (Aga Khan 1954: 203)

Elsewhere he writes:

> From all parts of the Ismaili world with which regular contact is
> politically possible a constant flow of communications and reports
> comes to me. Attending to these, answering them, giving my solu-
> tions of specific problems presented to me, discharging my duties
> as hereditary Imam of this far-scattered religious community and
> association — such is my working life, and so it has been since I was
> a boy. (25)

In the life and times of Imam Ali Shah we thus see the intensification of the drive to unify and consolidate disparate communities under a single common banner and the beginning of the process by which their introduction to the tenets of modernity becomes an imperative.

Under Aga Khan III, Pir Sabzali, a Khoja missionary, provided in 1923 one of the first modern connections between a distant imamate and the remote Isma'ili areas of the Himalaya, including Chitral, Hunza, Gilgit, and the Pamir. His journey, framed as one undertaken at the directive of the Aga Khan, appears as a survey of the Himalayan Isma'ili realm. At its center were the imperatives both of reporting back to the Aga Khan about the state of these communities and of informing the communities that he was their leader. Sabzali, traveling through the mountain communities, read the Aga Khan's *farman* as proclamation and explored with the local societies issues like loyalty, the tithe, and religious practice. This represents one of the first moments where the effort to bring those isolated societies into the fold, to ensure their loyalty and propose their inclusion, becomes visible. Even at that time, however, it was framed as a *renewal* of contact and a *revival* of unity—the alpine villagers were being *informed* of their connection to the imam. Some of the local Isma'ilis interpreted the visit as the prophetic return and remanifestation of the imam through his messenger. The visit is remembered and remains important even today in the Pamir, where it is recounted with some frequency.[12]

Michel Boivin (2003) paints a sweeping and detailed portrait of the primacy of rational humanism and modernization in the policies of the third Aga Khan. He delimits the features of a uniquely "aga-khanienne" view of the world in general and Islam in particular, develops a notion of Isma'ili "aggiornamento" (modernization or adaptation), details the Aga Khan's "projet humaniste" (in the interpretation of Islam among other domains) and "discours moderniste," and explores their manifestations in the imam's writings and speeches, as well as their consequences for the Isma'ili community. Boivin points out that it was a modernity not entirely isomorphic in its qualities with European modernity; indeed, though it borrowed heavily, it was often in opposition to the European version that the Aga Khan developed his own, patently unique Islamic modernity (263). Aga Khan III and Aziz (1998) note that Aga Khan III pointed his followers down "the path to a liberal and rational interpretation of Islam, the acceptance and practical interpretation of which would bring them into the mainstream of modern life without in the least betraying the fundamental tenets and injunctions of their religion" (xxvi).

Boivin (2003) makes note of the third Aga Khan's focus on his role in enabling followers' salvation and his expansion of the provision of *hidayat,* or guidance. Ubiquitous in his writings are the ideals of rational humanism, progress, and their various corollaries. Notions like "brotherhood," "pacifism," "humanitarianism," "liberalism," and "human rights" arise with regularity in his discourse, and they reveal the basic concern with social inequality and "advancement" that informs the subsequent proliferation of institutions of "development" enacted by Aga Khan III and IV. Of special note in this regard is the Aga Khan's emphasis on "cooperative capitalism," his interest in women's rights and girls' education, and his focus on healthy bodies. As we will see below, the concept of "cooperative capitalism" is still very much at work on the village level in the development projects of the current Aga Khan (IV) and forms a guiding principle in his global efforts at rural development (largely in Ismaʿili communities).

Of particular interest, as noted by Boivin (2003), is the Aga Khan's oblique discussion of an Ismaʿili state. Such a proposal is, in the contemporary Ismaʿili community, more or less off-limits, at least to outsiders, and considered both dangerous and subversive. But, as Boivin writes, "[c]'est parce que l'Aga Khan indentifie les aspirations ismaéliennes à celles d'une nation qu'il recherché un territoire et qu'il rêve de créer un Etat" (256). [It is because the Aga Khan identifies Ismaʿili aspirations with those of a nation that he seeks a territory and that he dreams of creating a state.] In his autobiography, the Aga Khan remarks upon the Ismaʿili quest for

> a national home — not a big, a powerful State, but something on the lines of Tangier or the Vatican — a scrap of earth of their own which all Ismailis, all over the world, could call theirs in perpetuity, where they could practise all their customs, establish their own laws, and (on the material side) build up their own financial centre, with its own banks, investments trusts, insurance schemes, and welfare and provident arrangements. The idea of a territorial state made no particular appeal to me; but in view of the strength of Ismaili sentiment on the matter I made my approach to the Government of India. For reasons which I am sure were perfectly just and fair, the Government of India could not see their way to granting our request. (Aga Khan 1954: 305)

Indeed, under the British Empire, like other princes the Aga Khan was given a degree of political autonomy. As perhaps the only "First-Class Ruling

Prince" with no state, he made a petition to the British administration to request a small land grant. As in the previously discussed Aga Khan case, the "experts" were dispatched to examine Islamic history to determine the empirical worthiness of the request. Not surprisingly, they found that Shi'i history revealed no precedent to justify such a grant. Moreover, as a sovereign, the Aga Khan would no longer be a British subject. Various territories around the subcontinent and the Indian Ocean, allegedly to be organized as small principalities like the Vatican, were rumored and proposed as possibilities; nothing materialized. And despite his grandfather's tendencies, explicit interest in and discussion of a territorial state seems fully to have vanished in the era of the current imam. Nonetheless, Boivin (2003) underscores a thrust toward centralization and hierarchization and seeks to locate the final success of the "Etat ismaélien sans territoire [non-territorial Isma'ili state]" (257). He concludes, ultimately, that no such thing came to be, but that the Aga Khan, all the same, did succeed in a project of secularizing and modernizing certain aspects of his institution.

Aga Khan IV: A Corporate Globality

Aga Khan III died after an imamate of seventy-two years. His tomb is in Aswan, Egypt, where the Fatimids built their empire — a choice indicative of conscious Isma'ili orientations to the past. Sultan Muhammad Shah played a critical role in starting the engine of modernization, institutional proliferation, and unification in the Isma'ili community. His grandson Karim, who became imam in July 1957, has maintained Aga Khan III's focus on rational humanism, the virtues of well-managed "collective" capital, and modern individualism.[13] He has intensified and expanded, moreover, the institutional scope of the imamate, to the degree that it reaches into the lives (in different ways in different places) of most every Isma'ili subject. But it was his predecessor that set, in an earlier moment, the tone and timbre for contemporary Isma'ili institutional globality.

The followers of Prince Karim al-Husayni, Aga Khan IV, refer to him as "Hazir Imam" or "Imam-e-Zaman," both of which roughly mean "Imam of the Time." In everyday speech in English he is usually denoted by "His Highness," or sometimes just "HH." According to Aga Khan III and Aziz (1998), he is the "architect of modern Ismaili institutions. On assuming the *imamate* of the Ismaili Muslims he set out to expand, develop and adapt to modern conditions the institutions he had inherited from his grandfather, with a view to their playing a new role in the service of independent nation states" (181). Certainly under his leadership the delicate relationship between Isma'ilis and individual states has been refined and redefined.

The Aga Khan Foundation (AKF), the subject of much discussion below, was established in 1967; the Aga Khan Award for Architecture, in 1976; the Aga Khan University, in 1983; and the Aga Khan Fund for Economic Development, in 1984 (Boivin 2003: 292–94). Under the current Aga Khan, a new constitution appeared. The Shia Imami Ismaili Constitution of 1962 established a regional Health Administration and a regional Education Administration. The universal constitution of 1986 institutionalized a complex hierarchical structure for Isma'ili communities throughout the world (applied to twenty countries), with its own educational, legal, political, and religious structures (Daftary 1990: 526–32; Kaiser 1996).[14] It also reinstitutionalized the authority of the Aga Khan over his subjects.

The constitution of 1986 regularizes and homogenizes the creation of councils in key Isma'ili areas, enumerated as Madagascar, Tanzania, Kenya, France, the United Kingdom, Canada, the United States, Portugal, Syria, the Persian Gulf countries (Bahrain, Kuwait, Qatar, Oman, Saudi Arabia and the United Arab Emirates), Singapore, Malaysia, Pakistan, and India.[15] In the intervening time, Tajikistan and Afghanistan have surely been added. Whether or not Iran or China will ever be added is unclear. The 1986 constitution also formalizes the Isma'ili Tariqah Religious Education Boards, creates financial monitoring bodies, and creates a new uniquely Isma'ili legal institution: National Conciliation and Arbitration Boards (Daftary 1990: 525–31). The national councils, their leaders appointed by the imam, constitute another medium for political participation in transnational Isma'ili institutions for influential urban elite Isma'ilis. Thus, the transnational structure contains constituent political forms on a number of levels (including that of the village, as we will see below).

The seat of the current Aga Khan at Aiglemont is, in an institutional sense, the "capital" of the Isma'ili community. It is the site from which the imam administers all of his institutions and constituent regions, the administrative and also religious center of the community from which all decrees and religious rules are issued. Aiglemont is a château located just outside of Paris near the old castle town of Chantilly. It is a secular, religious, economic, and social center of the Isma'ili jama'at, a hub of the Isma'ili socioreligious structure. As an administrative center, it encompasses and pervades all other institutions discussed here. It is the secretariat in Aiglemont that provides the crucial connection between those institutions. Aiglemont is a key institution in the formation of transnational connections, as it is critical in unifying and linking populations in vastly different settings.

The dynamics of Aiglemont reveal the charismatic role of the Aga Khan. They also shed light on the imamate's vision of its own political significance. AKDN-approved sources explain that as a "*statesman* and philanthropist, His Highness the Aga Khan" represents "a centuries-old *tradition of leadership*, associated with his office, to encourage human development, through individual self-fulfillment, as the key to social harmony and *progress*" (University of Central Asia 2004: 17; emphasis added).

Aiglemont evokes narratives of awe and transformation in Isma'ilis who are able to pay a visit. To some of them it can amount to the pilgrimage of a lifetime, a trip to the seat of their living spiritual leader. Even to elite and prominent Isma'ilis who are frequently invited to Aiglemont, the experience is considered profoundly auspicious and important; it evinces the centrality of devotion to the imam and the process in which status and prestige are gained by proximity to him. A visit to Aiglemont provides a basis for the development of shared experience among those who see themselves as privileged enough to be welcomed inside. A Khoja Isma'ili, one of the institutional elite, who visits frequently, described it to me as nothing less than "a court." The parallel is not insignificant.

Within Aiglemont, the Aga Khan is surrounded by an inner council of advisers who counsel him on social, political, and other practical matters. As mentioned, the key advisers are largely from the Khoja populations of Indian (and most often Gujarati or Gujarati-Kachchhi) ancestry; fewer seem to come from the Nizari populations of the Himalaya, which reflects that privileged status of Khojas within the community. Aiglemont has a number of departments, directed by various key advisers. Among these are a committee responsible for liaisons between Aiglemont and the Isma'ili Tariqah Religious Education Board (ITREB; see Chapter 3), between Aiglemont and the AKDN, and, notably, a department dealing specifically with Aiglemont's diplomatic relations.

The very existence of a diplomatic wing at Aiglemont is fascinating in the context of this discussion. It points to the status of the Isma'ili imamate on the global stage as a nonstate player, which nonetheless is recognized by and has the ability to interact with states.[16] The diplomatic wing at Aiglemont is responsible for the facilitation of extensive treaties, accords, agreements, and negotiations in which the signatories are usually the Aga Khan and a nation-state. How can we explain and account for the presence of a diplomatic wing in a nonterritorial global community? Why should it exist?

The Isma'ili institutional discourse on the matter usually suggests the following: after a long history first of resistance to the established powers in the world, and then of persecution by such powers, stable and sustainable diplomatic relations can help to secure the safety of subjects in their various and scattered situations across the planet and within (potentially unfriendly) nation-states. This is certainly valid. But it may not be the whole story: such processes and relationships also bestow upon the Isma'ili community a heightened status and a permanence in the eyes of other institutions and polities.

The imamate at Aiglemont plays a crucial socioreligious role; as we will see in greater detail in Chapter 3, its constituent institutions help to prescribe a standardized Isma'ilism. Some of first modern moves toward the creation of a broadly shared, standardized Isma'ili practice, now manifest in the institutions I am discussing here, can be located in the period of the first Aga Khan in Bombay, where in the face of conflict between Khojas and the imamate, the Aga Khan decided to demand an oath of loyalty (*bayat*) and to formulate a document that would prescribe the proper form of Isma'ili rituals, including those surrounding prayer, ritual bathing, funerals, and marriage (Daftary 1990: 515). The imamate and secretariat at Aiglemont also help to coordinate and prescribe the rules and processes that govern Isma'ili communities around the world. These bestow a certain amount of sociopolitical and legal homogeneity, unity, and shared process upon disparate Isma'ili societies.

This chapter aimed to illuminate the critically important place of empire, capital, and ideologies of modernity in the formation of a uniquely Isma'ili globality. I have used the rubric of the lives of the Aga Khans as (heuristic) markers of historical periods, but not as exclusive determinants of Isma'ili history. From the historical perspective, it is undeniable that colonial states played an essential part in determining the shape of the Isma'ili community, in unifying its disparate parts, and in establishing its channels of communication and movement. I have attempted, here, to trace pathways of connection between the imamate and the institutions that shape Isma'ili subjects' lives. In preparation for an examination of their role in local context, I now turn to an exploration of the conceptual geography of these institutions.

CHAPTER TWO

Fluid Cartographies

Isma'ili Institutions in Global Context

Spaces of Globality

No instrument has been more significant for the unification and consolidation of disparate communities under a single Isma'ili banner than the construction of common institutions. These institutions provide the basis for a shared experience despite diverse cultural backgrounds and help develop a sense of commonality or "simultaneity" (see Anderson 1991). They also provide a set of "publicly shared symbols" (Urban 2001) around which the community can rally.

But beyond this the institutions provide a vehicle to bring those distant communities into the fold of the imamate (and the sphere of the Khojas); to socialize them to ideologies of modernity and capitalism; to teach them how to be Isma'ili in a modern way, or modern in an Isma'ili way; to ensure their active, loyal, and enthusiastic participation; and to produce from a fragmentary constellation a unitary ecumene or polity. In these global institutions in part Isma'ili subjects (local and transnational alike) are made Isma'ili. They are sites for the production of certain types of identity. They are the spaces through which transnational Isma'ili subjects move and in that movement become global. They are themselves the spaces constitutive of the Isma'ili nonterritorial assemblage.

The significance of these institutions is, of course, not all about the consolidation of allegiance, socialization to modernity and capitalism, and the incorporation of communities into a centralized Isma'ili structure. The institutions serve many, and in the process, the survival of thousands of poor people is ensured. Like the Grameen Bank, the Aga Khan Foundation has been lauded for its efforts in sustainable, participatory development (including microfinance). It has frequently intervened in critical situations to save lives and enhance choices.

These institutions are key (but not the sole) elements in the formation of contemporary Isma'ili lifeworlds. To say that they are exclusively determinative of Isma'ili culture and identity, however, would be to represent Isma'ilis as being without agency, as mere pawns at the disposal of an institutional structure. In this chapter I present at least the basic social infrastructure of transnational Isma'ilism, the raw material out of which a vast and nonterritorial network is built. In the following chapters I focus on the institutions' critical engagement with Isma'ili selves and subjectivities, to reveal ethnographically the interstices of everyday lived reality and formalized structure, and to explore how they constitute for Isma'ilis everywhere a unique encounter with modernity.

States of Development: The Institutional Perspective

The formal secular (especially "development") institutions of the imamate, particularly AKDN, while comprising neither a state government nor a corporation, are engaged in the government and management of a borderless and scattered population. They address most every need of the individual and of the locality; no area of social or bodily life is left unattended. Moreover, AKDN and other institutions of the imamate provide a forum for political participation in a larger sphere. The ways in which the imamate governs the widely dispersed localities of the Isma'ili community are complex and diverse; this section is devoted to their ethnographic description.

I explore here the components that combine to form an integral and unitary institutional system, the wiring of the transnational machine that surrounds and involves subjects, the architecture of the system making deterritorialized participation possible. All of these metaphoric descriptions point to a process of interactive connection across space and through time. This chapter provides an inventory of interactive processes connecting subject and transnational community, a synchronic description of global process to complement the historical material elsewhere.

AKDN is the umbrella organization for a set of secular institutions created and administered by the Aga Khan and his imamate that provides services and helps to direct "sustainable development" in diverse areas around the world. It is not the case that AKDN serves Isma'ilis exclusively. Almost everywhere that it works, AKDN works with Isma'ilis and non-Isma'ilis, Muslims and non-Muslims. However, AKDN almost always works in areas where at least some population of Isma'ilis is present. Tom Kessinger, a non-

Isma'ili who served as general manager of AKDN at the time of my research (July 2004), defined the mandate of AKDN as "development, in the broadest sense of the word, *for* Isma'ilis." Moreover, he explained that locations for development work are chosen where AKDN has a "comparative advantage" — for example, where there is a receptive Isma'ili community or at least an Isma'ili elite. He noted that work with non-Isma'ilis can, of course, contribute to Isma'ili interests. For instance, AKDN work in non-Isma'ili communities may serve to legitimize their assistance to Isma'ili ones.

While it is also true that AKDN and its institutions are committed to secularism in their self-definition, the fact that they evoke religious associations among the Isma'ilis with whom they work is undeniable. The visual symbols of AKDN and its connection to its institutions are invariably tied to devotion to the imam. As Salmaan Keshavjee (1998) observes: "Necessary though it may be for Tajikistan's survival, the fervor with which local peasants have adopted new and foreign practices — have integrated these into their lives — is undoubtedly associated with the reappearance of the Imam" (73). Elsewhere he asserts that the enthusiastic reception given to AKF in Tajikistan because of its connection to the imam "contributes to the acceptance of the 'new world order' by the local community" (439). As a Shughni-speaking member of Khorogh's intelligentsia advised me about the inhabitants of surrounding villages, "when they see AKDN institutions they see the Imam." One of the implications of this association: while AKF certainly plays a role in introducing capitalism and other endogenous forms to remote regions like the Pamir, criticism of its policies is equated with criticism of the imam. Thus, by inference, criticism of the modernization and socialization to capitalism that these institutions bring can also be seen as criticism of the imam (Salmaan Keshavjee 1998: 92). The net effect may ultimately be the silencing of the articulation of some local critiques of social change.

AKDN certainly acts as a sociopolitical glue that binds together the scattered subjects of the Isma'ili transnational complex. Perhaps more than any other Isma'ili institution, it connects them to the central administration, creates the basis for shared experience, and forms a context for movement and interchange between subjects. As we will see below, it is the very medium through which Isma'ilis are able to come into contact with each other on a global level. AKDN is one of the key structures that facilitates the formation of a unitary, cohesive, integral global network, and this occurs both through its formal policies and its informal by-products, such as the flow of personnel through its network. Such integrality and cohesion means that there can be a single channel through which individuals move and in which interactions occur across the planet.

The question of the overall intentions and objectives of AKDN is an important one and points to a number of interesting areas for discussion. There is no doubt that it strives to some degree to achieve certain nearly utopian ideals, to effect a transformation and reinvention of the social fabric in the areas where it works. In many contexts it has accomplished such a transformation, reorganizing and reconfiguring aspects of local life from bodily practice and cultural ideology to political participation and decision-making, producing in the process a new social order. Salmaan Keshavjee (1998), in his broad exploration of "transition" in Tajikistan, including the imbrication of some of the Aga Khan's institutions with ideologies of capitalism, suggests that the "meta-narrative [of capitalism] is not just creating wealth and emphasizing individualism, but threatens to act as a great solvent, remaking fundamental values, and reconfiguring social relations" (4).

As I have explained above, AKDN is also importantly a conduit and an embodiment of modern discourses of "development" and progress; it both reflects and perpetuates the dominance of rationalist ideology through that liberal discourse of "development" that produces new social configurations, local realities, and modes of subjectivity.[1] Such a discourse espouses a certain view of the autonomous individual as the locus of decision making and accords a special status to rationality in the promotion of progress and self-improvement. The explicit fusion of liberal modernism and Islamic ideologies that this represents stands in stark contrast to the revivalist visions and revisions of Islam that so frequently command the focus of the media's attention.

Perhaps connected to this zeal for modern liberalism and rationalism is the central role AKDN plays in the socialization of localities and local societies to market capitalism. Participation in capitalist systems is enthusiastically endorsed by the institution, which helps them in the transition to engagement in regional and even global markets. Consider the following excerpts from an information booklet for AKDN's University of Central Asia (n.d.):

> Mountain regions almost everywhere *lag behind* the great down-
> country urban centres and agricultural flat-lands in economic and
> social development. Remote from capital cities and central govern-
> ments, they are easily neglected. Such neglect is deepened by the

fact that many high mountain regions are situated on distant border zones where security considerations outweigh the concerns of civil administration.

In such circumstances, modernity does not empower people so much as it threatens them. Old skills and practices wane under the growing impact of modern communications and transport, but adequate new ones are slow in coming. Millions of mountain people find themselves caught between two worlds, with the prospect of losing out in both. This situation exists across the mountain regions of Central Asia but also in other mountain regions of the world, from the Himalayas to the Caucasus, Balkans, Atlas, and Andes.

Deep poverty in the mountains has given rise to widespread suffering, which in turn causes a profound sense of hopelessness. Many mountain people flee to the major cities, where they become slum dwellers and swell the illicit labour market. Others find themselves forced to emigrate to find work, or to send their children to the capitals. The world seems to be telling mountain people, "You cannot participate in modern life by remaining where your forefathers lived; you must leave." As they do so, age-old mountain societies and cultures wither and die. And some of those people who stay may, in desperation, turn to the cultivation or trafficking of drugs or, out of sheer hopelessness, embrace extremist and militant causes. (1)

On the one hand, this text decries "modernity" for its exploitation of the traditional. On the other hand, it assumes the primacy of a teleological "development" and reveals the modernist, liberal, antifundamentalist orientation of the organization. AKDN, especially through AKF and the Aga Khan Fund for Economic Development (AKFED) has introduced basic market and business skills and processes to localities as remote as Chitral (Pakistan) and Murghab (Tajikistan). In yoking such places to systems of exchange, AKDN encourages a certain idea of "progress," values a certain vision of social happiness, and aligns remote peripheries with a global norm.

A striking aspect of the institutions of the imamate is their full provision of most services conventionally associated with the state. While he is skeptical about the applicability of parallels between these institutions and states, Salmaan Keshavjee (1998) writes that "AKF exemplifies a situation where private non-governmental organizations are acting in roles that in this century have generally belonged to the nation-state" (439). AKDN is neither a state nor a government, but in structure and process on the local level it sometimes plays an analogous role in people's lives.[2] The constituent organizations of AKDN in the Himalayan areas in which they work, including the Aga Khan Rural Support Programme (AKRSP) in Pakistan and the Mountain Societies Development and Support Programme (MSDSP) in Tajikistan, are often more present, visible, and prominent than the national governments in question.

It is perhaps in the area of infrastructural and ecological development that Isma'ili quasi-utopian aspirations are most visible. One of the major activities of AKF, the prominent arm of AKDN responsible for "sustainable development," is the transformation of local rural infrastructure and environmental conditions. In areas like northern Pakistan, southern Tajikistan, and western India, they are literally turning the desert green and altering local ecologies. In this realm of activity, the Aga Khan's institutions determine the very color of the landscape, the source of drinking water, the evening lights of the market, the plant life by the river, and even the material of the dwellings. In their alteration of infrastructure and ecology, AKF's services are analogous to the wiring of a nation-state; every service is provided, and the cumulative result is the creation of a complete sociopolitical environment, an environment created, in the impressions of its inhabitants, by their distant yet beneficent leader and by the global community of which they are members.

Among other landscape-altering and change-inducing infrastructural projects carried out by AKF in these Isma'ili Himalayan regions are many bridges. These are often built in conjunction with a large international NGO, an intergovernmental organization (e.g., the World Bank), or a governmental aid organization (e.g., DFID or USAID), and they are usually highly visible, colorful, and sleek. Many of the bridges in Pakistan's Northern Areas, for instance near Passu in Gojal, between Hunza and Nagar, or across the Ghizar valley to the mouth of the Ishkoman valley, have been built with the participation of AKRSP. By the turn of the twenty-first century, more than twenty had been built and more were in the planning in northern Pakistan by AKRSP (Aga Khan Rural Support Programme 1996, 32). In Tajikistan, the new bridges are even more prominent, in some ways, because they span the international boundary with Afghanistan and thus play a role in reuniting (or semiotically suggesting the reunification of) long-separated Isma'ili areas and ultimately in reinforcing and expanding the Isma'ili regional sphere of circulation and interaction. At the time of my fieldwork, border bridges had been built, for example, at Ishkashim and at Tem near Porshnev and Khorog. Another was in the process of being built across the border in Darvaz at Qala'i Khumb in the summer of 2003 when it collapsed. These bridges contribute to the formation of transnational contact even at the regional and local levels, bringing, for instance, Afghan and Tajik Badakhshani Isma'ilis into closer contact, and both of those in closer contact with aid workers (often Isma'ilis) who cross the border.

AKF is also involved in major programs of road construction in the Himalayan areas of Pakistan and Tajikistan. AKF's collaboration in road construction, particularly in connecting very remote valleys and villages, is notable in the transnational and transterritorial context. Through the construction of roads, subjects in different areas participating in common processes can begin to consciously formulate and discuss their commonalities and shared participation in historical processes. Thus roads contribute to simultaneity and the construction of collective identity. AKDN's construction of roads — traditionally another area covered by the state — is also significant because roads are often associated with "progress" and modernity (i.e., signifying whether the "modern world" and "progress" have "reached" a certain area), and with bringing remote areas up to pace with everywhere else. Roads are thus part of an implicitly teleological and linear "development" discourse and may be represented as a fundamental human need. Moreover, roads are linked to capitalism; they are part of the process in which isolated localities are connected to larger market systems, processes, and patterns.

The discourses and dynamics of progress, development, and capitalism enacted by the construction of roads in rural areas are obviously closely connected with each other. They are different aspects of a common set of discourses and processes that some theorists link to a transformation in the subjective, phenomenological experience of space and time that accompanies globalization (e.g., Harvey 1991). AKF's roads could be seen as an actual physical mechanism effecting such a change in the local experience of space and time. On a less abstract level, from the point of view of the relationships between AKDN and the world or its local subjects, roads are highly visible, good platforms for the foundation to publicly demonstrate its benevolence toward and involvement with local societies. Roads, moreover, are closely associated with the introduction of remote areas to larger markets. Finally, from the perspective of Isma'ili modes of globalization, roads are a way that communications from the imam and his institutions can reach remote societies more easily; they allow subjects to come into closer contact with Isma'ilism through their facilitation of migration and access to urban areas. In all these ways, then, roads are a channel of social globalization.

AKF's staggeringly vast role in shaping the physical, infrastructural context of people's lives extends, in the Pamir and the Karakoram, to the provision of electricity, especially hydroelectricity, as well as other forms of power. In Gorno-Badakhshan, for instance, AKF is involved in a major hydroelectric project near Khorog. Many villages in Pakistan's Northern Areas and Chitral have small "micro-hydel" projects. Another major infrastructural focus area of AKF is water; the foundation is actively involved in the provision of potable water in countless villages in Pakistan and Tajikistan (as well as the other areas it works). During the summer of 1995, I watched AKF staff channel drinking water from a clear spring to (Sunni) Faizabad Bala village in the central part of the Astor valley in Pakistan; another example of AKF's provision of a most basic service, one usually associated with governmental administration.

Water collection, purification, and distribution are critical issues in the high deserts of the Pamir and Karakoram ranges where AKF works. Local societies in these mountains have traditionally maintained a careful ecological balance by directing snowmelt water from high glaciers to villages along the mountainsides in carefully engineered traditional irrigation channels. Some of these channels are hundreds of years old and have long been the lifelines of the villages. Despite the lack of rainfall, as a result of this system many villages in the region appear as green oases in an arid and rocky terrain. In such a context, water is a profoundly political issue intimately connected with power and wealth. AKF's involvement with irrigation and the greening of the high desert thus becomes part of a larger project of social reorganization and takes on an even more utopian and visionary character.

AKF (through AKRSP in Pakistan or India or MSDSP in Tajikistan) is heavily involved in intensive irrigation projects, from small to large scale. This includes the restoration of old village irrigation channels and the construction of new ones, as well as larger-scale water distribution. Closely connected to this are programs of reforestation, or sometimes simply forestation, in areas where there has been no plant life within the range of human memory. In the Chapursan valley, in far northern Pakistan adjacent to the Chinese and Afghan borders, or in the remote village clusters of Phander and Teru on the boundary between the Northwest Frontier Province and the Northern Areas of Pakistan, these forestry projects (locally called "plantations") are highly visible for the colorful contrast they provide. Here again, what one might have thought was an impossible utopian vision is being realized. Such work begins to reveal the totalizing project of AKDN, whose activity re-creates the physical environment and in providing drinking water even enters the body.

The various branches of AKDN engage in a number of activities related to local and regional income-generation. As has been intimated, such activities amount to a process in which AKDN promotes and facilitates local socialization to the processes and patterns of capitalism and world markets. Salmaan Keshavjee (1998) identifies the emphasis of the institutional network as "defining a new path for Badakhshan: privatization, participation in the free-market, and pluralism" (89). This necessarily implies the promotion of certain values, ideologies, and modes of behavior. At the same time, it is, in many cases, a way for people to gain prosperity, greater freedom of choice, and improved health. Many such projects are very local in scale and involve the promotion of small business enterprises and entrepreneurship in villages to generate income and reduce poverty. Such programs, which often involve some kind of loan, might include, among other things, assistance with the formation of herds of livestock; this was particularly true in Tajikistan, where mountain people obtained nutrition from the deterritorialized and centralized Soviet system and had lost their traditional animal-based techniques. Other programs involve assistance for small businesses engaging in food production and sale, especially those utilizing the orchards and producing jams or other products from the abundant fruit that grows in mountain areas in northern Pakistan (particularly the Hunza, Gilgit, and Baltistan regions). Assistance is also provided for fisheries and poultry production.

Another major focus of local financial assistance is tourism and the marketing of indigenous crafts — one form of globalization encouraging the development of another. At the time of my research, for example, AKRSP in Pakistan supported crafts businesses in Hunza (Threadnet Hunza) and Chitral (Shubinak); they were meant to fight poverty, to enhance the status of women, and to generate tourist interest. In a very interesting process, they take a trope of local culture, simplify or polish it for mass production, and thus create a new form of representation of indigenous societies. In this way, programs like those in Shubinak and Threadnet Hunza encourage local people to consider what images of themselves they would like to publicize to outsiders, and in the process they choose new symbols and emblems of themselves. Such AKF projects can potentially foster a sort of locally generated reinvention of local culture.

AKDN also promotes large-scale economic participation in world markets. The main arm through which AKF conducts such work is AKFED, an organization that makes capital investments. Like the smaller-scale, market-based programs, the activities of AKFED can also be described as part of a "socialization to capitalism" process, both for localities and for less-wealthy regions. The economic activities of AKFED are meant both to help to counter poverty and to generate income for AKDN programs. The third Aga Khan, the grandfather of the current imam, established, in a precursor to AKFED, investment and insurance corporations favoring Isma'ilis to help increase the wealth of the community (Daftary 1990: 526; Boivin 2003).

AKFED is responsible for the administration of the high-profile Isma'ili-owned Serena Hotels, which are intended to energize and bolster local economies. Many of the hotels are in remote areas. Serena owns six safari lodges in Kenya and six in Tanzania; they also run six hotels in Pakistan (Islamabad, Karachi, Quetta, Hunza, Gilgit, and Faisalabad), one in Afghanistan (Kabul), one in Tanzania (Zanzibar), one in Mozambique (Maputo), and one in Uganda (Kampala). One of the stated goals of the chain is to promote "national growth" (⟨http://www.serenahotels.com⟩). The chain is closely linked with Isma'ili prosperity and business interests. Other AKFED projects include the development of large-scale hydroelectric and other energy projects, cell phone networks (such as Indigo in Tajikistan or Telecom Development in Afghanistan), food packaging companies, printing, manufacturing, insurance, airlines, and countless other endeavors. The portfolio is long and diverse.

This "economic development" activity is one way that the social processes of the transnational polity are connected to global norms and pathways of capitalism. Through such activity the institutions of global Isma'ilism encourage a culture of market capitalism and conformity with market systems. But perhaps more importantly, this area of activity demonstrates the material and monetary benefits that come with membership in the Isma'ili assemblage.

Bodies Politic

Among the areas of human relations transformed by the global Isma'ili institutional structure is that of gender. The Aga Khan's institutions, AKDN, AKF, AKES, and AKHS, along with other branches, are visibly concerned with the alteration and improvement of the status of women in the areas where they work. This too articulates with the entry of modern ideologies and concepts—including those of feminism and human rights—into the discourse of these institutions. It is worth noting that in this context the imamate is privileging the rights of the individual over the rights of the cultural group or area as a whole, a prevalent trend in post–World War II conceptions of political rights and statuses. This is relevant not only because it shows the incorporation of such European discourses into the language of a Muslim community, but also because many Muslim communities reject the very question of individual rights vis-à-vis the group by recourse to the language of cultural or communal rights, couched in part in the history of nationalism, communal law, and negotiation with imperialism. As mentioned before, a critical element of the modernist discourse of Aga Khan III was a concern with women's status.

It is largely in its rural development work in settings like Northern Pakistan and Afghanistan that AKF's focus on gender and on changing the disadvantaged and constrained situation of women comes into view. In Tajikistan it is also a focus, but the Soviets, in their radical transformation of gender roles, already did some of the changing. AKRSP has created a number of Women's Organizations (wos)—to parallel the men's Village Organizations (vos)—where women meet in a decision-making council to plan projects that are generally meant to assist them. Of course, we note that the men meet in a more universalized and generalized "*Village* Organization," and women, as a marked subcategory, are relegated to their own sphere in a "*Women's* Organization." All the same, the level of autonomy this process accords to women is unprecedented, the change is profound, and most of the alternative scenarios afford women even less power. In fact, some Sunni and Twelver Shi'i groups in the AKRSP project area have reacted adversely to its policies on gender.

The significance of this focus on women's rights should not be underestimated. Both the vos and wos represent a way that the Isma'ili global network is involved with social relations, the body, and bodily practice. AKF is not limited to the simple provision of services; here it is engaged in nothing less than the reorganization of roles and gendered subjectivities, of the relationships between women and men, of their differential statuses, and of the gendered division of labor in society. This change is on the level of the basic patterns and foundations of social organization; it is a major alteration in the social fabric, a reinvention of society itself, and demonstrates AKDN's significance in effecting real historical change in the lives of regions and localities.

The global Isma'ili complex (like other polities) thus takes as one of its starting points the body.[3] This means that a global sociopolitical structure, as institutional and massive as it is, is experienced on the most intimate levels of sensation and circulation. AKF's programs, in a sense, course through the very bodies of its subjects; they are relevant even to life and death, suffering and health, pain and pleasure. The Aga Khan Health Service (AKHS), another branch of AKF (and thus of AKDN), runs clinics and health care centers and employs doctors and nurses throughout their program areas. Almost everywhere that there are other AKF services, there are AKHS clinics. Here again the imamate is the primary provider of a service usually provided by national governments. This too could be important in encouraging local loyalty and enthusiasm for the benefits offered by this community in comparison to others.

The health care focus of AKDN is also relevant to my discussion of European notions of progress and rationalism that suffuse the language (and thus the underlying orientations) of the imamate. It represents not only an *involvement* with the body but also an active *socialization* to specific bodily *norms* of appropriate behavior and practice, from cleanliness to sexual health. Salmaan Keshavjee (1998) provides remarkable insight on the imbrication of the socialization of subjects to bodily norms through health schemes with the introduction of Pamiri societies to capitalism and larger market formations. An AKF Revolving Drug Program, he reveals, sought to "change the old ways of thinking" on medicine (145). Isma'ili health initiatives work to teach subjects how to take care of their bodies according to a certain perspective. Under a major initiative of AKF Tajikistan, for instance, teams of health educators in Gorno-Badakhshan travel to remote villages to teach children how to comport themselves and how to avoid illness. This is not without its absolute value, of course, as living longer and not dying of an avoidable illness are goals that are hard to argue with. Moreover, they are not outside of the rubric of Islamic tradition, all schools of which (including militant ones) have historically concerned themselves with proper bodily behavior and practice; what is unique here, however, is that traditional religious focus *combined with* specifically modern (but nonetheless universalized and naturalized) European and American values and norms.

Sites of Symbolic Production

Also significant, in addition to the development work of AKF, in the global semiotic process of the Isma'ili network, and in the generation of transnational signs, symbols, narratives, and meanings, is the work of the Aga Khan Trust for Culture (AKTC) and all its subsidiaries. AKTC assists in the creation of a specifically imamate-driven vision of Islam, of culture, of history generally, and of Ismaʿili history in particular. AKTC is responsible for the promotion of certain cultural and artistic activities, including those in the area of cultural heritage. One of the most visible activities of AKTC is the Aga Khan Award for Architecture (and the corresponding organization, Archnet).[4] The Aga Khan Award for Architecture honors significant architectural initiatives and restoration projects, largely in the Islamic world, but outside as well. The award for architecture also funds restoration programs.

The Award for Architecture is unusual in the context of Ismaʿili globalization and Ismaʿili history in that it seems to involve a recontextualization, reclamation, or reinvention of elements widely regarded as more generally Islamic. This fits well with an Ismaʿili tradition of opposition to mainstream discourses of Islam and its insistence on an alternative vision of the religion and its history. Moreover, it articulates with an image of the Ismaʿili imam as a leader (and *the* true leader, at that) of the Islamic world, an author of the meaning and history of Islam itself; in his involvement with AKTC, he intertwines his position with the heritage of Islam at large. In the process, he builds a connection between historic elements of the Islamic world and Ismaʿili contemporaneity.

Another initiative of AKTC, in cooperation with the U.S. State Department and the Smithsonian, is the Silk Road Project, which promotes the recording and marketing of music (in particular, but also other art forms) from the historic trade route known as the Silk Road. One of the effects of this project, of which the cellist Yo-Yo Ma is both the founder and artistic director, is that it institutionalizes the concept of the Silk Road as an entity, a regional identity, even an emblem that the peoples of (particularly post-Soviet) central and southwest Asia can mobilize and rally around in their reinvention of local culture. The project is not without its own transnational implications. On its website, Yo-Yo Ma writes, "as we interact with unfamiliar musical traditions we encounter voices that are not exclusive to one community. We discover transnational voices that belong to one world" (⟨http://www.silkroadproject.org/about/vision.html⟩).

AKTC constructs, beyond the Ismaʿili transnational social structure, an official *culture*, including a set of signs and symbols socially shared by participants across territory. Out of the activities of AKTC (and particularly the Award for Architecture) emerges a clear concern with the past, and more specifically, with the way that history is told.[5] The monuments, sites, projects, and areas chosen bear more than a tangential relationship to Ismaʿili identity and metacultures of history. In fact, in their intensive interest in the past, AKTC could be said to be involved in the creation of alternative historical counterdiscourses, in the recasting and retelling of history. Finally, the semiology of Isma'ili institutions, including AKTC, reveals an intense interest on their part in Enlightenment discourses and modernism and in their corresponding values of individualism, cooperation, rationalism, democracy, and industriousness (with reward).

The official photographs of AKDN are remarkable for their creation of a unique set of transnational Isma'ili signs, ideologies, and discourses, and play a key role in the consolidation of a global Isma'ili metaculture, in the visual semiosis of the Isma'ili transnational structure. They are essential in the synthesis of a coherent Isma'ili institutional self-image, an image that circulates within the community itself. A substantial effort goes into making these photographs, many by the photographer Jean-Luc Ray. Out of these images, which I reviewed in depth in northern Pakistan in 2001, emerges once again the focus on the values of the Enlightenment and modernity: individualism, democratic political participation and cooperation, "progress" and "development," virtuous leadership, health, education, and the benefits of capitalism. They reflect and help to produce a patent AKDN ideology, to exemplify an Isma'ili metaculture, the image that the community desires to fashion of itself as a historical and modern entity. At the same time, they reveal the kinds of orientalized images — exotic landscapes, poor but colorful villagers industriously directing their own development, primordial and isolated settlements — that play some role in motivating Isma'ili development efforts and that garner the interest of global audiences.

One of the key channels through which AKF and AKDN disseminate their unique set of ideas, signs, symbols, and discourses is their massive publicity and publication activities. Each year, almost every branch of AKDN (including AKDN and AKF themselves) publishes glossy and attractive books, brochures, and annual reports. These publications circulate widely through the world among Isma'ilis, visitors to Isma'ili projects, and potential donors. They too are part of the creation of a certain transnationally shared culture. Despite their nominal nonsectarianism, *within* the Isma'ili community and as a public image to the rest of the world *of* that community, these materials are key building blocks in the formation of an Isma'ili *metaculture* (Urban 2001) and thus help to mediate, filter, and formulate the community's self-image according to its collectively determined desires. Moreover, these publications exemplify the way that technologies of print and publication enable the synthesis of a sense of commonality across territory (Anderson

1991). They are also significant for what they reveal about the strict control of and interest in image and information by the central Isma'ili institutions.

AKDN distributes and disseminates its signs and symbols everywhere in the regions where it has some presence and sometimes farther afield. In alpine areas like Tajikistan's Gorno-Badakhshan and Pakistan's Northern Areas the implicit and explicit signs of AKDN are everywhere. Travelers in the Northern Areas especially are struck by their prevalence. Along every roadside, inside every village, next to bridges and water channels, in high pastures and by mountain springs, one sees signs bearing the Islamic hand symbol of AKF and indicating the presence of an AKRSP or MSDSP project, depending on the region. These are the most prominent (and often the only) signs in the landscape. They emphasize the ubiquity of the Aga Khan's organization and the extent of its penetration into every area of local life. They become a primary fact of the landscape.

The signs, then, also indicate the wide geographic reach of the Aga Khan's institutions into rural areas of the Pamir, Karakoram, and Hindu Kush. But the process in which the Isma'ili transnational complex distributes and disseminates its signs and symbols, with all of its efficacy in publicity, is not without its own social drawbacks. Because of their prevalence, the signs generate real tension between AKF, the nation-state, and other actors. Pakistan and Tajikistan are both concerned with maintaining total authority over their territory and with controlling their image among subject peoples. In light of this, social formations and institutions perceived to be competitors for their subjects' allegiance are not welcomed. Such outsiders may become the target of suspicion and may be seen as a symbolic threat or worse. For this reason, the state may regard the omnipresence of AKF's signs as a trespass on its own domain and role.

Not only the roadside and building-front signs but also the high-profile, expensive motor vehicles belonging to AKF play important communicative roles in transregional interactions, both as carriers of the institution's signs and insignias and as signs themselves. In poor rural areas of the Pamir and Karakoram, the clean, white, four-wheel-drive vehicles of AKRSP and MSDSP (usually Toyota Land Cruisers, Hi-Aces, or Jeeps), bearing the green AKF hand and the name of the institution (or the symbols of the Aga Khan Education or Health Services, AKES or AKHS) on both sides are readily visible. AKRSP and MSDSP drivers enjoy prestige and draw admiration for their skill in navigating difficult mountain roads in valleys as remote as Misgar (Kilik-Mintaka watershed, Pakistan Himalaya) or Yazghulam (Tajikistan Pamir). The vehicles, equipped with every necessity, including high-tech antennas for advanced communication, are known to be faster and more functional than any other in the region. They are a coveted resource and, in some contexts, a bone of contention. As a trapping or mark of privilege and enfranchisement, they can generate jealousy, competition, and resentment. They present an image of the prestige and power, as well as the prominence and even dominance of the imamate's institutions in the circum-Himalayan region.

Representatives of the imamate's institutions will generally argue that their symbols carry little specifically Isma'ili appeal. However, the consciously formulated denotations, the explicit meaning of the symbols, suggest otherwise. But even more important are their connotations, the implicit associations. My interviews in both Pakistan and Tajikistan suggest that even where not intended, AKDN symbols conjure the image of the imam to local Isma'ilis. The imam's institutions are, for Isma'ilis, inextricably tied to the leader himself, and despite the formally secular nature of the institutions, they associate them with him, his religious significance, and the resources he is thought to bring. In the wake of the Tajik civil war of the 1990s, the losing Pamiris were cut off from the rest of the country. Pamiris recount that it was their imam, the Aga Khan, who saved them, not the legally secular institutions he controls, which were the distributors of aid.

Architecture constitutes another important vehicle for symbolic representation in the Isma'ili community. Isma'ili structures are, in many settings, the most impressive and noticeable structures in sight. In particular, "Isma'ili Centres" in a variety of settings, including Lisbon, London, Dubai, Vancouver, and Dushanbe, are notable for their high profile and their symbolic richness. These centers usually house the central offices of Isma'ili *jama'ati* institutions, as well as a *jama'at khana* house of worship, a library, and so on. The University of Central Asia, with its planned campuses in Naryn, Kyrgyzstan, in Tekeli, Kazakhstan, and in Dasht-Khorog, Tajikistan, provides a good example. According to a publication of the university:

> Architectural planning for the three campuses is being carried out by Japanese architect Arata Isozaki. Born in 1931, Mr. Isozaki has won more than 20 architectural prizes in Japan, the United States, Britain, Italy, and Spain. Since 1963 his firm has created such major projects as the Olympic stadium in Barcelona, the Museum of Contemporary Art in Los Angeles, and the museum in Takasaki City, Japan. A visiting professor at Tokyo University, University of California

Los Angeles, Harvard, and Columbia, he is one of the premier expo-
nents of a contemporary international style in architecture, employ-
ing a language of design that speaks to modern people everywhere,
while remaining sensitive to the specific needs of environment and
climate.

Site designs for the three campuses and for the "university parks"
are being developed by a team of planning experts from the firm of
Sasaki Associates of Watertown, USA. (University of Central Asia
n.d.: 10)

AKDN's enthusiasm for liberal modernist values and for developing transnational connections is clear here. The presence of such high-profile and
strikingly visible structures in places like Khorog, with its utilitarian,
Khrushchev-and-Brezhnev-era architectural style, sends an unambiguous
message on the role of the transnational institutions in those localities: they
intend to be seen as important sociopolitical actors in the region.

The Isma'ili Centre in Dushanbe was still in its planning stages when I
left, but it promised to be one of the most modern and noticeable buildings
in the city. This visibility is notable in light of the ostracization of Isma'ilis
from national politics during and after the Tajik civil war; it represents a re-
entry of Isma'ilis into Tajikistan's politics as key (and wealthy) players. Unlike in other Isma'ili centers, religious and secular functions of transnational
Isma'ili institutions will be united here in a single space. According to staff
working for the organization in Tajikistan, AKDN attempted to acquire for
its center a restaurant and teahouse called Choixona Rohat, a Soviet-era
landmark and one of the most unusual buildings on Prospekt Rudaki, Dushanbe's central boulevard.

The Isma'ili Centre in London (not to be confused with the Institute for
Isma'ili Studies), another landmark, is an architectural showpiece suffused
with religious symbols, explicit and implicit. It contains carved calligraphy,
fountains, marble latticework, and a roof garden. Among other features,
the building contains an intricately ornamented *jama'at khana* worship hall
and a room specially designated for addresses by the imam that features a
podium bearing the official seal of the Aga Khan. In the *jama'at khana*, even
the carpets, walls, and columns bear esoteric symbols.[6]

Other significant types of buildings constructed by AKDN and by the
jama'ati institutions include schools, hotels, and the projects of the Aga
Khan Trust for Culture (AKTC). The school buildings receive professional
architectural attention and stand out in their locations. The AKES Girls'

School in Baltit (Hunza, Pakistan) and the lycée in nearby Gilgit are out-standing examples. The Serena Inns and Hotels are particularly noteworthy for their fusion of traditional and modern symbols. The Khorog Serena Inn, in Badakhshan, for example, is an iconic re-creation of a traditional Pamiri home. Like printed materials, these buildings are useful texts for the trans-lation of Ismaʿili metacultural desires and intentions. They show a conscious bricolage of symbols that contribute to the creation of a syncretic, global image and identity.

Secular Education in Muslim Modernity

The educational machinery of the Ismaʿili imamate is elaborate and exten-sive, and what I discuss in this section by no means covers the sum total of the educational resources and structures in the Ismaʿili global network. Here I only focus on the formal (and formally secular) educational insti-tutions of AKDN. I argue that these educational initiatives constitute one of the most significant of the many ways in which subjects are socialized to participation in a global society, a theme that I have been following throughout this chapter. The multitude of schools and universities of AKDN are primary sites at which the young are inculcated with enthusiasm for and even certain ideologies of the Ismaʿili transnational community's secular institutions. These educational institutions encourage students' participa-tion in that global community from a young age. They create (or produce) "enthusiastic subjects" (Foucault 1977, 1982). The curriculum promoted in the schools and universities of AKDN shows distinctive characteristics of certain liberal, modernist views of the world.

The distribution of schools established by AKES is at least as wide as that of the clinics and hospitals of AKHS, if not wider. Different schools accept girls or boys or both sexes, usually separately in Pakistan, according to cus-tom, and co-ed in Tajikistan, according to Soviet precedent. A number of places have "showcase" institutions and structures, with impressive archi-tecture and facilities unlike anything else in the region. The girls' school at Karimabad, Hunza, for instance, features manicured gardens, innovative architecture fusing indigenous and modern styles, and volleyball courts. Other highly visible schools include the lycées in Gilgit and Chitral (both in Pakistan), Khorog (Tajikistan), and Osh (Kyrgyzstan); they attract teachers from abroad and hold reputations as the best schools in the area. I have seen impressive AKES schools in areas as remote as Harf village in Thui valley (a tributary of Yasin, Northern Areas, Pakistan) and upper Ghizar.

AKF is also responsible for the creation of a number of extremely high-profile universities. The first of these is Karachi's Aga Khan University (AKU), Pakistan's only private university and arguably the best institution of higher education in the country. A co-ed institution, it boasts one of the top medical schools in the subcontinent. The second is the newer University of Central Asia (UCA), which serves "mountain peoples" and "mountain development" with campuses in Kyrgyzstan, Kazakhstan, and Tajikistan. UCA was established through an international treaty between the Aga Khan and the leaders of the three nation-states; here again we see the quasi-state character of the Isma'ili structure. The current and former directors of UCA are a set of prominent American academics and administrators, among them Vartan Gregorian, William O. Beeman, and S. Frederick Starr.[7]

UCA is unusual for its locations in Central Asia, which has no other universities of this sort, and in the rural locations of its campuses. I believe that it will profoundly alter the social patterns not only of the towns but even of the regions in which it is situated; it will become their defining institution. But beyond this, it will introduce new ideological norms and discourses to the region. The language of its promotional material is full of the discourse of the Enlightenment and modern concepts, even Anglo-American concepts of what a university and education are. In this sense, UCA will be responsible for the circulation of a new type of cultural language and a new type of institution in the area. Perhaps more important, however, is the central role UCA will play in transnational social interactions that combine to construct a connected global community. In particular, I see it as a critical and important site for the construction of a sense of commonality and simultaneity between individuals from widely separated locations. It will provide a shared experience for these subjects.

Some of the printed materials of UCA include an explicit discourse on transnationality and cultural diversity, as in this quotation from the Aga Khan's opening remarks in the front matter of an informational brochure (University of Central Asia n.d.):

Mountain peoples experience extremes of poverty and isolation as well as constraints on opportunities and choice, but at the same time, they sustain great ethnic, cultural, linguistic, and religious pluralism, and show remarkable resilience in the face of extraordinarily harsh circumstances. By creating intellectual space and resources, this university will help turn the mountains that divide the nations and territories of Central Asia into the links that unite its peoples and economies in a shared endeavour to improve their future well-being.

Most striking, however, is the following assertion: "Neither the problem of poverty in mountain areas nor its possible solutions are defined by *national borders*. In order to identify and build upon the common features and assets of mountain regions, an effective *trans-national institution* is called for" (5; emphasis added). This reflects what might be called a "metaculture of globalization," a conscious discussion of its process.

The same brochure also strongly reflects the imamate's favorable orientation toward capitalist processes and modern ideals of multiculturalism and tolerance:

> [The university] will provide mountain peoples with the skills necessary to generate income for themselves and their families and to create new jobs. It will give them greater leverage in their growing interactions with the down-country economic centres. It will provide skills and develop leadership that will enable mountain peoples to *participate fully in the modern world*. It will also help enable them to preserve and at the same time to benefit from the environment of which they are the guardians. All these changes will bring benefits that extend far beyond the mountains to the societies as a whole. . . .
>
> The new institution will help mountain people adapt to the emerging reality of *open societies and market economies*, in which individuals and groups are free to initiate activities and *enterprises outside the government*, as well as within it. This places a premium on understanding economics, finance, and an array of associated practical skills, including accounting and basic management.
>
> The new institution must also appreciate the very diverse cultural assets inherited from the past. Not only do these have a value in their own right but, because they embody all the skills and capabilities that people acquire over centuries, they are directly relevant to a successful *transition to modernity*. This creates a need for programmes that take account of cultural diversity and such key values as *pluralism and mutual understanding*. Together, such studies can foster responsible initiative *and enlightened leadership*. (3; emphasis added)

Consider also the following passage:

There are few, if any, opportunities for mountain peoples to gain access to a bachelor's degree programme that, in the words of the renowned twentieth-century educator Robert Maynard Hutchins, "prepares people not to do something but to *be anything*." UCA's bachelor's programme in the liberal arts and sciences is designed to enable young men and women to fill leadership roles in all sectors of the economy. By relating all studies to the specific conditions of mountain regions, the programme will empower graduates to function effectively and responsibly within mountain communities, while opening to them also roles at the national and international levels. . . . The teaching method at UCA will be *student-centered* and built around direct student-faculty interchange and new learning technologies rather than traditional lecturing and rote learning. (13)

We see an explicit juxtaposition between tradition and modernity here, with the privileging of a certain approach toward their mediation and moderation, a new paradigm for understanding the world. Discourse like this advocates the mobilization and promotion of modernist individualism and capitalism in the construction of an institutionally mediated transnational sphere. The university is charged to change not only the social fabric of the region but also its cultural fabric; its planners seek to introduce new concepts of education modeled on Euro-American modern and postmodern "liberal arts" traditions to the area. They seek to revolutionize the educational process itself by establishing forms that the region has never seen. Consider the syncretism portrayed by the following passage:

A *campus* (from the Latin word for "field") is a university community comprising classrooms, libraries, laboratories, faculty and staff offices, gymnasia and athletic fields, and cultural facilities. A *residential campus* is one in which students and many faculty members and staff are housed together and in close proximity with the other facilities and with each other to form a single, integrated *academic community*.

UCA will have residential campuses unlike anything now existing in the former USSR.

Why have residential campuses? The missions of both the Bachelor's and Master's programmes are broad, extending to many intangible elements — the development of practical leadership skills, the capacity to make ethical judgments, decision making in complex cultural settings—that are developed as much outside the classroom as within it. Residential campuses that have been carefully planned to form distinct communities will foster the mission of the degree programmes and of the UCA as a whole.

A residential campus can capture more of the waking moments of the students' day and channel them into educationally productive activity. Meals can be used for discussion, meetings, language tables, and study groups. Evenings in dormitories can be transformed into ad hoc seminars and discussions involving students who might not otherwise interact with one another. By such means, a residential campus greatly extends the formal curriculum and enriches it through informal learning.

UCA's international student body will be drawn from extremely diverse backgrounds throughout Central Asia and beyond. Some will come from regions that have experienced interethnic and intercommunal tensions. The skills required for intercultural living cannot be taught in the classroom. A residential campus that is distinct from any nearby town or city creates an independent environment that reduces or eliminates self-segregation by groups. The presence on campus of resident faculty members and advisors will further strengthen these processes, which are so essential to the region's welfare.

Each residential campus will be a kind of micro-polity, in which "best practices" in the realm of civic culture can be embodied in governance and everyday decision-making. Such a campus community offers rich opportunities for students to develop the many intangible habits of responsible citizenship.

Moreover, residential campuses of the sort envisioned for UCA inherently foster non-hierarchical and open communities. As economic liberalization advances and the distribution of income in Central Asia grows more unequal than formerly, the fact that all students are living under similar conditions becomes important. The expectation that every student will spend several hours each week working on tasks that serve the community as a whole will further minimize the importance of differences of wealth and status and foster a sense of common endeavour.

Finally, the campuses will serve as models of successful development. They will foster on a small scale the kind of social relations that graduates will be expected to promote in the larger community.

By this means, the campuses themselves will help communicate the institution's educational ideals to the general public. (6–9)

The language here is suffused with Western discourses on education and also with metadiscourses on what the educational experience should ideally be. Also interesting is the university's creation of the new social category of "mountain people" as a separate *type* of group with certain shared structural characteristics requiring special attention and institutional forms. Accompanying this is the field of "mountain studies" in which the university will offer a degree.

Occasionally AKF(often through a local wing like AKRSP) provides scholarships and exchanges for workers seeking to expand their knowledge of "development" processes. These scholarships are usually to Canadian or British universities with development studies programs such as the University of Guelph, York University, or the University of Sussex. Shamsuddin, a Wakhi Isma'ili friend of many years from the very remote Shimshal valley in Pakistan, was engaged for some time in a graduate program in a related discipline at Oxford. The recipients of such scholarships are usually Isma'ilis, and they usually connect with local Isma'ili communities in the cities where they are studying, providing them a sense of connection with other Isma'ilis worldwide in a process with parallels to Anderson's (1991) description of pilgrimage.

The Aga Khan Humanities Project in Central Asia (headquartered in Dushanbe, Tajikistan) develops curricula for existing schools and universities and trains teachers in the tenets of the "liberal arts." They strongly promote values of liberalism, individualism, and pluralism and reflect the general orientation of the imamate and the Isma'ili *jama'at* as a whole. Even in such symbolic activities AKF is thus working to alter the very foundations of culture and society in the region.

Incidentals and By-Products:
Institutional Impacts beyond the Institution

It is not only the institutions and texts of the Isma'ili community that encourage its existence and cohesion as a global, nonterritorial community. The importance in transnational processes of human flows and informal contacts, of extrainstitutional interaction between widely scattered sites and localities, cannot be overestimated. The community itself exists and functions without the institutions. There are countless connections, determined by migration or kinship networks or chance, between its subjects. The institutions themselves also act as spaces where informal social contacts are made; an Ismaʿili from Canada may come to work in the AKRSP office in Gilgit and in the process make a lifelong friendship with another Ismaʿili from London.

A critical mass, then, of individual and family social relationships is, in addition to the institutional processes, constitutive of the Ismaʿili assemblage as an integrated sphere of interaction; in fact networks of family and friends cannot be separated from institutional structure itself. These too are the building blocks of transterritorial polity, but as they either circumvent or transect (or even suffuse) the institutional structure, they are often invisible. Employment in Ismaʿili institutions provides a context for Ismaʿilis from widely separated areas to come together and develop a sense of common identity despite differences in language and culture. The institutions are an informal channel for the elaboration of transnational networks. An office like that of AKF in Khorog or Gilgit serves as a forum for the discovery of connections between Ismaʿilis who would otherwise never meet. Another context for the development of such connections emerges in global business contacts between the many wealthy members of the (principally Khoja) Ismaʿili community. Some of these relationships are fostered or subsidized by AKFED, but the key point here is that channels established by global market processes external to the community also lend themselves to the construction of intracommunity transnational relationships.

These contacts are, of course, not only incidental; they are enabled by the particular intersection of cultural meaning and economy that come together in AKDN. The vast machinery of AKDN demonstrates the status of the constituent organizations as absolutely critical regional institutions upon which the life of an area like Gorno-Badakhshan or the Northern Areas crucially depends, not least because of their role as primary employers. For this and other reasons, these organizations, like most institutions, acquire a life and momentum of their own; they need to survive, and they are also inextricably intertwined with local patterns and rhythms. A number of Aga Khan development organizations have tried to establish a self-sustaining development process in which the need for the central institution would eventually be obviated, but in almost every case, when the time came for the institution (notably AKRSP) to consider terminating its services, the conditions did not support such a change; the institution had become an absolutely integral part of the local context. The dynamics of these organizations thus suggests that AKDN institutions are now often permanent and central elements of local societies.

I see a process of "pilgrimage" as essential in the creation of a global Isma'ili social sphere of circulation and interaction and in the enhancement of consciousness about that sphere. Anderson (1991) describes a process in which individuals from a colonial outpost discover their commonality on their journey to and residence in the colonial city; this perception of commonality lends itself, he argues, to the formation of nationalist sentiment. He explains that among the pilgrims "a consciousness of connectedness ('Why are *we ... here ...* together?') emerges" (56). I argue that in the journey from remote Isma'ili localities to Isma'ili institutions in Europe, or to Isma'ili institutions in those remote localities *from* Isma'ili communities in European or American cities, a type of "pilgrimage" occurs in which Isma'ilis from distant areas become aware of and interested in the identity they share. This allows them to perceive the Isma'ili network as a worldwide unity despite its sociocultural diversity. It is not a nation-state that is under construction here, however, but something very different indeed.

This process of pilgrimage is engendered in particular through the value placed by the elite of the Khoja Isma'ili community on serving less-privileged Isma'ilis; this has become a widespread community practice, even a convention or a rite of passage not unlike organized journeys to Israel for Jewish youth (e.g., Birthright Oranim or Taglit Birthright). This pilgrimage is crucial in the construction of transcultural (but intra-Isma'ili) sharedness. It represents the flow of individuals throughout the polity, which serves to make Isma'ilis in disparate areas aware of their connection to it and to each other. A. Z., for instance, a Khoja Isma'ili of Indo-African descent who grew up in Vancouver, has developed extensive networks with other Isma'ilis in Tajikistan (through his work for AKF), in Pakistan (as an intern for AKRSP), and in Syria (as a coordinator for AKDN activities there). With each such journey a connection between him, Isma'ilis from those places, and Isma'ilis from other places who are working in the same location is enhanced and reinforced.

A caveat, however, emerging from the institutional situation: while Isma'ilis often display compelling allegiance to the imam, their relationship with him cannot be reduced simply to blind obedience.[8] Moreover, they demonstrate allegiance to the community itself less universally. In Tajikistan, for instance, discord between Isma'ilis was in plain evidence; critique of Isma'ili institutions (by Isma'ilis) was not uncommon. What forces stand in the way of transversal or horizontal allegiance, allegiance *between* Isma'ilis? Why does the allegiance so readily expressed by individual Isma'ilis to the Aga Khan (and even to the *concept* of Isma'ili unity) sometimes not translate into allegiance of individual Isma'ilis to one another? One explanation may be rooted in the contemporary nature of the Aga Khan's position within the community. His markedly central role focuses attention and allegiance toward him and diverts it away from the community. The charisma that has accrued to him as a result shifts the locus of authority and power out of the hands of the collectivity and into the hands of the imamate. Another explanation, however, can be found in the interethnic dynamics of the community.

This explanation deserves some careful consideration. The contradiction between the profound emphasis on unity, on the one hand, and an undercurrent of discord within the community, on the other, points to some critical questions about Isma'ili globality—and about the degree to which it in fact constitutes a single globality. The tension that emerges on the surface in the space of "development" institutions reveals larger rifts and fault lines. They in turn emerge out of the complex histories of Khoja interaction with non-Khoja Isma'ilis rooted in the colonial politics of community. As I discuss in the Introduction and in the Conclusion, Khoja interactions with Isma'ilis in the Pamir and Hindu Kush are sometimes fraught. Non-Khoja Nizaris in Tajikistan (and, less frequently, in Pakistan) express concern about the imposition of Khoja institutions, norms, and practices on their societies. The institutions are themselves objects of contestation, aspiration, and sometimes resentment. Himalayan Isma'ili subjects are, moreover, sometimes critical of imbalances of power and influence (and wealth) between themselves and the Khojas within those institutional spaces. The unsettling new configurations of class and status that the Khoja arrival in the Himalayas brings can produce anxiety.

The institutions discourage this type of conflict and encourage ethnic harmony in Isma'ili interaction. Such focus on unity, for instance through the institutionally generated notion of "frontierless brotherhood," can of course mask and obscure the real significance of these seemingly trivial tensions. All this does not negate the value of institutional services and community-building in Isma'ili borderlands. It also does not suggest that the interactions they introduce are defined by conflict. Indeed, for many Isma'ilis these changes are overwhelmingly positive, even life-sustaining. But that does raise the question of whether assumptions of the unity of

Ismaʿili globalization is an interpretive superimposition on a more fractured landscape. Could there be multiple Ismaʿili globalizations (i.e., diasporic, institutional, religious) in operation here, their overlapping interstices hidden in the seemingly simple encounter between remote societies and the institutions of the Aga Khan Development Network?

CHAPTER THREE

Universalizing Isma'ilism

Institutionalities of Devotion and Regimes of Standardization

Global Religious Institutions

Constituting its own separate sphere in the social life of the Isma'ili transnational structure is a complex of formal institutions whose job is to provide religious advice and to prescribe and regulate proper religious practice. Among the most important of these institutions is the Isma'ili Tariqah Religious Education Board (ITREB), or Committee (ITREC), as it is known in Tajikistan, which provides religious education and guidance to Isma'ilis everywhere. ITREB offices and locations can also act as important community meeting centers. A related institution, also very prominent in the development of global Isma'ilism, is the Institute for Isma'ili Studies in London (IIS), which we discuss below.

Jama'ati religious institutions like ITREB and IIS are significant in encouraging a certain degree of uniformity and homogeneity in the practice of Isma'ilism across the planet.[1] This, in turn, is significant because it engenders a sense of social connectedness and commonality between practitioners of Isma'ilism from distant areas. ITREB, generally with the backing of the imam and some help from IIS, works in widely variable cultural settings. In many of these settings, Isma'ili religion displays great diversity and includes many local elements. Sometimes ITREB's prescriptions are not entirely well received in local contexts because they come into conflict with long-established local traditions and lifeways.

This is not to say that the *jama'ati* religious institutions constitute a strict orthodoxy; the imam's dicta trump their prescriptions. However, they do prescribe and decree what are considered to be the current proper forms of worship and of personal practice. They are often the acting emissaries of the imam in remote areas of the world, in that they carry out and enact his religious directives and interpretations on the ground in those areas. In that

way, along with the *jama'at khana* structure and in concert with the imamate, they comprise a central formal, institutionalized religious structure
of Isma'ilism.

But the significance of ITREB/ITREC, IIS, and related institutions is not
only religious; it is also more broadly social. ITREB and IIS play central roles
in creating a globally and regionally shared sense of Ismaili commonality;
while religious in content, the outcomes that they produce are often fundamentally social and relational. I see them as critical in the formation of an
Isma'ili global ecumene. The *jama'ati* institutions are central in the creation,
negotiation, and refinement of Isma'ili images and imaginings of self. They
are interested in and focused on the Isma'ili past, particularly as it relates to
themes of 'Alid descent and the Fatimid Empire. As is the case with many
communities, for Isma'ilis history has become a central motif or emblem of
contemporary identity.

A final important function of the *jama'ati* institutions reveals their central role in binding the community together across territory, in creating a
pan-Isma'ili sense of connection: they are often responsible for making first
contact with Isma'ili organizations on behalf of the global community.[2] I
was told that in sensitive and politically unstable areas, it makes the most
sense for the *jama'ati* institutions to initially establish a link with what are
called "uncontacted" Isma'ili societies. The *imamati* institutions, for instance
those of AKDN, usually operate through official, bureaucratic processes that
require too much preparation time for them to move very quickly into a
problem area. And the *jama'ati* institutions can also provide services exclusively for Isma'ilis without having to make a gesture toward wider inclusion
of groups in the region, whereas *imamati* institutions must, in the name of
legitimacy, present themselves as inclusive and universal, even if they generally only initiate projects in areas where Isma'ilis live. Making initial contact
through the representatives of IIS or ITREB also keeps the official responsibility in the hands of individual community members.

Focus Humanitarian Assistance is a *jama'ati* institution run by Isma'ilis
and usually for Isma'ilis (although it sometimes includes non-Isma'ilis in
its programs) that provides swift aid and relief to the community in disas-
ter areas, particularly where it is impossible or unwise for AKDN to work.
Well before AKDN had established itself in northern Afghanistan, during
the years of civil war and the Taliban-centered conflict, representatives of
Focus crossed the river secretly from Tajikistan on rafts at night and delivered supplies there. Focus workers were among the first to show up in
Tajik Badakhshan. There is an element of high adventure and almost self-

sacrificing devotion in the narratives of such campaigns, described as clandestine and exclusive. Focus also worked for some time with resettling Isma'ili Afghan refugees in Karachi.

Mention should also be made of a formalized system of Isma'ili missionaries, often consisting of preachers (*waezeen*) and teachers (called *mu'allim*) who even now operate from religious schools or in settlements. I have seen such missionaries in both the Hunza and Yasin valleys of Pakistan. These functionaries, their title derived from the "mission schools" of British India, have been characterized by Daftary (1990) as "comparable to the *da'is* of the earlier times" (528). The arrival in Gorno-Badakhshan, Tajikistan, shortly after the disintegration of the Soviet Union of three prominent Isma'ilis, Rafique Keshavjee (a Khoja),[3] Sayyid Jalal Badakchani (an Iranian), and Ali Muhammad Rajput (a Shamsi or Panjabi Isma'ili), is now fabled. Among the first Isma'ili outsiders to visit the area in this era, they were likened to the three *qalandars*, the three wandering dervishes who were fabled to have originally brought Isma'ilism to this mountain region. The return of Isma'ilism, embodied in these figures interpreted as emissaries of the imam, was such a momentous event that it was quickly mythologized and rendered supernatural.[4] Safdar, my interpreter, says that they were "the connectors . . . the founders of the [current] connection."

Charismatic leaders operating outside the purview of official Isma'ili institutions have a special place in the local iterations of Isma'ili globality. Like various other forces and figures, they complicate the neat geographies of connection the institutions endeavor to build. One such figure in the Tajik Pamir is the same Ali Muhammad Rajput just mentioned. From the institutional point of view, at least, he was a dissident and an agitator. Rajput opened in Khorog (capital of Gorno-Badakhshan) an unofficial *jama'at khana* that, despite its illegitimate status, became quite popular.[5] More than once, while I was in the Pamir, Rajput's illicit activities came up in discussion. The attendance of his *jama'at khana* by Khoja elites (and some Pamiris) in the area certainly highlights some contradictions between ideology and practice, explicit and implicit levels of discourse.

Note should also be made here of Nasiruddin (Nasir al-Din, or "Nasir") Hunzai (b. 1917), a most prominent theological philosopher and poet from Hyderabad, Hunza, about one mile from the homes of Sher Ali and Sultan Ali in Pakistan. In addition to his intellectual contribution to the refinement of certain philosophical concepts and his role in promoting a corpus of literature in his native Burushaski, "Allama" Nasir participated in mid-twentieth-century proselytizing activities in Chinese Sinkiang, for which he spent years in a Chinese jail in Yarkand (Shache) (Boivin 2003: 296–97). Like Rajput, he was a "free agent," known for his independence from Isma'ili institutions. Unlike Rajput, his renown was such that he was tolerated by those institutions. Interestingly (or perhaps ironically), he is also the father of Izhar Ali Hunzai, a general manager of AKRSP in Pakistan.

What can be made of the stories of such dissenting voices? They point to the presence of resistance, contestation, dissent, and agentivity in the formation of Isma'ilism. Isma'ili subjects actively shape their community and religion; despite the prominence of Isma'ili global institutions in their lives, they are not without autonomy. They are neither determined nor controlled by those institutions. They also problematize the depiction of global Isma'ilism as unitary, seamless, and homogenous, as passively accepted by all adherents. The reality, it seems, is more fragmentary and more turbulent (see my discussion of Badakchani in Chapter 2). Their various local histories (which are certainly not insignificant on the global level) underscore some tension between an explicitly formulated official Isma'ilism and the creative interpretation and formation of practice and tradition by individual Isma'ilis. These figures seem to have a unique role in producing a dynamic and imaginative vitality in Isma'ili life.

The Production of Isma'ili Knowledge:
Emergent Subjectivities from Khorog to Euston Square

Boivin (2003) explores the role of Aga Khan III's emphasis on "research" as a means of developing a parallel between a glorified Fatimid past and modern Isma'ili contexts. The real connection between those pasts and the present is tenuous; it is difficult to establish continuity. That said, however, the effort itself reveals a great deal. The significance for Isma'ili globality of the Institute for Isma'ili Studies (IIS) in London must not be underestimated. Underlying the explicit goal of IIS to create a discipline or a field of "Isma'ili Studies," in part, is an effort to gain public legitimacy and recognition; to institutionalize it as an academic discipline requiring its own educational apparatus, bestowing upon Isma'ilism a special epistemological status that reinforces the view that it has objective historical significance (Foucault 1972). Such views may be informed, as we have noted with other elements of Isma'ili culture, by imaginaries and collective memories of the Isma'ili past. IIS institutionalizes that past and gives it a greater sense of permanence. The existence of IIS also reflects the imamate's interest in Western-style liberal arts education (and, by association, simply in Euro-American liberalism).

But more important, perhaps, than the explicit mandate of the institution is the part it plays in transnational social interaction. It is, crucially, a global social hub, one of the most important spaces in which Isma'ilis from vastly different backgrounds come together and begin to see each other as part of the same community. To IIS come Isma'ilis from Pakistan and Tajikistan, India and China, Iran and Syria, Canada and the United States, Tanzania and Madagascar. And they are all there, talking about Isma'ilism, consciously reflecting on their Isma'ili identity. So it could be said that a new reflexive Isma'ili metaculture is being created and negotiated in that very place. Part of this is the *creation* of Isma'ili images and discourses of the past, and the selective emphasis on certain elements of this past. For example, publications put a great deal of emphasis on the Fatimid era (e.g., Halm 1997), the philosophy of Nasir-i-Khusraw (e.g., Hunsberger 2000), and even on the philosophy of cyclical time (e.g., Corbin 1983). Even cosmologies and religious views that may no longer be active in Isma'ili religion are remobilized as important parts of its present self-image.

Students from poorer countries usually receive scholarships to enable their study at IIS. These scholarships are generally publicized and made available through local ITREBS, which have a subsidiary relationship to IIS, the umbrella institution. This means that IIS in London is in constant contact with remote Isma'ili localities, as well as with the secretariat in Paris, AKDN institutions, and other educational institutions. It is consequently a very important node in the Isma'ili transnational institutional structure, a key hub from which many connections radiate like spokes. It also helps students find places to live, has a canteen and seminar rooms, and provides students with orientation and graduation exercises like any other university. A student at IIS can stay there for several years, studying one or another aspect of Isma'ilism, conducting fieldwork, archival research, or both. The institution funnels its graduates into degree programs at prestigious universities (e.g., Cambridge, Oxford, Uppsala).

Among the many activities held at IIS, prominent scholars, both Isma'ili and non-Isma'ili, have been invited to speak on topics related to Islam and Isma'ilism. In fact, IIS both hires and publishes the work of prominent scholars of Isma'ilism of diverse religious and cultural backgrounds. In this way it may take some ownership and even exercise some influence over what is written about the community. The institute also develops and prescribes the multilingual curriculum materials distributed by the local offices of ITREB/ITREC. And, importantly, it is actively involved in preserving, cataloging, and translating a large corpus of historical Isma'ili texts from all parts of the traditional lands of Isma'ilism, including India, Egypt, and Central Asia. These texts are stored in an extensive library, and the project is seen as an important one in taking care of the Isma'ili cultural heritage. This too can be connected to the institutionalization of Isma'ili culture and history by giving the community an image of its legacy's perduring importance and permanence. Finally, IIS helps to organize conferences, events, cultural programs, and even summer camps for youth.

Who comes to IIS? Amirbek Janmamadov, from the very remote region of Roshorv in the Pamir, studied at IIS, then pursued a master's degree at Cambridge, and is now working on a doctorate in Sweden. Amanullah, a Sarikoli Pamiri Isma'ili from Tashkurghan in China (where he is called a Tajik)—the only one from that country when I was there—is a scholar at the institute and a great source of information on his own region. Hadi Mirshahi is one of several staff members from Mashhad in Iran. Anise Waljee is one of several Indo-Isma'ilis of East African birth. Ghulam Abbas Hunzai, who was also at the Khorog conference I describe below, a religious scholar from Hunza, in Pakistan, offers a valuable perspective on the communities of the Karakoram. These people all help each other imagine (and sometimes romanticize) the lives of Isma'ilis in their country of origin. Amanullah helps Hadi, for instance, develop an image of what the lives are like of Isma'ilis in the Kunlun Shan mountains, and Hadi can offer the same thing to Amanullah for the Isma'ilis of Iran.

I think that the theories of Benedict Anderson (1991) are not insignificant in the analysis of what goes on at IIS. To begin with, the process by which individuals from such radically different and distant settings come together in this context is closely tied to the idea of a shared identity despite cultural differences. This global forum is critical in engendering the imagining that is necessary for the creation of this nonnational "imagined community." At IIS, students and scholars are imbued with a sense of the simultaneous existence of the other members of their community in many countries. They begin to be able to envision themselves as part of a community defined not only by loyalty to the imam but also by connection to each other. Moreover, the patterns that characterize movement and communication to and from IIS are not unlike what Anderson refers to as "pilgrimage." Here too we have the same process of subjects from hinterlands coming to an urban center and discovering their common identity. Here too that experience energizes the subjects' enthusiasm for membership in the community. However, *this* pilgrimage helps to synthesize a global, nonterritorial, nonnational formation and not a nation-state. A final similarity with Anderson's observations connects to the extensive publication activity by IIS. Although this is not "print-*capitalism*" it depends on the same technologies and serves a similar function in binding together individuals of different backgrounds in a single polity (see the analysis of an Isma'ili children's book, *Murids of Imam az-Zaman*, below). So we see that IIS is critical in facilitating a global sense of commonality.

One important function of IIS seems to be the creation of a transnational Isma'ili intellectual elite. Students come in as villagers educated only at Khorog State University or Peshawar Agricultural University, and five or six years later they have doctorates from Cambridge. During this period they become the most highly educated Isma'ilis in their country. Their class and status are altogether transformed in this experience. Moreover, the experience reinforces the primacy of Isma'ilism as the central idiom of their identity and, underlying that idiom, a vision of Isma'ilism as fundamentally unitary. At IIS, local modes of identification are blurred (although appreciated on the explicit level); it is the fact of being "Isma'ili" that is shared here. There is also a shared experience of being in the city, one of the most cosmopolitan cities in the world, which engenders a sense among students that they are a select (and privileged) group. The material and social benefits are great. Sooner or later, they will move into positions of prominence and authority in their countries, especially in the Aga Khan's institutions in those countries. So the specialized training often feeds back into the operation of the institutional network itself. And in the mix, new dynamics of social class are produced in localities around the world.

It is there, at IIS, then, that a set of standardized and prescribed symbols are created and a cadre of Isma'ili intellectuals is produced. And it is there (among other sites) that a new mode of Isma'ili global subjectivity is formulated. In this fertile and cosmopolitan space, a new type of Isma'ili self (and a new experience of being a modern Isma'ili) emerges. I continue here with an example of how this occurs.

Inculcation in Action: Reading Discourses of Global Community in a Contemporary Isma'ili Children's Text

I have found no text that better conveys the Isma'ili community's own emphasis on building global relationships, their own metaculture of transnationality, than *Murids of Imam az-Zaman*, a children's publication of IIS designed for use in Isma'ili educational programs around the world (probably in particular for use by the ITREBs, to which it will be distributed). In this section I will analyze the discourse contained in the book to show that it seeks to enact, perform, and actualize in young Isma'ilis a sense of the simultaneous existence of other young Isma'ilis elsewhere with whom they share a common identity. As with Anderson's (1991) nascent nations, here too print materials are essential in the creation of a polity of people who, although they have never seen each other, are assured of the existence of an imagined community of people with whom they are closely connected.

The back cover of the book specifies that it is part of a series, "*Ta'lim* [Education]," an "international programme in religious education for Ismaili Muslim students." It describes the series' function in education on Islam and particularly Isma'ilism, explaining that it "seeks to promote self-development, learning, and a moral engagement with society." Here we can see already the fusion of Euro-American liberal values with Islamic ones. The book is aimed at broadening "the children's understanding of the Ismaili community today. The book introduces the readers to Ismaili children from around the world who talk about their countries, their jamats [communities], and their own hobbies and interests. The young readers also learn of the special relationship that exists between the imam of the time ['imam az-Zaman'] and his murids [disciples] all over the world." We can see here an apparent focus on diversity ("their countries, their jamats") that underlies the focus on commonality and connection ("*Ismaili* children from around the world," "the special relationship that exists between the imam of his time and his murids all over the world").

The book begins with the image of a girl wearing clothes that suggest a South Asian style who is marking days on a calendar. "At last," it reads, "the special day Sadia has been waiting for has arrived. It is the thirteenth of December. Today is Mawlana Hazir imam's birthday. It is Salgirah!" Sadia and her brother sit together and discuss the upcoming occasion. They wonder what present they can present to the imam: "They think and think. 'It has to be the best gift in the world,' Nizar says" (2).

On the next page we see an image of families gathering at an ornate South Asian–style mosque underneath stars, a moon, and a palm tree. Consider how the following excerpt aims at developing discourses of connection across territory, of people connected by their common devotion to the imam, and of their common engagement with the same practice and the same experience. In describing this uniformity of experience, it also enacts and perhaps even prescribes it. The writing conveys a sense of enchantment. I have added italics for emphasis:

In the evening, Sadia's family joins the jamat for Salgirah. Jamats *all over the world* are celebrating Mawlana Hazir imam's birthday.

Hundreds of people, young and old, make their way to the nearest jamatkhanas. The volunteers have spent a long time decorating the jamatkhanas. The coloured lights on the walls glimmer in the night.

The jamats offer special prayers of thanks on this night. They recite ginans, qasidas or manqabats [devotional poem or praise poem] in praise of the imam.

They listen to a special farman of Mawlana Hazir imam.

And they think of all the years the imam has spent improving the lives of jamats *everywhere*. (3)

Hence the individual, Sadia, represents a much wider experience. Notice that Sadia is the only individual in the story whose home location is unnamed. She is the universal Ismaʻili, the vehicle for the story's content.

We turn a page, now, and see a picture of a boy (Nizar, Sadia's brother) watering plants in a peaceful garden with flowers, butterflies, and birds. The text continues with an explanation of who the imam is. Halfway through the page the official view of his identity is described:

Mawlana Shah Karim al-Husayni is our Hazir imam, our present living imam. He is our imam az-zaman, the imam of our time.

Mawlana Hazir imam belongs to the Ahl al-bayt, the family of Prophet Muhammad. He is the direct descendant of Prophet Muhammad, Mawlana Ali and Hazrat Fatimah.

We love our imam deeply. What can we do to make our imam happy? What gift can each of us give to our imam on his birthday?

Mawlana Hazir imam has said to us: "The jamat can give me one happiness—that they should be united, that they should be regular in all jamati work, and that they should live in the best tradition of my spiritual children."

Sadia and Nizar have searched hard for a gift to give to their imam. Now they know what gift will make Mawlana Hazir imam happy. They will do their best to follow the farmans of imam az-zaman. (4–5; emphasis in original)

Page 5 shows the girl (Sadia) in a similarly utopian (possibly Mughal-inspired) garden with fountains. The intention would appear to be not only to introduce Ismaʻili children to the philosophy of the imamate (for there is certainly an emphasis on obedience here), but also to begin to engender in them a sense of shared experience. On pages 6 and 7 (beginning with "Sadia loves going to jamatkhana whenever she can") we see a spread of many people in a Mughal-style *jama'at khana* with fountains and arches. Unveiled women, men, and children fill the courtyard. The emphasis here, as before, is on the numbers, the ranks of people *sharing* this moment ("She recites ginans and qasidas with *everybody in the jamat*"; "Sadia knows *many people* in her jamat"; "And there are her *many* friends"). The text continues:

> The jamat is like one big family. All the people in the jamat are the spiritual children of Mawlana Hazir imam. We are the murids of imam az-zaman.
>
> A murid is one who gives his or her bayah [oath] to the imam of the time. When murids give their bayah, they promise to be loyal to Mawlana Hazir imam. During the time of Prophet Muhammad, the Muslims gave their bayah to the Prophet. Today, we give our bayah to our imam az-zaman.
>
> Sadia is a murid of Mawlana Hazir imam. She loves and obeys Hazir imam. She remembers the farmans of imam az-zaman and tries to follow them every day. (7)

Here we see an interesting use of repetition that begins to emerge in the text as a whole, a continuing focus on obedience and allegiance, and a parallel that is drawn between the place of the Prophet and the imam. We also hear repeatedly the imperative of following the *farman* as a global directive regardless of location. On the next page we have another spread, this time of prosperous-looking families in mixed Western and South Asian garments sitting by a mountain river and having picnics.

> All the murids of the imam are spiritual brothers and sisters. Mawlana Hazir imam wants us all to *live and work together as one family*, as one jamat.
>
> There are many jamats around the world. Our jamats live in different countries and speak different languages.
>
> Mawlana Hazir imam *guides all the jamats around the world*. He is the spiritual father and mother of all the jamats.
>
> We will now visit some of our spiritual brothers and sisters living in different countries. We will learn something about their countries and ways of life. We will also find out *what unites us as one jamat all over the world*. (8–9; emphasis added)

That last sentence almost sounds like the thematic of *this* book. The text is self-consciously transnational and cross-cultural and is clearly working to build those horizontal connections *among* Isma'ilis in addition to the vertical ones between the imam and his subjects. The description of the imam as "father and mother" is of particular interest in capturing the doctrine of the imam as a particular example of an eternal and timeless reality.[6]

The first chapter is titled "Hasan Lives in Syria," and it elucidates some details on the life of a boy growing up in Salamiyya (Salamis); the global is illuminated here through the regional examples. The individuals depicted are vehicles for conveying certain values, obligations, and principles and for developing a sense of connection across space. The description of Hasan's life now moves on to a description of the Isma'ili population in the country and continues with another linkage with the Isma'ili (this time Nizari) past: "Hundreds of years ago, some of our imams lived in Salamiyya. There were also times when Isma'ilis lived in forts on the mountains" (11). This again shows the centrality of the imaginary of the past to Isma'ili identity. Hasan is shown, like Sadia, attending *jama'at khana*, but also engaging in his own personally and culturally specific activities. His profile ends with a *farman* excerpt on service to the community, one's family, and, notably, the country.

The next chapter is "Ramziya Lives in Tajikistan." Ramziya is from our familiar town of Khorog in Badakhshan. These pages include some rosy images of Khorog, of the Pamirs, and of Badakhshani villages, along with some wildlife. On the next page we see Ramziya walking to school and read about her classroom duty: "When the pupils come into the classroom, we have to inspect them. 'Show us your hands,' we say to them. 'Are they clean?'" This reflects a focus, already established in the book, on representing Isma'ilis as modern. It also reveals an interest in modern discourses of hygiene, self-regulation, and the body, in norms of self-comportment and cleanliness (Foucault 1973, 2003). This is also evident in AKDN's many health education programs that seek to socialize diverse societies to shared norms. Ramziya's chapter ends with an appeal to cosmopolitanism: "When I grow up, I hope to visit many countries around the world" (17).

The chapter titled "Aziz Lives in Iran" raises issues of migration: Aziz has moved from a traditional-looking village to the large city of Mashhad. Again here we have the emphasis on fraternity: "We have a large jamat in Iran. Our Ismaili brothers and sisters live in big cities such as Tehran and Mashhad. They are also to be found in small villages" (19). The focus is also on the Isma'ili past, highlighting continuity with the present: "Iran was the home of many of our imams for hundreds of years. Some of them lived in the fort of Alamut. The fort was built on top of a steep mountain. If you travel from Tehran to the mountains, you can still see the ruins of the fort today" (19). Once again, reflecting a rhythmic repetition throughout the book, we have a description of the *jama'at khana* and the practice of praising the imam — a point that suggests an emphasis on standardization and the creation of a uniform worldwide (Khoja-inflected) Isma'ili culture, with an acceptance of diversity but also certain shared features.

"Karima Lives in Pakistan" depicts a girl in Karachi. All of these children do things that make them accessible and familiar to children in other countries (playing soccer, going to school, living in a city, being a youngest sibling). After a description of Karima's life and of the sociocultural diversity of Pakistan, Karima's case reflects the all-encompassing aspect of Isma'ili social services that we have discussed, and their *religious* association with the imam:

> Pakistan is home for many Ismailis. Our jamats live in Karachi, Islamabad, Peshawar and other cities.
>
> Many more Ismailis live in small towns and villages in the north of Pakistan, such as Gilgit. The lands here are full of mountains and rivers. *Mawlana Hazir imam is helping people in these areas to build roads, canals, schools, and clinics.*
>
> *Mawlana Hazir imam has built* a large number of schools in Pakistan.
>
> The school I go to in Karachi is one of the biggest. It is called the Sultan Muhammad Shah School. Here, I learn to read, write, and count. I also learn about my country and about people who live in other lands.
>
> *Mawlana Hazir imam has built* a large hospital in Karachi. It is called the Aga Khan University Hospital.
>
> A few months ago, when grandfather fell ill, we took him to the Aga Khan University Hospital. We visited him every day while he was ill. There were many people at the hospital. Some of them had come from far away to be treated by the doctors.
>
> Luckily, grandfather soon got better. Now he is almost his old self again. I walk with him to jamatkhana every day. (24–25)

There is thus an Isma'ili religious resonance to the presence of the secular social institutions. It is the imam *as* religious leader who motivates these institutions, who is the agent and the engine behind them. We also see the degree to which these institutions are meant to be interwoven with the fabric of people's everyday social lives. Here as in other parts of the book we also see the emphasis on late-modern thematics of diversity and multiculturalism and again the trademark Khoja *jama'at khana*.

The next story is "Akbar Lives in India." Akbar, like the other children, is accessible and "normal": "Of all the places near my home, I love this garden the best. I sometimes hide behind the shrubs when I do not want my brothers and sisters to find me. But somehow, they always do!" (26). As with the other children, Akbar expresses vaguely Islamic motifs: "I like to listen to the nightingale singing in the garden, away from the noise of cars, buses and rickshaws in the streets" (26). The nightingale is a common symbol in Persian poetry. Akbar continues with a description of Isma'ilism in India, and again we return to the common theme of social services provided through AKDN:

> Mawlana hazir imam has set up special programmes to help the
> farmers in Gujarat.
>   Our imams have helped the jamat to make great progress over
> the years.
>   Our forty-eighth imam, Mawlana Sultan Muhammad Shah, lived
> in Bombay many years ago. He guided the jamat in India to build
> schools, hospitals, clinics, and houses. Mawlana Hazir imam too
> is preparing the jamat for a better future. He wants the children to
> grow up to be educated and healthy. (28)

Akbar's family is *modern*: his father is a computer scientist and his mother a lawyer. Akbar wants to be a pilot. This shows the Isma'ilis' favorable orientation to capital and notions of progress.

The final story is "Salma Lives in the United States of America," an interesting way to culminate the case histories in light of the interest in progress and modernity. It also adds a crucial element to the book: Salma is connected, through parallels in narrative structure and repetition of content, to all the other children, whether in Tajikistan or Iran or India. Salma's world is represented visually with skyscrapers and interstate bypasses: modern. But she is part of the same worldwide collectivity as all the other children. Salma lives in Chicago, and she explains her ultramodern life presumably to an invisible audience of children like those described elsewhere in the book. On the next page is an image of the Golden Gate Bridge and the United Nations building. The migration situation, although a global one in this case, is apparent here too: Salma moved here from Pakistan at age three. She also conveys the emphasis on both connection to other Isma'ilis and on pluralist cultural diversity:

> There are many other Ismailis in Chicago. They too have come from different countries like India, Pakistan, Kenya, and Tanzania.
>
> Some of my friends are children from these countries. I also have good friends at school. My best friend, Hannah, is from Brazil. She knows all kinds of songs and poems. (32)

The concluding section, "Mawlana Hazir Imam Guides the Jamats," surrounded by fifteen, ethnically diverse faces, sums up the book's message:

> In this book, we traveled to many countries around the world. We visited our jamats in Syria, Tajikistan, Iran, Pakistan, India, and the United States. We met children who live in these countries. And we learned something about each of them.
>
> Our jamats have their homes all over the world. Ismailis live in Asia, Africa, Europe, Australia and North America.
>
> Wherever they live, Ismailis are the spiritual children of Mawlana Hazir imam. It is our imam who unites us as one community all over the world. Our imam guides the jamats to make spiritual and material progress. (33)

The text ends with a parable about a tree planted by Sadia's father. The parable ending is also a form common in Persian and Indo-Muslim poetry and literature. On this Salgirah day, Sadia's father comes home bearing a new mango sapling. The children ask about another mango tree in the garden. He says that he and his father planted it on the day that the current Aga Khan succeeded to the imamate. Each year on imamate day, he says, he could see its progress, and now it has become a healthy tree bearing much fruit.

The main themes are commonality across the diversity of the Isma'ili community, modernity and progress, membership and citizenship, liberal modes of plurality and unity in multiculturalism, disciplines of loyalty to the imam (through following the *farmans* and attending *jama'at khana*), and the importance of the past in the present. The book is meant to drive home in children (through widely distributed print materials translated into many languages) what Anderson (1991) describes as "simultaneity"—the belief that, though you have neither seen nor met them, and although they live in different areas, you are part of a unitary and homogeneous community of people like you (and like each other). In Anderson's conception, most citizens of a state never meet each other, and yet each is aware of the perpetual functioning of the collectivity: he or she "has complete confidence in their steady anonymous, simultaneous activity" (1991: 26). The point in *Murids* is: "Isma'ilis live everywhere in diverse cultural contexts, and wherever they live, they share a common identity and set of practices." But it is not a nation-state that is being produced here: this is a text of transnationality, a document that seeks to enact, perform, conjure, and actualize a sense of global belonging across both time and space.

Globality beyond Institutions: Ritual and Devotional Practice in the Making of Transnational Isma'ilism

Absolutely central to the cohesion and integrity of the Isma'ili transnational community are devotional processes; these shared practices and patterns bring Isma'ilis from diverse regions in contact with each other and help to establish a sense of connection between subjects. Certain critical rituals, doctrines, and discourses provide powerful anchors of sharedness. They can play key roles in the formation of simultaneity, commonality, and intersubjective shared experience; they provide a context for finding similarities in personal identity and experience despite cultural differences. To Isma'ilis, moreover, they are of paramount importance and at the heart of belief and practice. From the perspective of most Isma'ilis the religious life is the whole thing, more crucial than any other aspect of life. Those other aspects, such as involvement with AKDN, may be seen by Isma'ilis as simply contributing to one's *religious* worth and virtue. Success in the AKF may thus be intertwined with understandings of devotional self-worth and service to the imam.

The complex of rituals, practices, and doctrines, much of it secret, appears to exist outside the institutional infrastructure. A closer inspection, however, reveals a more complex interaction between these strains and domains of Isma'ili activity. It can be said, at the very least, that religious doctrine occupies an orthogonal relationship to institutional architecture. Isma'ili cosmology and visions of history certainly play some role in informing institutional development. Moreover, the politics of proper practice and belief penetrate deep into the policy of the religious institutions. While I describe here the connective force of ritual practice, in this, as in other areas, there is contestation. Prescriptive questions of practice constitute a basic and prominent object of contention between Khojas and Himalayan Nizaris. The ITREB efforts to standardize religious ritual and belief according to Khoja norms (i.e., to establish *jama'at khanas*) is met with real resistance (and sometimes resentment). This does not mean, of course, that practice is nonnegotiable, nor that it is ever really standardized.

Among religious elements of Isma'ili life, none is more central than devotion to the imam. Such devotion is the single most significant fact of Isma'ili religion. It could be described, in fact, as itself constitutive of Isma'ilism. And it is not that Isma'ilis are devoted simply to *this* imam, Prince Karim the Aga Khan, and to his particular personality and traits. Certainly they are devoted to that, also, but more importantly, they are devoted to the timeless *institution* of the imamate, to the reality that underlies any particular imam who is but a manifestation of that institution. Devotion to the imam can thus be seen as a central pillar of horizontal Isma'ili fraternity. According to Isma'ili doctrine, the presence of an imam is a fundamental property of the cosmos itself. Devotion to the imam is the most essential act in life. Moreover, throughout the history of dissidence and schism, people who rejected the imam did not stay in the community as critics but tended to form a new sect; thus total devotion is seen as a criterion of membership. Nondevotion is by definition nonmembership.

Another practice key to the formation of a transnational Isma'ili sense of commonality and shared experience, and one that deserves more attention, is that of *didar*, which translates loosely from Persian as "audience" (as with a king), or "vision," which for Isma'ilis is a peak experience and the subject of numerous narratives. Marsden (2005) writes that "'catching a glimpse' (*deedar korik*) of the Aga Khan is a moment when Isma'ilis feel themselves to be in the presence of 'spiritual truth' (*haqiqat*); and it is a religious event that is without comparison for Isma'ili Muslims" (16). The *didar* consists of a formal religious ceremony in which the imam visits a certain area and addresses his adherents. During the address, the imam provides guidance and advice, often relating to the political situation of the community in a certain area, or to proper behavior, to his followers. For many Isma'ilis, it is a dream to be attained, a goal more valued than any other; this is the moment of contact with the imam, the holiest living person and the intermediary between God and humans. Isma'ilis see *didar* as a transformative and pivotal moment in their lives.[7]

The *didar* narrative of a Badakhshani woman, Zuhro, demonstrates well the level of devotion and loyalty that is given to the imam. Zuhro is a member of an old Badakhshani elite and now works for the provincial government. She described with great emotion the *didar* as one of the highlights of her life, a peak experience. She waited on the airport tarmac for his arrival.

Upon seeing him she wept profusely and tried to hide. She searched for English words to say to him as he came to speak to her, and stumbling over her words, finally came out with "all the best!" Afterwards, however, she was struck with intense anxiety over the meaning of "all the best" and realized she didn't know what she had said or what it meant. She was suddenly regretful. Ultimately, however, she expressed a sense of having received a blessing from heaven and an entirely extraordinary experience. *Didar* is also important because it is for Isma'ilis a religious experience unmediated, or less mediated, by institutional process and bureaucracy. For Zuhro, the *didar* was the "jewel of [her] life."

Among the earliest texts discussing the Isma'ili *didar* is the *Pandiyat-i Jawanmardi*, the advice of Imam Mustansir bi'llah II, dating from the late 1400s. This imam emphasized the *didar* voyage and audience as one of the most important religious duties and experiences (Daftary 1990: 469). In *didar* (as in Hindu *darshan*) it is significant both that the devotee see the imam and that the imam see his devotees; to the devotee it is a powerful blessing. Isma'ilis also believe that there can be a nonphysical *didar*, in which subjects' can attain a mental or spiritual vision of the imam in his ideal form. This emerges out of the Isma'ili division of the world into internal and external phenomena, as discussed in relation to *ta'wil, zahir,* and *batin.* Thus even Isma'ilis who are not able to receive the worldly *didar* can receive the blessing of an inner *didar* in which the imam appears to them in their prayers. The Isma'ili notion of a "physical *didar*" is thus contrasted with a *didar* in the mind's eye; it is assumed that even Isma'ilis who do not have the privilege of a direct experience will be paid a spiritual visit by the imam. Isma'ilis in Tajik Badakhshan spoke frequently of their inner vision of the imam, even during their long "isolation," before his first official visit after the break-up of the Soviet Union.

Besides the subjective experience of *didar*, the ritual also has a wider global social significance. Narratives of the power of *didar* are found across Isma'ili regional cultures, from Syria to the United Kingdom. It is described as fantastical, as a dazzling spectacle, by its witnesses. The ritual form followed is largely the same everywhere. For this reason, and because of its intensity, *didar*, like some of the other religious rituals discussed, is important in the formation of a shared Isma'ili global identity and of Isma'ili personal identity; as a public speech event, a face-to-face interaction between the imam and his subjects, *didar* is a critical discursive moment (Spitulnik 1997; Agha 2006; Urban 2001). It provides an unparalleled encounter in which Isma'ilis can formulate their own sense of themselves *as* Isma'ilis and a central emblematic symbol around which this subjective identity can be formed. But it has an even wider social implication in the transnational context. The experience, because of its intensity and uniformity, becomes a focal point not only within any given local Isma'ili community but also across global Isma'ili cultures. Thus, like other shared religious experiences, *didar* acts as a critical process in the formation of a global sense of connection and simultaneity.

But even non-*didar* audiences with the imam produce the same intense reactions in followers. At the imam's visit to Khorog (Gorno-Badakhshan) on August 21, 2003, villagers lined the streets, waited for hours, processed, and wept upon his arrival, even though he was only there for about an hour to survey a potential site for the University of Central Asia. AKDN functionaries wore suits; competition for a place in an AKDN vehicle to the various sites was fierce. The visit itself engendered profound and intense displays of devotion. Particularly moving was the sight of an elderly woman who, after the Aga Khan had left the scene and the excitement had calmed, lay prostrate and traced in the long light of early evening his entire path, touching her veil to the ground repeatedly everywhere that she had seen him walk, bringing it to her lips, and lowering it to the ground again. For some time after the imam's departure, the townspeople in Khorog who had seen him could be heard congratulating each other on the blessing of such a vision.[8]

Another major element in the creation of Isma'ili transnational connections is the *farman* (or *firman*), shared by Isma'ilis all over the world, which Boivin (2003) characterizes as constituting "par excellence l'instrument de la modernisation [the signature instrument of modernization]" (277). The *farman* is a spoken (or sometimes written) directive, decree, pronouncement, or edict of the Aga Khan that provides guidance and advice for followers. *Farmans* became a part of modern Isma'ilism under Aga Khan III, who provided advice on trade, gender, religion, proper behavior, and social issues. Many early *farmans* focused on the role of women in sociopolitical life, including the Aga Khan's desire that Isma'ili women stop wearing the veil (Daftary 1990: 526). *Farmans* generally circulate to Isma'ili communities once a week; wherever possible, they are transmitted as vocal recordings to be played in *jama'at khana* houses of worship. In settings where there are no *jama'at khanas* (e.g., Khorog as of 2003), *farmans* may be transmitted as faxes to be read by interested subjects. As with the discursive content of the *didar*, the *farman* helps Isma'ilis make sense of historical developments. It is through the *farman* more than anything else that the imam fulfills his

Villagers weeping at the sight of the Aga Khan, their imam and spiritual leader, Porshnev village, Gorno-Badakhshan, Tajikistan.

mandate to continually update and interpret, through *ta'wil*, the meaning of Islam. Non-Isma'ilis are not allowed to hear the *farmans*. From a discourse-analytic point of view, *farmans*, like *didars*, are important, large-scale, real-time, interactive speech events (see Spitulnik 1997; Goffman 1981; Agha 2006), which, through incorporating Isma'ilis in such different areas, can also generate a transterritorial sense of simultaneity—a sense that Isma'ilis in different places are experiencing the same thing at approximately the same time and are thus part of the same community, despite the distance between them.

Besides the *global* and officially sanctioned religious practices that help to provide connections and a sense of commonality between Isma'ilis from different regions, Isma'ilis from diverse backgrounds also sometimes share in each other's specifically *local* practices. When this occurs, the elements of local religious tradition, even the differences in tradition, become emblematic of Isma'ilism itself and important additions to the shared experience. For example, visiting Isma'ilis from Canada, Europe, and the United States travel to and participate with local Isma'ilis in the rites of important shrines (called *oston* in Tajikistan, *ziyarat* in Tajikistan or Pakistan), such as those of Baba Ghundi in Chapursan (Gojal, Pakistan) or Bibi Fatima in the Wakhan (Tajikistan), and both visitors and hosts see it as a way to commune with each other. Correspondingly, Badakhshani or Hunzakuts Isma'ilis living abroad in London or Houston participate in the *jama'at khana* culture of such urban areas.

It is to the special role of locality that I now turn, to the profoundly rich meanings of all of these global forms in the lives of real individuals, homes, and places. I seek to complicate the relatively straightforward descriptions of the preceding pages with a concern for the multiplicity and ambiguity of their meanings, and for their profound polyvalence and contextual contingency.

CHAPTER FOUR

Into the Fold

Himalayan Borderlands and Isma'ili Modernity

Ethnographic Triangulations: (Re)Locating the Subject

My perspective to this point has been bound by Isma'ili institutional structures; I have explored Isma'ili life so far entirely from within their boundaries. I now shift my perspective from the institutions themselves to their
messier, more complex cultural contexts: to the localities they inhabit, the
moments they effect, and the subjects they engage. Getting a grasp of the
institutions involves a much simpler task than discerning their meaning in
lives and localities. But Isma'ili globality must be situated in the context
of personal experience and rendered meaningful through the lens of local
cultures; abstracted from contestation and interpretation, from aspiration
and ambition, from pleasure and desire, we are left only with the work of
the powerful and the affluent, and we cannot make sense of the varied and
polycentric landscapes of transnational space.

The historical and social dynamics of such a vast phenomenon must
be illuminated through the intimate lens of individual lives, of subjects'
own stories. Thus, at the heart of this chapter (and, if I am successful, of
this book) are narratives of the lived experience and emotional history of
Isma'ili subjects (and places), their stories of movement through and incorporation into a global community, and their construction of self through
the institutional structures and semiotic lexicon of the global network of
which they are taught to feel themselves members. I write in dialogue with
them and, I hope, with their willing participation. I have tried to be respect-
ful of their words, their feelings, and their realities. History, change, and
upheaval are, after all, fundamentally experienced on the most personal of
levels. Thus, the life of almost any Isma'ili can reveal a great deal about the
transnational dynamics of the global institutional structures in which they
are encouraged to participate.

But the Isma'ili subject that I seek is not entirely easy to locate. She is rarely the subject of major works of scholarship (and I have certainly not done her justice here). She is seldom at the helm of the institutions she navigates, nor in the highest levels of advisers in Aiglemont or Geneva. She is absent from the pages and pages of Islamic history that explore her beliefs and propose her past. And yet, she and her compatriots constitute the Isma'ili "community" whose characterization I have attempted and whose unity I have assumed. She is situated, most crucially, in the life of the local. She shares a lot with other Isma'ilis. But not everything; she has her own opinions and her practice is idiosyncratic.

I started with Sher Ali and Sultan Ali—subjects whose lives are imbricated with the Isma'ili global project, but whose control over its processes are minimal. We have perhaps come to understand (or at least identify), at this point, the larger forces, historical and institutional, that help to shape their lifeworlds. But on the local level, how can we make sense of their profound and intimate engagement with Isma'ili globality? How does it intersect with other regional formations and processes and other modes of globality? And what ability do they have to shape or sway the Isma'ili institutional web?

In this chapter I focus the scope of the discussion with a more careful consideration of the Himalayan Isma'ili region—the site of my fieldwork. This allows me to explore with greater ethnographic texture the lived realities of the institutional infrastructure I have described and to interpret more credibly its ramifications for the construction of self and for the socialization of remote areas to ideologies associated with capitalism and modernity. My hope here is to shed light on the real implications of the abstracted architecture of the imamate for living places with unwritten histories. Where the primary significance of an institutional form is in the Himalayan region, I have kept it here.

In this chapter we will explore the living backgrounds, contexts, and settings in which Isma'ili global institutionalization occurs. In the next chapter, by virtue of an ethnographic emphasis on the fabric of local life, formations and processes that are less easily characterized, simplified, and defined—such as public performances, tense relationships, ambiguous moments—also come to light. And yet, the same issues explored elsewhere also resurface here: the transformation of sovereignty and citizenship; the complex encounter between diasporic Khoja elites and borderland subjects; the role of empire and nation-state in transforming social subjectivities; and the very active recruitment and incorporation of distant societies into the Euro-American institutions of the imamate. What emerges here as new and different, however, is the role of international boundaries (and the territorial units whose peripheries they denote) in dividing populations and in determining their differential trajectories. The presence of a tangle of borders in the region under consideration renders the reconnection of adjacent societies through the Aga Khan's structures more visible and more significant. It marks (and charges) the process, bestows upon its interpretation (and reality) a special gravity and intensity.

Of Peripheral Histories and Historical Peripheries: The Isma'ili Himalaya

The Isma'ili communities of the western Himalayan ranges were the core ethnographic focus of my research. While my emphasis was on the Isma'ilis of far northern Pakistan and southern Tajikistan, the contiguous Isma'ili area of the Himalaya also encompasses a section of western China and northeastern Afghanistan. This area, which forms the largest territory occupied predominantly by Isma'ilis in the world, is interesting precisely because of its status before the establishment of national boundaries, when culturally and religiously it formed a relatively unitary zone, despite its striking ethnolinguistic diversity (Stein 1907, 1921, 1928; Kreutzmann 1996; Roy 2000; Shahrani 1979; Dani 1989; Jettmar 1975). In the past two hundred years, however, it has been at the center of extensive geopolitical activity and transformation (Hopkirk 1991; Kreutzmann 1996). The political borders that were drawn across this mountain area separated long-connected areas from each other and created divergent social conditions and even distinct cultures. This situation is of particular interest to us in a global moment: before the borders were created, the region was characterized by a translocal connection, one of whose bases was the Isma'ilism of another time. This translocal connection was both an internal aspect of the region and an element of its interactions with larger Isma'ili networks. The arrival of institutional Isma'ilism and its discourse of a common, unifying global connection shared by the people of the region, regardless of the nation-state they live in, has created new social, religious, and institutional linkages and new elements of shared identity across borders. This globalizing process transforms the primacy of nationality as the dominant criterion for identification in the area and remobilizes some of the processes and patterns of the past.

Despite their apparent isolation, the deep valleys, river gorges, and glaciated peaks of the western Himalaya have long been major thoroughfares for human movement, trade, and conquest. Invaders from Kanishka to Timur, travelers from Hsüan-Tsang to Fa-Hsien to Marco Polo, missionaries preaching the Dharma and the Shariʿa, and traders bearing silk, spices, or jewels have all come this way. Petroglyphs in almost every valley attesting to the constancy of human movement through the region across several millennia are well-documented, much of it in Karl Jettmar's (1989) *Antiquities of Northern Pakistan*. The area has passed in and out of the hands of countless empires and polities and has often been ruled by small, autonomous principalities or emirates.

Before the arrival of Islam, the Karakoram, Hindu Kush, and Pamir ranges were, some 2,500 years ago, an important area for the Scythian and Khotanese Sakas, Iranian-speaking pastoral nomads with distinctive burial practices and material culture. Many place-names, including Ishkarwaz (Afghanistan), Ishkaibar (Yasin), and Ishkashim (Tajikistan) still bear the root *ishk*, meaning "Saka." Alexander the Great passed through the region in the process of his Indian invasion around 326 BC. Lore surrounding Alexander remains a major element of local culture: many ethnic groups attribute their origin to him, and Sikander or Iskander remain popular names for boys. Moreover, among Ismaʿilis Alexander as *Dhu'l-Qarnayn* or *Zulqarnain* (the two-horned one) holds mystical power. Not long after Alexander, the valleys of this region made significant interregional connections with the Bactrian areas of northern Afghanistan and the Sogdian areas in what is now Tajikistan and Uzbekistan. More significantly, it was incorporated into or at least associated with the Greco-Buddhist polities of Gandhara (in the vicinity of Peshawar and Taxila) beginning with the Kushans (or Yüeh-Chi) under Kanishka. In this period, these mountain valleys became a major route for the transmission of Buddhism to the rest of Asia and were thus connected into an early organized translocal network (Stein 1907, 1921, 1928, 1929; Biddulph 1880; Jettmar 1975; Sinor 1990; Tucci 1977). The evidence for these past flows and processes is archaeological, linguistic, toponymic, textual, and ethnological. Local traditions also resonate with historical observations.

In the centuries leading up to the arrival of Islam, and particularly in the sixth and seventh centuries, the Chinese and the Tibetans vied for control of these mountains at the western extremities of their power. With the invasion of the subcontinent by the Ghaznavids, the high valleys here became a refuge area for the Rajput Hindu-Shahi dynasties, which now ruled the plains at their base. Southern areas like Gilgit transitioned in this period from Buddhism to Hinduism, but their religion was more accurately a fusion of Hinduism, Buddhism, and local mountain cosmologies. Islam arrived in Central Asia with Arab conquests in 712–13 (Lapidus 1988: 41), but it probably did not penetrate these mountain areas until significantly later. Some areas of Badakhshan seem to have been fertile ground for early radical forms of Shi'ism.

The introduction of Isma'ilism to the region is attributed to Nasir-i-Khusraw, who after his time at the Fatimid court in the eleventh century, became a da'i (missionary) in Central Asia, faced persecution in the Marw area, and fled to Badakhshan, where he spent the rest of his life and converted or reformed much of the population.[1] Nasir remains very much a living part of the culture of Badakhshan and northern Pakistan. He is revered as a hero, as a saint, and as an important religious teacher, and has become an emblem of local Isma'ili identity (see van den Berg 1997; Hunsberger 2000).

After their conversion to Islam, these areas were still subject to the vagaries of shifting dynastic borders. They interacted very little with the Seljuqs and the Ghorids and saw little of the upheaval experienced by other areas at the hands of Chinghiz (Genghis) Khan and the Mongols. Timur (i.e., Tamerlane) passed through these mountains, and some local rulers entered into alignments with the Timurids, a development that presented some difficulties to the Isma'ilis of the area. But for the most part these mountains were for centuries ruled by hereditary Isma'ili dynasties of *mirs* (hereditary rulers) who controlled their small, autonomous principalities and occasionally entered into alliances with larger polities. Thus, despite their isolation, these principalities were part of larger transregional networks of exchange, religious intercourse, and political alliance. With the decentralization of Isma'ilism that came with the Mongol destruction of the Nizari state around 1256, the circum-Himalayan Isma'ili region, like Syria, western India, and elsewhere, became isolated from the centralized Isma'ili leadership of the imamate and began to be led by Isma'ili *pirs* (hereditary religious leaders), who became the primary religious authority (Daftary 1990). For this reason, Himalayan Isma'ilism began to develop its own unique traditions, which has led to some tension as global Isma'ili elites attempt to standardize religious practice.

The Isma'ili region of the Himalaya spans some of the highest mountain ranges on earth. These young ranges, formed by the collision of the Indian subcontinent with the Asian continent (as well as an island archipelago that was between them) are rising at a remarkably fast rate, as is evidenced by perpetual tectonic activity like Pakistan's earthquake of 2005. They form a vast region characterized by deep gorges (most of whose rivers predate the collision of the subcontinent with Asia), jagged peaks, and glaciers. Ismaʿilis inhabit the Karakoram, Pamir, Hindu Kush, and Hindu Raj ranges of the Himalaya. The Karakoram (Mongolian for "black rock") contains the most concentrated area of glaciers outside of the poles and is divided between India, Pakistan, and China. The Hindu Raj (southern Chitral, Ghizar, Yasin, Ishkoman) is a spur of the Hindu Kush, which is itself split between Afghanistan and Pakistan. And the Pamir is contained in Tajikistan, Afghanistan, China, and small parts of Kyrgyzstan and Uzbekistan.

The ecology of this area, which generally lies in the rain shadow of the subcontinent's monsoons, consists of high mountain desert, an arid and harsh environment for human habitation not unlike the Altiplano region of the Andes or parts of the eastern Caucasus. Most habitation in the western Himalaya is along the river valleys; Ismaʿilis live primarily in the watersheds of the Indus (including the Kunar, Gilgit, Hunza, and Ghizar tributaries) and the Amu Darya, formerly the Oxus (including the Shiwa, Kokcha, Panj, and Rushan tributaries). More specifically, Pakistani Ismaʿilis live in the northern valleys of Chitral, including the Yarkhun, Turikho, Arkari, Begusht, Mulkho, Laspur, and Lutkho tributaries; in most of the tributaries of the Hunza River, including the very remote Shimshal, Chapursan, Misgar, and Kilik-Mintaka watersheds; and all through the Ghizar area abutting Chitral, including the Yasin, Ishkoman, and Bashqar valleys. In Afghanistan they occupy the upper valley of the Wakhan and the area downstream along the Panj-Amu Darya, as well as the long Munjan valley adjacent to Nuristan, the Shiwa River, the Sanglech River, and a good portion of the Kokcha. There are also isolated Ismaʿilis in the Afghan part of the Kunar-Indus watershed in Laghman.[2] In Tajikistan, there are Ismaʿilis on the other side of the Wakhan and Panj-Amu Darya; in the Badakhshani tributaries of Shahdara, Ghund (of Shughnan), Rushan-Bartang-Roshorv, Khuf, Barju, and in Yoged, in the Darwaz division. The Vanj and Yazghulam streams are Sunni-inhabited. In China, Ismaʿilis live in the area traditionally known as the Taghdumbash Pamir and specifically in the area called Sary Qul or Sarikol around the settlement of Tashkurghan (Tashi-kuer-kan). They also live in the cities of Kashghar (Kashi) and Yarkand (Sha-che); an isolated population resides in the Guma-Pishan villages in the Kunlun Shan spur of the Karakoram at the edge of the Taklimakan desert near Khotan (Ho-Tien).

Trees are extremely scarce and the landscape is rocky and dry in most of the region; some high-altitude areas, such as in southern Hunza, are at the very edge of the monsoon belt and have coniferous forests. Cultivation in these areas is achieved, with great labor, through a traditional system of channeling water from glacial streams. The channels, which can be five hundred years old or more, are carved out of the mountainside; water gradually zig-zags through them into the villages' fields. The effect, as I have mentioned, is that settlements appear as splashes of green in otherwise brown and grey rocky landscapes. The channeling practice seems to have been abandoned in most areas previously under Soviet administration, probably because of the deterritorialized provision of resources to those areas, which had little need for self-sufficiency. Tall, white poplar trees (Persian *shamshad*, Shughni *arar*) line lanes and pathways in villages throughout the entire area; they are used as windbreaks and erosion control, cut down for firewood and fodder, and they are a common motif in poetry and folklore.

Herding is practiced widely across the region and forms a central element of local cultures. High mountain areas provide plentiful grasslands for the grazing of cows, yaks, dzos (a cross between a cow and a yak), sheep (especially in the Pamir and the Iranian-speaking areas; see Parkes [1987]), goats (more in the Indic-speaking areas), horses, and occasionally camels. Herding is much less common in Tajikistan than in the other areas, again perhaps because of the Soviet transformation of local economies. In the Soviet part of the region, in Tajikistan, the division of labor was utterly transformed by the Communist system. Local people's occupation was not dependent on the imperatives and exigencies of local subsistence; instead food came from elsewhere and people worked as doctors or teachers or nurses.

The economy in the mountains of Pakistan has been radically transformed by its incorporation into the nation-state, the roads that have been built in the past twenty-five to thirty years, and the consequent elaboration of trade and tourism. Tourism has become a major component of the local environment in northern Pakistan, and it has radically altered local social conditions. With the construction of roads in Pakistan that cross into China there has also arrived a thriving commodity trade and an explosion in the number of roadside shopkeepers and providers of services for truck drivers and automobile drivers. The main market towns for Ismaʿilis in Pakistan are Gilgit, Aliabad (Hunza), Sost (Gojal), and Chitral. Smaller market centers within the Ismaʿili area include Gahkuch, Gupis, Mastuj, and Dainyore. In Tajikistan, the center of gravity for Ismaʿilis is the old Soviet garrison town of Khorog, although their traditional center was at Qala-ye Bar Panja, which is now in Afghanistan. Porshnev, across from and traditionally part of the latter settlement, also trumps Khorog in pre-Soviet historic significance.[3] Other important Badakhshani market towns are Murghab (in the Eastern

Pamir) and Qala-ye-Khumb (Kalaikhum) in Darwaz. Isma'ilis in China use Tashkurghan and Kashghar as their economic bases. And Afghan Isma'ilis gravitate toward Zebak, Jurm, and Faizabad.

The Isma'ili area of the circum-Himalayan region can be said to form a *sprachbund*, a geographically contiguous area of stunning ethnolinguistic diversity. Of particular interest here is the fact that many of the languages spoken display features associated with the archaic ancestral forms of their groups. For instance, many of the eastern Iranian or Indic languages of the region display a case system that has been lost in other Iranian languages. Many of the Indic languages display features of Iranian, and vice versa, which may suggest that these languages split off from the Indic or Iranian groups not long after the two split from each other. Among Pakistani Isma'ilis are found speakers of Indic languages of the "Dardic" group, with a case system characteristic of Old Indic languages, including Shina, in southern Hunza, the Gilgit region, and the western part of Ghizar (including lower Ishkoman, Gahkuch, and Gupis); and Khowar, spoken throughout Chitral, western Ghizar, including some of the population of Gupis, parts of Yasin and Ishkoman, and the Phander-Teru cluster. The Isma'ilis of northern Yasin and Ishkoman and the central Hunza valley speak Burushaski, which, as I mentioned before, is an isolate language unrelated to any other on earth. A small peripatetic Isma'ili population in Hunza speaks Domaaki, a New Indic language. In far northern Chitral, Yasin, and Ishkoman, including Baroghil and Karambar, in Chapursan, in the Ghujerab and Khunjerab watersheds on the Chinese border, in Shimshal, and in the part of northern Hunza known as Gojal, the Isma'ili population speaks the eastern Wakhi, a Pamiri language that is said to be the closest living relative to the language of the Zend-Avesta, the Zoroastrian sacred text written some three millennia ago. The Wakhi seem to be exclusively Isma'ili, and live in all four states of the Himalayan Isma'ili region. In far western Chitral there is an Isma'ili population speaking the eastern Iranian Pamiri language Yidgha, which is very close to Munji, spoken in Afghanistan.

In Tajikistan, Isma'ilis speak the Pamiri languages of Shughni, Rushani, Roshorvi, Khufi, Barjuvi, Wakhi, and Ishkashmi-Sanglechi, known in Tajikistan as Ryndagi for the one village in which it is spoken there (Ryn). All except the last two of these languages (Ryndagi and Wakhi) are mutually comprehensible and vary only slightly. They are thus more like dialects than separate languages. Isma'ilis in Yoged, near Qala-yi Khumb, and in the Garam Chashma area of Ishkashim district, speak Tajiki. In Afghanistan some also speak Ishkashmi-Sanglechi, Wakhi, Shughni, Rushani, and Tajiki

Young Wakhi-speaking Isma'ilis, Chapursan valley, Pakistan. This is one of the most remote Isma'ili areas of Pakistan, close to both the Afghan and Chinese borders.

or Dari. Further south there is a sizeable community that speaks Munji, which, like Wakhi and Ishkashmi, is not mutually comprehensible with the Shughni group of dialects. Afghan Munji and Yidgha, spoken in Pakistan, are mutually comprehensible. Finally, in China Isma'ilis speak Wakhi, Sari-qoli, closely related to Shughni, and sometimes Uyghur.

The linguistic situation of this region relates on some level to its status as a *refuge area*, a hinterland where historically people may have fled to escape disasters and invasions. It may also be that the linguistic map of these areas was determined by long-dead empires, and that in their isolation languages wiped out elsewhere survived there. There is a clear and marked similarity between the Indic languages of the southern part of this region and the language of Greco-Buddhist Gandhara (Fussmann 1972; Morgenstierne 1929), and it is known that the Hindu Shahi Rajas took refuge here during the Ghaznavid invasions. The northern regions may have acted as refuge areas for peoples of the Scythian, Bactrian, and Sogdian periods. The topography of the region, moreover, lends itself to linguistic diversity and rapid divergence, as in the past many of the language communities had little contact with each other.

This linguistic diversity corresponds to marked cultural syncretism. The cultural practices of the peoples of this region are markedly and visibly different from those of neighboring regions. This is particularly true of Ismaʿilis, who tend to be more willing than other Muslims to accommodate pre-Islamic practice. This pre-Islamic practice is rarely understood *as* pre-Islamic by local people and is often instead understood by them as Islamic. Nonetheless, it has been labeled un-Islamic by Sunni radical movements (like the Sipah-e-Sahaba in Pakistan) who seek to rid society of such elements. Ismaʿilism accommodates syncretism on the local and even on the official doctrinal level. It incorporates Neoplatonic, Zoroastrian, Manichaean, and Judeo-Christian belief even into its most fundamental cosmologies. But on the local level in the Himalayas, it adds Hindu, Buddhist, Bön, and indigenous practices and symbols to its already-diverse repertoire.

Many indigenous rituals and beliefs in the region are firmly rooted in an altitude-based cosmological complex that spans the Pamir, Karakoram, and Hindu Kush. The high places are associated with purity and goodness. These spaces are the domain of fairies, with their herds of ibex and markhor (wild goats, called *payaro* in Shina, *nakhchir* in Pamiri-speaking areas) along with snow leopards. It is for this reason that ibex horns so often adorn the apertures of sacred spaces. The valley floor and the village, in contrast, are considered impure and defiled, the zone of human activity. Demons and witches also abound here. In this altitude-based, vertical system, various domestic animals are assigned values according to their level of purity. Moreover, as different subsistence activities are carried out at different elevations, and since such activities are divided according to gender, the worldview has major implications for village life and gender relations. But Pamiri migrants in postwar, post-Soviet Dushanbe told me, in September of 2003, that *pari* (or *peri*, i.e., fairy, mountain sprite) beings no longer come down to their villages because humans have, in the modern moment, become impure and corrupted (as, they say, has Pamiri society), and the *paris* are now afraid. But, as we will see, what also emerges is that the *people* are afraid to pursue rituals involving forces deemed as pre-Islamic, local, and deviant from emergent institutional Ismaʿili norms.

Villagers from Chitral to Badakhshan (and even beyond, from valleys like Yaghnob and Yasin) attested to the vitality of these beliefs across the Pamir and Hindu Kush. Their fusion with Islam in local discourse is remarkable. For example, according to Safdar Alibekovitch, an Ismaʿili from Shughnan, the Ismaʿili missionary Nasir-i-Khusraw was surrounded by the *nakhchir* animals when he struck the ground to reveal a spring; locals saw it as a sign of his authenticity. A tradition in Porshnev tells of a villager who killed one of the *nakhchir* animals while hunting only to find, once it revealed itself in the form of a beautiful woman, that it was really a *pari*. His family was cursed to the seventh generation. Religious practitioners from the same village were said to wrap (Muslim) amulets (bearing written prayers) in the hide of the *nakhchir*. Safdar explained that the magical male spirit *vouj*, pre-Islamic in origin, "can only be seen by the pure who follow the tenets of Islam"!

Himalayan Isma'ilis generally incorporate pre-Islamic tradition more visibly into their practice than their Shi'i or Sunni neighbors. Many pre-Islamic traditions become emblems of shared identity among Isma'ilis and markers of boundaries with other groups. Such traditions might include the adornment of shrines with ibex horns; the sacred architecture of Pamiri houses, with each pillar having its own religious signification (see Salmaan Keshavjee 1998); the altitude-based cosmologies of northern Pakistan where the highest zones are the abodes of fairies and the most pure; rituals involving fire (such as *chiraghrawshan* (candle lighting), or Nawruz (the Persian New Year; and the use of shamans (i.e., *bitan* in Hunza or *dayal* in Gilgit).[4] One individual from Porshnev even spoke of these rituals as "Islamicized or *Isma'ilicized*." Thus, because of their local and regional associations, certain pre-Islamic practices and forms come to be seen *as* "Isma'ili", both by Isma'ilis and others, rather than as indigenous or pre-Islamic. They become recontextualized markers or emblems of Islamic Isma'ili identity. This is not something that occurs only on a local level; it has also been seized upon as an important symbol by the global Isma'ili institutional structure and its leadership. These emblems constitute a special focus of interest in the transnational Khoja milieu, marking as they do a certain type of authenticity. For instance, I discovered in the course of my research an unpublished report on the pre-Islamic practices of the Isma'ilis of the Pamir, produced by IIS and officially commissioned for a special seminar by the Aga Khan's brother, Prince Amyn. A set of practices identified as *non-Islamic*, then, come to index and stand for a certain *Islamic* identity.

A number of these ritual practices, including *chiraghrawshan* and those involving the *ziyarat* shrines, are unique to Himalayan Isma'ilism. Institutions like the ITREB that regulate and standardize the practice of Isma'ilism have made some of these practices objects of contention and contestation. As the villager from Porshnev explained, they "are politicizing everything nowadays." Certain local practices are now discouraged or proscribed; moreover, regional offices of the ITREB regulate even the standard regional

A village shrine in Porshnev, Gorno-Badakhshan, Tajikistan, adorned with Arabic calligraphy and featuring the distinctive architecture considered emblematic of Pamiri houses and sacred structures.

version of certain religious practices. Thus, there is now an ITREB/ITREC-approved version of the local *chiraghrawshan* ritual.

Moreover, a little-known group of Isma'ilis around the village of Darmorakht and a few other locations in Shughnan, Tajikistan, known as the *Panjibais*, practice a divergent variety of Isma'ilism that is distinct from that in Badakhshan as well as from the rest of the worldwide community. The written work of one scholar from Porshnev on the subject of regional shrine beliefs and practices of the Panjibais was reportedly censored first by state authorities and later by ITREC. As I describe in the next chapter, a documentary made by a Pamiri on the diversity of customs surrounding shrines, which depicted a broad range of nonstandard local practices, was also the object of strong disapproval by the ITREC. Even the subject matter of the film appeared to have been impacted: while editing the film in a studio in Dushanbe, the Pamiri filmmaker reported that "until the interference of ITREC, [the villagers] came to this shrine and they were singing these songs." Now, she explains, they are afraid not to follow the standardized ritual forms. So it is not only global Isma'ilism, but also regional

Isma'ili practices, that are now regulated and institutionalized. The long post-Mongol period of isolation created widely divergent communities. The current global context reveals a centralized attempt on the part of the imamate to end that isolation and disconnection.

The pre-Islamic practices of the region are of particular interest in the social context because they become an emblem of Isma'ili Muslim identity in relation to other groups. The Isma'ilis visibly and comfortably retain these practices even while some other Muslim groups seek actively to purge them from their societies. Thus, shamanism or saints' tombs or *chiraghrawshan* or rituals involving *peri*, although not Islamic or Isma'ili in their origin, become markers of Isma'ilism and thus distinctively Isma'ili practices. This is especially true when these practices are named and targeted by purist groups (e.g., the Sipah-e-Sahaba or the Tablighi Jama'at) as indicators of Isma'ilism. In such contexts, practices unique to the Isma'ili community become charged and politicized sites of contestation (see Comaroff 1985).

Himalayan Isma'ilis traditionally had no *jama'at khanas*; its spaces of worship were homes, meadows, shrines, public squares. However, Khoja missionaries brought *jama'at khanas* to northern Pakistan over half a century ago, and they are now well-entrenched there. The religious institutions of the imamate are currently in the process of establishing *jama'at khanas* in Tajikistan, which has never had such spaces for worship and where it took place secretly and in homes. The imamate is also currently constructing a new Isma'ili Center in Dushanbe. It will be the first structure and institution of its type in the city and the first official *jama'at khana* in former Soviet Central Asia. This dissemination of patently Khoja religious culture, particularly the trademark form of the *jama'at khana*, is at the core of enormous tensions. It is the object of significant resistance, particularly now in a post-Soviet Tajikistan, where religion had long been forbidden. Thus the introduction of Khoja culture forms connections in practice and experience between Isma'ili populations just as it introduces new fissures. In part due to imbalances in power between Khojas and others, the drive for unity is simultaneously the catalyst for fragmentation.

Carving the Landscape: National Borders and the Limits of Cultural Solidarity

After a long period of great isolation, in the 1870s some of the Himalayan Isma'ili areas now in Tajikistan and Afghanistan (especially Darwaz) came to be part of both the Emirate of Bukhara, which soon came under the influence and control of the Russian Empire of the Tsars, and the Emirate of Afghanistan. With the British expansion of their territories in India, the two empires began to clash in the very lands inhabited by the Isma'ilis. Russia and Britain thus faced each other in a complex set of maneuvers and machinations of espionage that came to be called by Rudyard Kipling, and then in popular parlance, "the Great Game." It was this encounter, which drew in Afghan, Iranian, and Chinese polities, that produced the borders that would divide the Isma'ili areas of the Himalaya. The Anglo-Russian Boundary Commission of 1895 created the state of Afghanistan as a buffer between the two empires and demarcated the current boundaries.[5] But it was also the incorporation of these areas into empires that ultimately engendered the improved channels of movement, trade, and communication that allowed increased contact between Isma'ili populations and the imamate. Now the imam's emissaries could once again travel to Hunza or Chitral or even Badakhshan to prescribe standard Isma'ili practice, to deliver the imam's decrees, and to establish Isma'ili social services in the area. This was helped by the special position in the British Empire accorded Aga Khan I, II, and III. Thus empire once again served as a channel and a vehicle for translocal connection and the incorporation of remote areas into an Isma'ili network.

The Russians formed a base in Khorogh in 1897–98 and began to gain control of the area. In the 1920s, when the Soviets established themselves as the region's major power, Islamic *basmachi* rebels began to flow across the border in one of the first transboundary movements (Akiner 2001: 10–12; Centlivres and Centlivres-Demont 1998:3; Shahrani 1979). A Shughnani resident of a border town explained to me that before 1917, there was moderately free movement across the border, but that after 1929 movement began to be more strictly controlled and was regulated in a system of required authorization. Violators could be severely sanctioned or even killed. Moreover, this process divided families, some of whom even now retain knowledge of their relatives on the other side. In 1937, according to locals, the border was closed completely.

The transformation of Himalayan Isma'ili society with the arrival of new national borders was of such a magnitude that it created new forms of divergence among the cultures of the Afghan, Tajik, Pakistani, and Chinese sides. What was previously a unitary, territorially contiguous sphere of interaction and movement (or at least one whose diversity was organized by ethnolinguistic or geographic elements) became now multiple societies divided by national borders, moving in new and very separate directions.[6] Afghan and

Tajikistan and surrounding states. Reprinted with the permission of the UN Cartographic Office, Tajikistan, no. 3765 Rev. 10, January 2004.

Tajik Badakhshan, for example, though adjacent, were no longer recognizable as a single sphere of circulation, both to outsiders and to the inhabitants of the respective sides. In the late 1800s, then, the area was carved up into Russian and British portions. By the 1920s parts of it were in the Soviet Union or Afghanistan, and by 1947 the British portions were in Pakistan. The parts of the Ismaʿili Himalaya that were in either British territory or later in Pakistan were the most accessible to globalizing forces and contacts. Major paved roads, most notably the Karakoram Highway built in 1982, reached northern Pakistan in the latter portion of the twentieth century and brought with them tourism, large-scale trade, and heightened connections with the rest of the world. Portions of the Ismaʿili region in China and the Soviet Union were part of translocal circulations confined to the borders of those polities alone; moreover, the bases and substance of translocal circulation in these areas were circumscribed by the restrictions on interaction imposed by the various states. Translocal circulation in the Soviet Union was in most cases limited to the orchestrations and machinations licensed by state Communism. Thus Himalayan Isma'ili societies came to be defined and divided by their allocation to a national territory.

Much is revealed by local perceptions of the border. A native of the border village of Porshnev, for example, put it in the following terms:

> The old men and women who are still alive say that it was the border that separated two undividable sides, the thing that separated the homogeneous culture of a blood-related people into two parts. They don't even call the people of the opposite side Afghans. If in front of them you call the other part Afghanistan, they will remind you that Afghans are different and that the name of the opposite side is not Afghanistan but rather *wiruya* [a Shughni word]. Some of them even nowadays might get angry when one calls the people of the other side "Afghans" and they might again remind you of a better equivalent for them as *wiruyayej*, i.e. the ones from that side. They usually anchor what they say in the fact of having close relatives there who have the same language, culture, and religion, some of whom left there since 1895, the time when the border was divided by Russia and Britain and others of whom settled there because of Stalin's repressions in the thirties.

A native of the Rushon Valley provided the following characterization:

> Afghans: backward, barbaric, conservative, traditional. Tajiks: progressive and civilized, modern. Some people—mainly with a background in Soviet propaganda—looked at the Afghans negatively, as hostile, uneducated, barbaric, backward. They said the Afghans cause trouble—sell weapons, and drugs, torture and kill people, and bring infectious deceases like malaria, typhoid, diarrhea, etc. Other people—mainly people who grew up before the Soviet time—said the Afghans are similar to Tajiks, having similar culture, language, religion, traditions, and that the Soviets are just separating Tajiks and Afghans because they are afraid the Afghans will make the Tajiks fight against the Soviets.

During the Soviet era even discussion of Afghanistan was forbidden. Tajik Pamiris from Khorog, Porshnev, Ishkashim, and Rushan corroborate that locals could be and were punished for pointing across the border, questioned even for looking across. Thus, the border was, as it is now, simultaneously a looming, pervasive presence and a forbidden topic. My guide characterized verbal reference to the border during that period as "extremely risky." He continued: "There was 100 percent likelihood that you would suffer from talking about the border and that side. And people used to remind their children to avoid talking about the border and that side." Afghanistan was absolutely taboo.

If framed in terms of a teleological evolutionism as embodied in locally incorporated popular doctrines of Marxism, Afghanistan was at an earlier stage of history, somehow stuck in the past. It could thus be constructed as a savage place, one where the laws of society were not only different but somehow broken down or underdeveloped. Afghanistan had yet to reach the perceived postrevolutionary apex of Communism that had been achieved in the Soviet lands. These views, while finding their origin in European evolutionist philosophies by way of the Enlightenment, Hegel, Marx, and Lenin, did in fact entrench themselves into emergent political belief systems of the Soviet Union, European and non-European. Thus, Marxist concepts, including revolution, progress, and cultural evolution, became facets of local worldviews in places like the Pamir. They found their ways into individual and collective subjectivities, where they remain, even in this post-Soviet moment.

Afghanistan is thus even now seen as the primary source of local pollution and pestilence. Tajik Pamiris have described it to me, variously, as the source of scabies, disease in general, a vicious dust-bearing wind known as *afghanets*, destabilizing narcotics, dangerous arms, Islamic fundamentalism, violence, and general disorder. In addition, this characterization extends to the past. One Shughni subject referred to "the violence and misdeeds that the Afghans did on our side," including stories of "raping virgin girls and gathering virgins and small boys for Afghan amirs for sodomy." Other stories recounted (somewhat disapprovingly) by Pamiris who have visited the other side refer to fertilization of fields with human excrement, the polluting presence of animals and their droppings in the house, and disrespectful treatment of bread, considered sacrosanct on the Tajik side. A Pamiri who had crossed the border, in an interesting conflation of patriarchal and political metadiscourses, explained that (despite an expectation or at least a suspicion of beauty) the "girls" of the Afghan side were in fact not beautiful because of the degree to which they must work the land from a young age. Another informant expressed that there is "chaos there: no law, no development, no education, no rights for women, child labor, poor health, and lots of drugs."

In general, the construction of self in relation to this other is intimately bound up with conceptions of time and history. A temporal-spatial equivalency is formed in which it becomes possible to say, "that space is in another time" (cf. Fabian 1983; Gupta and Ferguson 1992). Afghanistan becomes a chronotope (Bakhtin 1981) of a particular kind. A Pamiri informant explained simply that "Afghanistan resembles Tajikistan before 1917," and another informant said that the Isma'ili Muslims on the far side still follow the religion in the "old spirit." Perhaps most fundamentally, this other is constructed as an earlier version of the self as it existed in its own past; that other represents the self at an earlier stage of "progress" and "cultural evolution." The photonegative other is thus also a primordial, wild, organic imagining of self.

In the perception of the Pamiris of Badakhshan, as described above, Afghanistan remains the locus of anarchy, poverty, and tribalism. It is the site of militant Islam, drug trafficking, and violence. A stark difference between the two sides is in fact visible; on the Afghan side, there is no electricity, almost no motorized transport, few schools, and little built infrastructure. Buildings are constructed in traditional style. It is this which motivated my Pamiri guide to say, as we drove along the border, "It's a medieval landscape, huh?" Later he explained: "They are a backward folk with medieval houses, with animals and humans in the same house. That side of Afghanistan is very different from this side, the Pamir. First of all when one looks at the opposite side, he will discover that there is a medieval scenery in front of him: unpainted houses without roofs, darkness from sunset till dawn." Consider the following comments on a trip to Afghanistan provided by a Pamiri scholar while showing film footage of that trip: "Lake Shiva is paradise. . . . You had to be there and feel the weather. It is so fresh and so clean, you know. . . . I was in paradise at that time. I was in the paradise at that moment. . . . It is beautiful here on TV, but the reality is so . . . The language is the same but their attitude is different. Psychologically, they are quite different. . . . You had to be there." The complement of the discourse of pestilence and contamination is an orientalist and nostalgic discourse of exotic and pristine purity, a primeval and romantic vision of one's own perceived past.

Recent historical conditions have played some role in the partial disruption of those orientalist and evolutionist discourses, opening up the possibility for new formulations of identity and new orientations of each side toward the other. The civil war and its aftermath and the arrival of the Aga Khan's institutions, in particular, have played a role in transforming and disintegrating some of the ideas of evolution and progress that define Tajik discourses of the Afghans on the other side. An anecdote from postwar Tajikistan, recounted to me in 2004, exemplifies this: An expert driver in the employ of AKDN, known to many as the best driver of the Pamir's precipitous roads, broke down in an isolated area between Ishkashim and Khorog on the road that runs along the river that forms the border. After trying unsuccessfully to solve the problem, his only option was to walk the long distance to the next town. The driver began walking on the desolate paved road along the border. As he walked, an Afghan Pamiri approached on the dusty path running along the mountain slope on the other side. As is common in places where the two sides come into very close proximity, the Tajik Pamiri driver and the Afghan villager shouted greetings at each other. Considering the isolation of the location, the Afghan then inquired, "why are you walking?" The driver of course relayed his predicament. The Afghan, in response, laughed: "Ha! Look at you! At least we have donkeys!"[7]

This story reflects a subversion of supposed order, an inversion of the notion of progress so central to the sense of difference between the two sides. In a situation where the social fabric has been torn, where humanitarian aid agencies are now at the heart of local society, there is a sense that the treasured "advancements" of the Soviet era have been reversed. This process itself brings the denizens of the other side into closer imagined proximity, breaking down some of the orientalisms and romanticizations that allowed the Tajik Pamiris to hold themselves up as so much more advanced and cultured than their neighbors, increasing the potential for contact on a more equal footing, and bringing the two sides into closer contact.

The change in the status of the border of course reflects deeply transformed orientations toward capital on both sides. In the Soviet era the focus in Tajikistan was on keeping capital out at all costs; capital was a contamination, a polluting force. Now Tajikistan is making its first tentative steps toward participation in a capitalist system, although many Communist institutions remain, at least informally. And Afghanistan, long cut off from global capital by its long saga of violence, has also changed its stance toward the world economy. Afghanistan, thrust into the public eye by the events of 9/11, has suddenly become a focal point for capitalist activity, virgin ground for market exploitation and exploration. The border cannot help but reflect these changes. My Pamiri informant Safdar Alibekovitch remarked that the other side is now "a potential way to world markets." Rather than an impermeable barrier dividing political worlds, the border may now become a line marking transition from one zone of administration and trade to another, from one (diminished) sovereignty to the next.

In Badakhshan, divided populations are now being intensively drawn together through the shared structures of Isma'ilism and the expansion of AKDN. The populations, historically unified and then divided, are now being made to see each other once again as part of a single sphere.[8] The significance of the border is transforming, and territory might better be formulated as organized into something like what Aihwa Ong (1999) describes as "zones of graduated sovereignty" (217) rather than exclusive and self-contained domains of activity. What will happen to the perceptions engendered by the historical separation of peoples when they are reconnected and begin again to mix and interact (cf. Balibar 2002: 85)? Perhaps the dialectically constructed image of the other will merge with that metadiscourse of the self that it once differed so radically from. Alternatively, perhaps the opening of the border will create new fractal forms of nested inequality: the Tajik Pamiris to the Afghans as the Khojas to the Tajik Pamiris?

The Tajik Civil War: A Primer

Travelers who drive across Tajikistan on the M-41 road from Dushanbe to the Gorno-Badakhshan Autonomous Oblast, the Pamir Highway, will see the abandoned and decaying skeletons of tanks and bombed-out structures lining the entire route. Going farther, they will notice that the road deteriorates, and even seems to disappear at times, as they approach the autonomous region and begin seeing the remains of the Tajik civil war: tanks and shells left just where they were when the tide turned one way or another, or maybe when the machinery failed; roads intentionally left by the government to decay and wash away in an effort to cut off rebellious areas; villages abandoned entirely; and minefields marked with a sign or two. If the travelers don't try, they won't see much more. Tens of thousands of lives were lost in the Tajik civil war, and it lasted for four full years. It was vicious and brutal. It involved ethnic cleansing and mass graves, and the world hardly noticed it.[9]

The exclusion of Isma'ilis in Tajikistan must be framed at least in part in the context of the Tajik civil war, which itself cannot be understood without some review of the Tajik incorporation into Russian and Soviet polities. By 1917 Basmachi rebels had mounted a fierce resistance to Russian rule. In 1921 Tajikistan became part of the Turkistan Autonomous Soviet Socialist Republic. Three years later, in 1924, it was made into the Tajik Autonomous Soviet Socialist Republic of the Uzbek Soviet Socialist Republic. In 1929, Tajikistan was made into to a full-fledged republic of the Soviet Union, in part because the Soviets wanted to make a showpiece of Socialism to send a message to the Persian-speaking peoples in Iran, Afghanistan, and British India. Stalin never really trusted the rebellious and remote republic: until 1941, the Communist chiefs of the Tajik SSR were of Russian and Moldovan origin. After that, the Soviets co-opted Tajiks from the more "loyal" and industrialized Leninabad (Khojand) area to do the job. They became the controlling ethnic group.[10]

With its divide-and-rule policy, the Soviets had always favored certain Tajik clans over others. Between 1941 and 1991, native Communist bosses in the Tajik SSR came from Khojand-Leninanbad clans, while their junior partners from Kulob staffed the police and the army. The clans from the mountainous regions of Karategin, Zeravshan, and Badakhshan — the latter the home of the Isma'ilis — were largely excluded from the power system. Between 1949 and 1960, the Soviets forcibly relocated thousands of families from mountain areas for intensive labor in the cotton plantations in the hot and malaria-ridden Vakhsh valley. Many remain.[11]

The disadvantaged and dispossessed people of this system, especially the mountain people, started to mobilize themselves around politicized forms of Islam and, to a lesser extent, democratic and nationalist groups: "Culturally distinct, more purely 'Iranian' subgroups, whose mountain origin underlay both their relative ethnic homogeneity and their lack of access to the assets of the Soviet state and economy, took advantage of the weakening of the state to seek a radical break with the imperial heritage" (Rubin 1998: 128). Once Gorbachev's *perestroika* set in, the most important opposition movement became the Islamic Renaissance Party (IRP).

After a failed coup attempt in Moscow, Tajikistan declared itself independent on September 9, 1991. The coup was carried out by Communist hardliners to take control of the Soviet government, now perceived as lax. Elections were held soon thereafter. Rahmon Nabiev, a Communist functionary from Leninabad-Khojand who had once been a party leader, was elected head of state with a majority of the votes. Opposition candidate and film director Davlat Khudonazarov, a Pamiri Isma'ili, came in second with 30 percent. The Supreme Soviet at this point elected a new neo-Soviet government, keeping the regional inequalities in the political power structure. Government officials came from the Khujand, Kulob, and Hisor regions, whereas the opposition was based in the southern Qurghonteppa (Kurgan-Tyube) region, the Garm (Gharm) valley to the east of Dushanbe, and Gorno-Badakhshan (the Pamir) in the east. Under pressure by the dominant regional structure, the urban Pamiris of Dushanbe began to organize.

Discontent at policies like this, and Nabiev's reluctance to share power, triggered more than seven weeks of opposition demonstrations in Dushanbe in March and April 1992, by which time Islamist Gharmis had joined secularist pro-democracy Pamiris. Olivier Roy (2000) writes that "the real issue was the rising power of the excluded regionalist groups (Gharmis and Pamiris) against the Communist establishment" (140). The details of the political power struggles between Nabiev and others are beyond the scope of this account; it is sufficient to say here that the regional galvanization of the government now intensified, and that the country reached the point of no return in May of 1992 when Nabiev had thousands of machine guns distributed among his supporters and formed the Popular Front. The Kulobi opposition, defeated, retreated promptly.

The Uzbekistan-supported Popular Front was at first a ragtag army, though soon it would form the bulk of the pro-government forces. The first battles between opposition fighters and government forces now began near Dushanbe. Fighting quickly spread. In September of 1992, Nabiev was arrested and forced by a group called the "Youth of Dushanbe" to resign. At this point Akbarsho Iskanderov, a moderate opposition leader from Darwaz in Badakhshan, took his place. The Islamic-democratic alliance formed a military coalition called the Popular Democratic Army and held control of Dushanbe until December. They agreed to hand over the city when the new government was formed, but militias loyal to the government attacked and captured the capital anyway.[12]

In reaction to all this, and in rejection of the coalition government, temporarily dispossessed pro-Communist forces appointed Imomali Rahmonov, until then a relatively unknown state farm manager from Kulob, as head of state and the Supreme Soviet. Tajikistan now entered full-blown civil war. The pro-Communist Popular Front seized Dushanbe in December 1992 and overthrew the coalition government. Fighting spread to Kulob, Kurghonteppa, Karategin, and Badakhshan. The opposition retreated to the mountains of Karategin and Badakhshan and to Afghanistan, from where it continued to mount a guerilla war. The violence of the civil war killed tens of thousands and created hundreds of thousands of refugees through early 1993. The Pamiris, acting primarily as "Pamiris" and not as "Isma'ilis," maintained control and autonomy over Gorno-Badakhshan. They recognized Dushanbe, and they accepted the presence and regime of Russian peacekeepers. The area became a central station on the drug route. The power of the Soviet classifications of territory was too much for anyone to overcome, even the power holders.

As the government cracked down on the press, the supreme court officially banned all opposition parties in June 1993, leaving the Communist Party of Tajikistan as the only legal party in the country. In 1993 there was a Peace and Reconciliation Conference in Khorog, but even after it Badakhshan was subject to campaigns by helicopter gunships and fighter jets. In early 1994, the IRP, the Democratic Party, and a selection of other groups formed the United Tajik Opposition, or UTO. Later that year the two sides reached a temporary cease-fire accord and agreed to seek reconciliation through political means. The United Nations sent an observer mission to monitor it. Late in 1996 an official cease-fire was declared, followed up by several rounds of talks and a peace agreement in June 1997. The agreement set up a power-sharing body. The final toll: between 50,000 and 90,000 lives, 600,000 forced from homes, 80,000 forced to leave the country, and billions of dollars' worth of destruction (Akiner 2001). All the while, the ex-Communist elite, embodied in Rahmonov, extended the domain of their power, stretching terms, shutting down civil liberties, rigging elections, and practicing ethnic exclusion. This is one of the points where AKF's privileging of the Pamiris gains extra significance.

What was the Tajik civil war fundamentally about? Olivier Roy (2000) writes that "this was a savage war: massacres, rape, torture, looting and summary executions. The lower Vakhsh valley was the scene of Serb-style ethnic cleansing. The houses of Gharmis and Pamiris were systematically destroyed and the civilian populations fled towards the border with Afghanistan" (140). Perhaps most important, Tajikistan was one of only a few post-Soviet places where an opposition mounted a serious challenge to the old Soviet guard. The war was about the massive and swift reaction to that opposition. It was at least in part about punishment for rebellion against the Soviet elite, which entrenched itself firmly after the war.

The Soviet nationalities policy played a central part in this story. Not surprisingly, the major parties to the conflict were divided according to the Soviet division of nationalities in Tajikistan, with the Pamiri rebels occupying what had been an autonomous region for a separate nationality during Soviet times. Related to this is the role of *ethnicity*. "Pamiri" as a unified ethnicity didn't exist before the Soviet period—people in the mountains categorized themselves according to their location in various mountain valleys. Even "Tajik" was a category that simply referred to speakers of Iranian languages in contrast to speakers of Turkic ones—Tajiks were more likely to describe themselves by the name of their clan than as Tajiks; they were unlikely, then, to see themselves as members of a centralized group. So the

Soviets in effect *created* the ethnicities that came to see themselves as fundamentally opposed and primordially different unified ethnic groups in the civil war. Their censuses and nationalities policy produced the groups that formed the war's parties.

The implications for the Pamiri Isma'ilis have been profound and manifold. The war played a key role in furthering the distinction, first of all, between "Pamiri" or "Badakhshani" and "Tajik," and in bolstering the notion of a unitary "Pamiri" identity. Perhaps more important was its role in engendering the emergence of "Isma'ili" as a major category of identity in Tajikistan. During the war, the government had cut off supply lines and let the roads badly deteriorate. The Pamiris found themselves, cut off as they were from the rest of Tajikistan, on the edge of famine. It was the Isma'ili network, at first through the Pamir Relief and Development Program (PRDP), that saved their lives. Thus resources, no longer derived either from the Soviet Union or from Tajikistan itself, were provided by a global assemblage. Badakhshan itself became a floating territory, for all intents and purposes part of no national state at all. The Isma'ili complex became far more involved in their administration and daily needs than any state. As Salmaan Keshavjee (1998) writes, "Imamate-sponsored non-governmental organizations are expected to take on a leadership role in areas that were previously under the purview of the state, fulfilling a role left open by the government's inability to carry out its traditional function" (67). The words of two of Keshavjee's Pamiri ethnographic subjects express it well. "AKF and PRDP," explained the first, "should do the job of the government because the government seems unable to do anything. The Huqqumat survives because of AKF/PRDP. The government only functions with the fuel of AKF" (66). The second put it even more simply: "Then the imam came and now we are happy to have him do what the state did" (69).

Some of this dissatisfaction was attributable to the degree to which people had grown accustomed to obtaining food through the Soviet system of distribution; they essentially forgot how to cultivate crops and subsist on what they grew. Food had come from Moscow and other places throughout the USSR. Villagers were doctors and engineers and academics and had no need to learn how to farm and herd. The system provided. So when the region was cut off from trade and commerce, they began to starve. They didn't know how to herd goats. They didn't know how to irrigate the hillside anymore. The Aga Khan's subsidiary organizations consequently trucked humanitarian convoys in from Osh, in Kyrgyzstan.

The Tajik civil war effected and cemented the exclusion of Pamiri Isma'ilis, which motivated them to seek resources and membership in a new formation that accorded them higher status. For the first time, they were placed at the center, rather than the edge, and they were allocated material and symbolic resources that gave them a comparative advantage over the neighbors and competitors who had disenfranchised them. In the wake of the war, as we will see below, the primacy of AKF has remained. In the mountains of Tajikistan and Pakistan, the Isma'ili global assemblage constitutes an administrative and symbolic entity in many ways more significant than the state itself. The implications for sovereignty and citizenship are significant. Who really governs the inhabitants of these regions? Of how many formations are they members?

Intersectarian Violence in Northern Pakistan

Isma'ilis in neighboring northern Pakistan are for a variety of reasons the objects of marginalization and persecution, and within both the region and the nation their status as citizens is less than complete. They are, to begin with, inhabitants (except in Chitral) of the region referred to as the "Northern Areas," a portion of disputed Kashmir long claimed by India and administered by Pakistan. Due to the disputed status of the region, it was at the time of my research administered directly from the Islamabad, the capital of Pakistan. Many Pakistanis claimed that the reason for this was related to national policy on Kashmir: to give the Northern Areas the status of a province would be to cede to the division of Kashmir, to settle for only a portion and recognize that one part is officially held by Pakistan and the rest by India. The implications of this for local life were significant; the military was ubiquitous, the regional council weak and ineffective, and the bodies of local government underdeveloped and with little power. The local people had little to no parliamentary representation and no right of petition to the supreme court. Many locals expressed a disillusionment with Pakistan and perceived that it had not fully incorporated the Northern Areas into national life, that inhabitants of the territory were less than citizens, and that they correspondingly had fewer privileges and rights.

Serious violent conflict broke out in the summer of 1988 around the celebration of Eid, which falls at the end of the month of fasting, Ramadan. Members of the Shi'a sect in the town of Gilgit, the administrative center of the Northern Areas, are said to have broken the fast a day earlier than the local Sunnis due to what appears to have been a difference of doctrinal interpretation. Shi'a celebration in the main bazaar was reported to have sparked the tension; a fight broke out, and a young Sunni man was shot dead. Soon after this incident, according to locals' reports, Sunni clergy had mobilized huge informal militias from the Sunni-populated mountains south of Gilgit, calling for "retaliation." Thousands of armed men from these populations reportedly moved towards Gilgit and the predominantly Shiʿa and Ismaʿili areas that lie north, east, and west of the town in the regions of Baltistan, Ghizar, and Hunza. Shiʿa and Ismaʿili residents of the Northern Areas interpreted this attack as persecution in Pakistani national society: they report that police checkpoints not only failed to stop but were complicit in letting the armies pass.

According to these accounts, the militias attacked Shiʿa villages, encircling, burning, and pillaging them.[13] They shot villagers, burned houses and trees, and slaughtered livestock. Local makeshift resistance forces were reportedly overwhelmed. An essential element of the narratives I gathered from locals on this matter is that the regional military knew about and was complicit in the attacks, doing nothing to bring them to a stop for several days and reporting nothing to newspapers. At least ten villages — mostly Ithnaʿashari Shiʿi — were attacked; many people fled their homes for the safety of upper valleys, but as the internally displaced people arrived, the fear had spread to these Ismaʿili areas as well. Many villagers described their loss of loved ones; one told a story of an elder who refused to leave the village and was slaughtered. Others described what they perceived as senseless and excessive violence — the destruction of livestock, the burning of houses after their residents had fled. In the end, the military imposed a cease-fire.

Many eyewitnesses to the conflict tie it to the existence of the military regime of Zia-ul-Haq. They interpret the conflicts according to a desire on the part of that government to instigate clashes and then "create" peace, thereby legitimating its own power and the need for a police state. Narrated histories were full of accounts of administrators and officials admitting their participation. Moreover, numerous villagers connected this attack to foreign nation-states: Zia was backed by the American government, as he was an important ally in the channeling of funds, *mujahidin*, and weapons to resist the Soviet invasion of Afghanistan. So some residents of the Northern Areas tie the massacres to the United States through Zia-ul-Haq, and others claim that the United States was involved to counter Iranian influence. Others point to involvement by India, Iran, and, unexpectedly, the timber industry.

In the aftermath, the government constructed "relocation villages" (like

Jagote Sai) for victims of the massacres. Residents of Jalalabad, the worst-affected village, say that they received "commando training." Local sectarian violence and tension has repeated itself year after year in the Northern Areas, even in the last decade, with ensuing government-imposed curfews. But in terms of the number of deaths, and in the memory of the people on this borderland, nothing compares to "1988," whose very utterance (*atthasi*) has become a potent icon in itself.[14]

It was the Ithna'ashari Shi'a of the area that suffered most deeply and directly because of the incident, but it represented to Isma'ilis a moment embodying a structural paradigm in which they also understood themselves as the potential targets of violence and persecution, and indeed increasingly in subsequent years they were. The Isma'ilis, seeing the Shi'a refugees, understood clearly the significance of the moment: they too, it was clear, were at risk. The fragile and shifting alliance between Pakistani governments and radical Sunni movements is accurately seen by Isma'ilis as a perilous element of uncertainty in regional life. The presence of the AKRSP (discussed in Chapter 5) generates even greater tension: it can be a source of jealousy and resentment, and it can also draw attention to the perception of Isma'ilis as non-Muslims.

The primary source of discomfort for Isma'ilis in northern Pakistan is the focus by Sunni revivalist groups on their conversion — and sometimes on their violent elimination. Groups like the Sipah-e-Sahaba of Pakistan (SSP) seek to frame Isma'ilis as non-Muslims and work actively toward their subordination. Missionary groups like the Tablighi Jama'at, widely active in Gilgit and throughout the Northern Areas (see Metcalf 1993, 2004; Masud 2000) while superficially nonviolent, also play a role in representing the Isma'ilis as *kafirs*, infidels. This engenders a sense in the populations of places like Hunza and Ghizar that they are always the potential victims of violence, exclusion, and even massacre. For our purposes, however, the key fact is that such a structural position motivates local Isma'ilis to seek security — symbolic and material — in regional *Isma'ili* institutions where, unlike in the domains of public Islam, the Pakistani state, and local ethnic relations, they are the beneficiaries of great privilege.

Marsden (2005) shows, however, that tension between Isma'ilis and others in Pakistan is not always a direct product of the charged national or global politics of Islam, but rather of village relationships and "sectarian boundaries." His rich study of the Muslims — Isma'ili and Sunni — of Chitral's Rowshan village reveals the way that multiple modalities of conflict between the two "communities" emerges out of local boundary-making projects and efforts to construct contrastive and dialectic identities. AKDN and larger Sunni movements like the SSP, he shows, do indeed contribute to the tension, but it seems that their role is largely symbolic and that their relevance is in their local mobilization. The conflict, writes Marsden, "is about underlying anxieties about inner dimensions of life and self shared by both Ismaʿilis and Sunnis . . . [and] what it means to live an emotionally legitimate and intellectually significant Muslim life" (249). At the heart of all this are the expression of religious emotion, the maintenance of secrecy, and the pursuit of debates over the nature and content of faith. In the next section, we will see that these concerns, despite the radically different course of events in former Soviet areas, are not themselves absent from the politics of identity in the Pamir.

Pamiri/Ismaʿili: A Fluid Calculus of Identity

The definition of identity in the Tajikistan Pamir is, like everywhere else, fluid and subject to the ever-shifting exigencies of political power. Identity in Badakhshan is clearly a product of the conceptions of status dictated by relations with the larger post-Soviet polity in which the territory is situated. The relationship between local community, language community, and religion are essential in the formation of identity, but the relationship between these three in Badakhshan has changed profoundly. Their relative configuration is, in fact, defined by change. They have changed so frequently and with such magnitude that one generation hardly remembers the ethnonyms and self-appellations used by the last. An Ismaʿili who grew up in Kashgar and then in Tashkurghan, China, for example, explained that the term "Ismaʿili" itself is very new and only came into vogue in eastern Turkestan after the Aga Khan visited the Id Gah mosque in Kashgar in 1982. Before that, Ismaʿilis used the term *Panchtani* (of the Five Bodies: Ali, Fatima, et al.) to contrast themselves to Uyghur Sunnis, whom they referred to as *Choryori* (of the Four Friends: Abu Bakr, Usman, et al.). However, they did not hide their identities, as they wanted to remain distinct not from Han Chinese but from Uyghurs themselves. Consider what he had to say on the matter (I am labeled "J" and the respondent "A," for Amanullah):

J: Well when did you learn that you were Ismaʿili?
A: I inherited it, as if I knew it from the time of my childhood.

J: And you, did someone explain it to you, or it was just part of your family life?

A: Yeah, we didn't question that, no. There was no need to explain it. I was just told when I was a kid, "you're Panchtani." Even Isma'ili is a new term we adopted in the '80s after the route was opened into Pakistan, it's a new concept. Now the people call themselves Isma'ilis. We used to call ourselves Panchtani to contrast with Sunni.

J: What is Panchtani?

A: Panchtani means Shi'a, you know, the followers of 'Ali's family, "Panch Tan," Muhammad, 'Ali, Fatima, their two sons Hasan and Husayn.

J: And what is Choryori?

A: Choryori is the followers of those two guys, that's what we, Abu Bakr, Usman, what was the third guy . . .

J: Abu Bakr, Usman, 'Ali . . .

A: Before 'Ali, Choryori, because for us, 'Ali is the rightful successor to the prophet, so Choryori means Sunni for us.

J: And Panchtani . . . So, when you grew up, and you had this discourse of the Panchtani, I mean did people know that there was an imam out there, or not?

A: Yeah, it was kind of a mutual consensus reached by the community. They thought the imam is actually himself a god to some extent, even physically is a . . . You see when we were kids they used to tell us these stories about the imam: never eats food, you will never see him eating food, you never see him sleeping, and he is just, how can I say, omnipotent, everywhere?

J: Omnipresent?

A: Omnipresent, and there was the story that once the imam went somewhere to a Sunni mosque and he walked seven steps forward and turned back and started to speak the language of the Uyghur people, this kind of thing . . .

J: Magical stories . . . but did they know who or where he was in fact or not?

A: Yeah, until '82 we thought he was in Bombay, because that's where we broke the communi-, our communication broke. That last *farman* was received in 1947 from Sultan Muhammad Shah when he was still in Bombay.

J: In Bombay.

A: Yeah.

J: How did it come?

A: No idea, maybe he sent it through a messenger.

J: Horseback?

A: Horseback, definitely, yes, and that's where every communication stopped, because in '49 the Communist government took charge of the border, and the border was closed. Until then it was very loose, there was no border checking and all these things like today, the political border was kind of very loose and porous; everyone could cross, especially the nomad people from that area. So there are a lot of families with some parts in northern Pakistan, some in Afghanistan, and some in Badakhshan, Tajikistan. At that time it was just, we separated those other parts from Tashkurghan by local names; they wouldn't say they were from Pakistan or Tajikistan but rather they would say Hunzai, Wakhani, or say Badakhshani place names, not the very new names of the countries.

J: Were you told to keep, I mean, were you told to keep quiet about being Isma'ili when you were growing up—

A: No.

J: By your family?

A: No, we were very proud actually of presenting ourselves as Isma'ili because we looked at the Sunnis as a—

J: Panchtani?

A: Yeah, looked at them as not Muslims and we laughed at them and even if they were praying or calling for the prayer. . . .

J: How do Chinese Isma'ili children know that they're Isma'ili, just from parent to child?

S: Yeah. They have, they had *jama'at khanas*, it's an inherited religion actually, it was not very widely practiced, but in Yarkand, Karghalik and that area where they live among the Sunnis they practiced because it was again a part of that whole society surrounding them. The Uyghurs are practicing, and it was becoming only normal, to distinguish yourself from non-Muslims, from Hans, by practicing, and the Isma'ilis did not want to fall behind the Sunnis, and they were also keeping the faith alive due to these, maybe there was another reason, but I see this as one of the major rea-

sons for them to keep going even during this very hard and difficult time.

The example demonstrates the fluidity and contextuality of identities rooted
in specific localities.

The following excerpt from a recorded discussion with a native of the
remote Roshorv village in Tajikistan's Gorno-Badakhshan further indicates
this fluidity ("A" is for Amirbek).

J: Well first of all let me ask, how would you describe your identity?
    Who you are . . .

A: Oh, who I am?

J: Yeah. What are the things . . .

A: Who am I now.

J: Yeah. What are the things that would come to your self-
    description first?

A: First I am . . . Well if you would like would like to put things this
    way, then I can . . . Identity can be changed, can be subject to
    change, every time I — At the moment what I want to describe
    myself as is someone from Gorno-Badakhshan.

J: Mm hm.

A: From that area, from Badakhshan. Um, coming from, ethnically
    maybe I belong to "Tajik." They call us most of us "Pamiris" but
    I myself call us "Badakhshani." I came from Badakhshan, my
    mother language is Roshorvi, which is one of the Pamiri lan-
    guages. My religious background is Isma'ili and I myself am a fol-
    lower of this sect of Islam, so I cannot describe my . . . I can't say,
    yes, I am Badakhshani, and coming from Tajikistan, but ethnic —
    religiously I am Isma'ili. Ethnically I am just, called . . . depending
    on who you . . . Pamiri. They call it Pamiri.

J: Would you have described yourself as Isma'ili, you know, during
    the '80s, when it was still the Soviet period?

A: During the '80s?

J: Yeah.

A: That's part of my, my family background. I knew, I knew some-
    thing about it. I knew. I mean, I wouldn't. We called ourselves by
    Panchtani, Panchtani.

J: Panjibai?

A: Panchtani.

J: Panchtan.

A: Not Panjibai, Panchtani.

J: Five bodies.

A: Yes.

J: What does it mean, what is it?

A: Panchtan is like the five members of the Prophet's family; that's what I always learned from my family.

J: Your family is in that lineage . . .

A: I mean, I don't want, they called us, we referred to ourselves as Panchtani and Ismoiliyya [Isma'ili], and then, the term *Isma'ili* is coming right now, you know, right now becoming much more popular. We knew that we were Isma'ilis but we also called ourselves Panchtanis, but my dad was telling me that whenever he meets a person from the Pamir or wherever, you know, some people called Choryori, the followers of the four rightly guided *khalifas* in Islam, we were called "five," panchtanis, five bodies, like Muhammad, Fatima, Hasan and Hussein, Fatima, and Ali.

J: Right.

A: And in our family the pillars are also like this.

J: Um, but, so Choryori, is, all of these terms mean Isma'ili, right?

A: Yeah, Panchtani means Isma'ili, Choryori are like the Sunnis, we called them, but we called ourselves Panchtani, we were Panchtan—and Shi'a, and all these terms, and all of these were there. Not the Isma'ilis that now we call ourselves. Now this . . . became something much more, you know, it carries many more connotations and much more connection and it is much more dominant now.

J: Who did that? Who are the agents of that? I mean, who made, who is, how is it that it became more dominant physically, like how . . .

A: Oh well, physically, the connection is with the global community of Isma'ilism and the arrival of the Aga Khan, of the Imam of the Time to Badakhshan. The connection with the Imam of the time. That's what physically made it possible for "Isma'ili" to be dominant.

The Tajik civil war had a profound impact on the roles of local community, language community, and religion. The Soviets created the concept of "Pamiri" as a separate category of identity, and the civil war galvanized it. It is not clear at what point this occurred, but the consensus in Badakhshan is that "Pamiri" and "Tajik" are not only utterly different and distant, but diametrically opposed. Pamiris will not abide being called Tajik. They tend to express antipathy toward Tajiks and make a considerable effort to set themselves apart from that ethnicity. Among Tajiks, "Pamiri" is, for its part, a word with some charged associations. So-called Tajiks who live in Badakhshan (i.e., Darvaz, Ishkashim, and Vanj) are an exception to that setting apart, likely because they were with the "Pamiri" opposition forces in the civil war.

However, within Badakhshan itself such sentiments are of course not entirely uniform. Shughni (or Xughni, or as most people call it, Shughnani), is now clearly the prestige language. While its center of power has shifted from the old seat at Qala-ye Bar Panjah, across from Porshnev, to Khorog, it is still clearly the elite language of the elite group. Any prestige that Persian once had (perhaps at its height during the Emirate of Bukhara period) seems more or less gone. It is extremely rare to hear Tajiki on the street in Khorog. Persian/Tajiki is now largely the domain, in central Badakhshan, of official interactions and religious rituals: the *madoh-khon* mystical bards use Tajiki to recite poems from Rumi (Balkhi), Hafiz, and Nasir-i-Khusraw (van den Berg 1997), but in central Badakhshan you will rarely hear it otherwise. In Ishkashim and Qala-i-Khumb it is quite common, but locals there will default to Shughni when an official from Khorog comes. Most public addresses and local governmental interactions in Khorog and around it are conducted in Shughni. However, some of the peoples on the margins of Badakhshan are at least somewhat aware of their marginal position in relation to the Shughnanis. Moreover, despite the prestige of the Shughni community, the capital town of Khorog is, according to its inhabitants' own descriptions, in disarray. At night it is run by drug gangs and it is full of heroin addicts. Its infrastructure is crumbling.

Russian, however, and Russians retain their prestige. At a conference I attended in Khorog, Yuri Rybakov, a prominent Russian academic, began his address with something like: "I hear the people here in Badakhshan speak excellent Russian." The audience responded with electric applause and cheering. At the same conference I submitted, according to convention, an anonymous, handwritten note to the Russian academic after his talk on "The East" and "Oriental Studies" that read, "Is 'The East' a unity? And are the systems of knowledge upon which oriental studies are based not connected to the history of domination and colonialism?" This question, when read by the moderator, immediately caused a stir and an air of disapproval. I immediately recognized my mistake: I had raised the question of anticolonialism to open discourse, in the presence of a representative of the colonial metropole. It was assumed that the note was written by a restive Pamiri intending to "cause trouble." On another occasion a Tajik in Dushanbe told me excitedly about the Georgia-Russia soccer match that night. When I asked him who he would root for, he seemed shocked: "The Russians, of course," he said. "Russia is so much more like us!" He was surprised at, but interested in, the thought that Georgia, as a former mountainous borderland of the USSR that had also experienced some civil war and political upheaval, was indeed a lot like Tajikistan — structurally, at least, more so than Russia.

But the feeling toward Russians is nonetheless deeply ambiguous in Isma'ili Tajikistan. Many Badakhshanis seem to have chosen to identify more with Russia than with Tajikistan, as it is essentially the other model available for replication — an alternative to "Tajik." In Khorog, one may see self-consciously "Russian fashion" more than in other areas of the country (i.e., other mountain areas or even Dushanbe). Despite this, however, there is a good deal of tension between Badakhshanis and the Russian border guards, who at the time of my research had recently begun their withdrawal. There are mixed feelings about this withdrawal itself. While Badakhshanis see Russians as the vanguard of style and prestige, they are deeply ambivalent about their actual relationship with Russians. Most, however, see them as metonymic with a much better (Soviet) time, which they miss deeply, and with what in their view was a gentler and more beneficent form of political rule.

The nostalgia for the Soviet period is pervasive. Many local communities gained their current structures and adopted their current patterns of interaction in that period. Those internal structures remain, but the engine that drove them has disappeared. For example, herds are still distributed according to the same rules of collective resource sharing decreed by the small *kolkhoz*, the collective farm. In fact, those who held power in the *kolkhoz* itself are still prominent. Even decisions on the local level seem to be made in ways established during the Soviet period.

Channels of communication have also changed greatly. During the Soviet period, there was constant interaction between Dushanbe and Badakhshan. More recently, there have been periods in which communication with Osh, in southern Kyrgyzstan, exceeded communication with Dushanbe. Moscow remains a very important center for Badakhshanis, and there are numerous migrants living there and in other Russian cities. Many Isma'ilis born before the entry of the Soviets insist that growing up they did not know they were Isma'ilis, or that their parents waited to tell them until they were deemed mature enough to keep the secret. Salmaan Keshavjee (1998) notes, however, that some still practiced Isma'ilism during the Soviet period (59). He maintains that some tithes were collected from within the USSR during the Soviet period, and that they may have even heard about the accession of the current imam through a secret emissary; the Soviets, for their part, were anxious to minimize the influence of the Aga Khan. Official contact was allowed to resume in the late 1980s (64–65). There was thus at least some awareness of a sociocultural division and difference between the Isma'ili and Sunni communities within Badakhshan; these communal divisions were reinforced by the Soviets. With a great deal of effort and attention from the Aga Khan, religion has now become a primary criterion of identity. It has greatly gained in importance in social interaction. The divide between Isma'ili and non-Isma'ili has, consequently grown, even within Badakhshan. The national divide between Isma'ili and non-Isma'ili has also grown, as it has become clear that the beneficiaries of AKF are generally the people of Badakhshan and Garm, both on the losing opposition side of the civil war. This has engendered at least a degree of resentment.

"*Isma'ili*," like "Pamiri," is a new term in the region, but the idea of being Isma'ili has quickly become deeply important in Badakhshan and now plays a major role in regional relationships with Sunnis. Relations between the two, while not always warm, are at least cordial—much more so than relations between people from the Gorno-Badakhshan Autonomous Oblast as a whole and Tajiks from the rest of Tajikistan (especially Kulobis). In general, the people of Gorno-Badakhshan as a territory have, from the civil war, gained a certain degree of regional cohesion.

The categories are thus rapidly changing, and the region's people know it. A villager from Porshnev ("S" for Safdar) said the following:

J: So these things continue maybe in Ishkashim, Wakhan . . .

S: Yes, the farthest places. But they . . . as my father says, even the new generation of Wakhan, even they are forgetting.

J: It seems like that's a theme that runs through the, that's running throughout the area, the difference between the generations.

S: Yeah.

J: Do you think the younger generation is less serious, or more serious about religion?

S: I think that it is less.

People are highly conscious of the changing currency of terms like "Shughni," "Pamiri," "Badakhshani," "Tajik," "Isma'ili," "Musalman," and even "Komsomol." They are accustomed to the changing tides of interaction and identity and discuss it freely. Some of them have seen several prevailing social orders in the course of a single lifetime, and for this reason they expect it.

As I was walking through the alleys of Khorog one afternoon, a boy, perhaps six, issued an enthusiastic "hello" in my direction. I returned the greeting and asked in Tajiki if he spoke English (no), Russian (no) or Shughni (also no). "So," I said, "what language *do* you speak?" His response: "Pamiri!" The calculus of language, locality, and religion is enormously complex and fluid. The relative values and meanings of classifications like "Isma'ili," "Pamiri," and "Badakhshani" (and even more carefully delimited categories like "Shughni") are profoundly contextual in their formulation and reliant upon shifting historical contingencies. Local subjects understand that the appearance of fixity is itself fleeting.

CHAPTER FIVE

Living Globality

Local Modes of Transnational Experience

Moments, Subjects, and Spaces: Confronting Complexity

It is in certain moments, and in the spaces they occupy, that the intersection between violence, identity, the global assemblage, and the state comes into its clearest resolution. In such fleeting settings as conferences or children's plays, suddenly the meaning of the Ismaʿili arrival in remote borderlands comes into focus and begins to make sense. The ethnographic richness of such glimpses reveals the complex negotiations and interactions that constitute the Ismaʿili subject's encounter with the community's global institutions. Much of what I describe here could be characterized as mechanisms (or interactions) of assimilation and inculcation, the purposive alignment of Ismaʿili metropole and periphery. However, unlike in the abstracted descriptions above, it comes across here wearing fewer of its institutional garments, in its less-dressed, more informal iterations.

In the last chapter I explored the larger regional dynamics and contextual settings that characterize Ismaʿili institutional globalization in the circum-Himalayan region. In this chapter, I confront what I have referred to as "messier" realities: the real meanings of Ismaʿili globality on the ground, the material embodiments of the incorporation and induction of remote societies into a centralized infrastructure. It is never as simple as it appears; as I have emphasized, these institutions are not simply imposed from above. They are objects of contestation and negotiation, spaces of desire, power, and symbolic production. The people the institutions interact with have their own ideas.

I have privileged here the qualitative (and sometimes fragmentary) methods provided by ethnographic participation. While in the process I have likely neglected in their favor the value of surveys and samples, I believe ethnography is well-suited to such sprawling formations as the Isma'ili global complex. Through a selection of thickly described events, subjects, spaces, and structural forms, a clearer image of the real meaning of Isma'ili transnationality begins to clarify itself. The image is rather like a mosaic. But so is the phenomenon itself.

The Isma'ili Tariqah Committee, Khorog: The Worldwide Network's Local Office

I look in some detail first at an institution critical for the translation of official institutional activity into local activity. The Isma'ili Tariqah Religious Education Committee, under the auspices in part of the Institute for Isma'ili Studies, is a key mediating institution in the relationship between remote Himalayan Isma'ili societies and Euro-American (Khoja) Isma'ili institutions and norms. It also plays an important role in the effort to standardize and universalize Isma'ili practice.

ITREC (the Tajik variant of ITREB, the worldwide form taken on by the Tariqah Boards in local settings) plays a central social role in Khorog town and in the Gorno-Badakhshan Autonomous Oblast. Located in Khorog's city park, it acts as a community hub, especially for people heavily involved with religious activities. It is at ITREC that Isma'ilis, particularly ones that are interested in the fact of being Isma'ilis, come together and formulate their concept and discourse of self and community. It is here that some of the meanings of Isma'ili identity are synthesized, developed, and navigated. It is also here that Pamiri Isma'ilis are taught how to comply with universalized Khoja standards of ritual and belief.

ITREC Khorog is, from dawn to dusk, teeming with Pamiri Isma'ilis with questions about religious practice and doctrine. They come from far and wide, often visible in their own valley's style of garments, for advice on proper conduct and comportment. They come with questions on weddings, funerals, and other rites of passage; they come to hear or read the *farmans* of the Aga Khan (which emerge from the fax machine); they come for general advice on life decisions; and they come, simply, for company with other Isma'ilis. I never saw the ITREC office empty. Isma'ilis from Badakhshan explained to me that the function of ITREC is to prescribe the proper form for some Pamiri Isma'ili rituals and to discourage the practice of others.

Sometimes, as we will see in more detail below, ITREC feels that it is necessary to specifically sanction certain local Isma'ili practices that seem to come into conflict with standard practice (which even has an allowable degree of deviation). In Gorno-Badakhshan, for instance, there is, as discussed above, a group of Isma'ilis living in the region of the village of Darmorakht (Shughnan) who are called *Panjibais*. Though my primary guide believed that this was a corruption of "Punjabi," because of the origins of this group in the activity of Indian Khoja Isma'ili missionaries, the term, as mentioned, comes from *Panjebhai* (meaning "hand brother"), the name of a type of Khoja committee developed by Aga Khan III in Africa and India. They are said to engage in practices closely resembling those of Indian Isma'ilis, including recitation of *ginan*-like songs. The term's arrival in this area can likely be attributed to the missionary activity of Pir Sabzali during the period of Aga Khan III, or perhaps to Pamiri visits to Bombay.[1]

ITREC Khorog, like ITREB offices in other locations, also helps facilitate, plan, and coordinate cultural events and programs. Such cultural events or programs can include film screenings, conferences, community plays, and summer camps, all of which I had the opportunity to witness in Badakhshan. Cultural events are generally focused on depicting some element of Isma'ili history to make it relevant to social life in the present. It should be noted that there have been no official *jama'at khanas* in Badakhshan up to this point, and that, in other areas where they exist, *jama'at khanas* carry out many of the activities administered by ITREC in Tajikistan. The proposed establishment of *jama'at khanas* in Tajikistan is the source of significant contention and conflict; it embodies the perceived imposition of Khoja styles of worship onto the Pamiris.

IIS and ITREB/ITREC also organize other types of international scholarships and exchanges for young Isma'ilis in which the London institute is bypassed. Khorog's Khurshedsho Konunov, for instance, who became the manager of the Khorog English Program (KEP) organized by IIS, was sent on a one-year exchange to Vancouver;[2] his friend and colleague Masud, who is also involved in KEP, studied at the London School of Economics. During these scholarships and exchanges the students live in Isma'ili host communities; transnational bonds are formed between Isma'ilis from different areas, and the sense of commonality and global simultaneity is encouraged. The common ground is that of Isma'ilism. These individuals are becoming the intelligentsia of Khorog, and KEP, as a meeting place for them and a forum for local, highly educated political progressives, is now central to that process.

KEP is an intensive residential English-language program. Admission to the program is highly competitive; many see it as a way out of Badakhshan and as an unparalleled opportunity. During their tenure at KEP the young women and men of the student body try to live entirely in English. A satellite feed brings in CNN, the BBC, and MSNBC, and there are extensive film resources. They are eventually taught to read literary classics; my guide Safdar had read Western scholarship on Islam (e.g., Hodgson, Said, and Ruthven), along with an impressive corpus of classic English-language literature. With his roommate, an Isma'ili from the distant village of Yoged in Darwaz, he spoke only English. Even this could be said to contribute to the development of a sense of trans*regional* connection; the curriculum in sum could be understood as contributing to the socialization of the future educated classes of Isma'ilism to Western values of the Enlightenment, liberal traditions, and global mediation. He characterized it as follows: "Before KEP we just accepted everything we read. KEP changed everything—we learned critical thinking there. We learned to be concerned with Western society's image of Isma'ilism."

Students report their time at KEP as an intensive bonding experience wherein Isma'ilism becomes the key idiom of commonality. KEP in fact serves as a sort of feeder for IIS. Every year the students eagerly wait to find out if they have been selected; only a few students are chosen from the program to go to London as resident graduate students at IIS and eventually, more often than not, to other universities. The competition is fierce and sometimes unpleasant. The passage to Europe is seen as a prize of the greatest magnitude, a ticket out of the "beautiful prison" (in the words of Khurshedsho Konunov) that they describe Khorog to be. So KEP, like other programs of the *jama'ati* institutions, is a small but important node in transnational community-building. This too is a site for the formulation and negotiation of an emergent identity. More important, perhaps, is its role, like other Isma'ili institutional forms, in the promotion of Euro-American (corporate-inflected) discourses of modernity, rational individualism, liberal humanism, and academic discipline.

Millennial Ghosts in the Dompolit:
Conference-Hall Conjurings of an Isma'ili Saint

In September of 2003 the town of Khorog, capital of Gorno-Badakhshan Autonomous Oblast, played host to a conference celebrating the one thousandth birthday of Nasir-i-Khusraw, the missionary who brought Isma'ili Islam to the region. The gathering, "Nasir Khusraw: Yesterday, Today, Tomorrow," billed itself "The Conference Devoted to Nasir Khusraw Millennium Celebration" and was the culmination of a longer summer of millennial events and celebrations organized by AKF and the provincial government to commemorate the missionary-hero. Exactly what this *millennium* is, how Nasir-i-Khusraw has been constructed and deployed as a post-Leninist cultural hero, and how it plays into the formulation of Isma'ili identity on a most marginal post-Soviet borderland, is the focus of this section.

As I interpret it, this millennial commemoration, more than simply reflecting a historical reality, *creates* and *generates* through discourse a new post-Soviet hero around which local societies long alienated from the central Tajik polity can rally. Conferences, plays, and other events centered on Nasir-i-Khusraw manifest, materialize, produce, and bring to life the importance of this figure in Pamiri society. Such events are performative rather than descriptive; they conjure Nasir-i-Khusraw as a living figure in daily imaginaries and a guide for local political organization.

But even more important, the canonization of Nasir-i-Khusraw as a local hero, as revolutionary as it seems in the light of what came before, allows for the creation of an emblematic regional figure whose position in local society is firmly rooted in the ideal form of the heroes manufactured and provided for "peoples" by the Soviet nationalities system. A central focus of this section is an exploration of how the role of such national heroes endures in areas rapidly entering global markets. What is new in this, however, and where we see a break from the Soviet system, are the notions that a Soviet-defined people or nation, a *narod* or *natsiya* in the Soviet terminology, can choose their own hero, that the hero can be a religious figure, and that a hero's objective importance can be validated by currency and circulation in other cultures and polities, that the transnational somehow affirms and constructs the local.

I thus seek here to excavate the meaning of "millennium" and the genesis of new "heroes" in a moment of massive historical change on the very peripheries of the former Soviet polity. The polity is vanished, but the forms it so successfully entrenched and established persist, phantom institutions and spectral discourses deeply pervading the social fabric. I aim here to interrogate the historicity of a particular type of cultural revival in an "out-of-the-way place" (Tsing 1993), the moment in which Pamiri Isma'ilis are witnessing what John and Jean Comaroff (2000) describe as a "millennial capitalism" that is "both capitalism at the millennium and capitalism in its messianic, salvific, even magical manifestations" (2). We can discern in all this the insistent assertions of a group shunned and scorned, of Tajikistan's Pamiri Isma'ilis choosing a symbol for themselves, claiming an emblem, taking ownership over history. While the vocabulary they have for such a choice is ultimately derivative, circumscribed and delimited by practice rooted in a Soviet approach to culture, such designation and construction of new heroes nonetheless represents the articulation of a cogent critique of the agents and circumstances that underlie the violence and misery of their recent history.

Nasir himself, born in Qubadiyan (in current-day Tajikistan), was a Central Asian. He was from a privileged and influential family, worked as a political functionary, and was apparently a bit of a hedonist until he reached middle age, when he underwent some kind of a personal transformation that prompted him to become a renunciant with an almost ascetic orientation. In the time of al-Mustansir, in the mid-eleventh century, Nasir (who was probably by this point already a convert to Isma'ilism) set off from his Seljuq-ruled homeland across western Asia to Mecca and on to Cairo, where he visited the Fatimid capital and court. All of this is recorded in his famous *Safar-Nama*. He stayed for a few years there, was trained, and became a prominent *da'i*, or missionary. He took a southerly route back, visiting many Isma'ili locations, and upon his return to his place of origin became the head *da'i* (and in his descriptions, the *hujja*, lit., "proof of God," i.e., a high-ranking dignitary who can represent the imamate) of Khurasan in eastern Iran, disseminating and promoting Isma'ilism from Balkh, now in Afghanistan. He also spread the *da'wa* (the Isma'ili cause) to some of the Shi'i areas of the ranges of Caspian Iran. In Balkh he was the focus of much suspicion and animosity on the part of the local Sunnis. He ultimately was compelled to leave Balkh and found sanctuary in Yumgan in the Pamir ranges of what is now Afghanistan, adjacent to the Tajik Pamir and not far from Pakistani Chitral. Nasir was received by a local ruler who was already an Isma'ili. He remained in exile in Yumgan for the rest of his life, producing many important literary works from his remote home. He became the chief *da'i* of this mountainous region and continued his line of connection to the network of *da'is* and the chief *da'i* in Cairo; he is responsible for the conversion of most of the region and is still revered as a saint (and sometimes even an "imam") by the villagers of the area (Daftary 1990: 215–18; Ivanow 1956; Hunsberger 2000).

Nasir's commanding ghost even now resides in the many sacred sites of the Pamir, a description of which can contribute to an understanding of Nasir's mythic status in the Pamir. The Midenshor Nasir-i-Khusraw spring in Porshnev village, for example, a site of major regional pilgrimage, received before the millennial conference a great deal of attention; as I will describe below, a well-known Georgian sculptor unveiled there during the conference a sculpture of Nasir-i-Khusraw. It is thought to be auspicious to drink the water of the spring at the shrine, whose presence Nasir is said to have divined and that reportedly erupted from the earth with a strike of his rod. Once, according to local legend, he stopped there to rest and asked a girl carrying a jug for a drink. The girl gave some to him, but she gave none to some bystanders who were sitting right there. Nasir asked why the others received none. The girl responded that she only gave Nasir water because he was a stranger, but in general people fetched water from the river, some ways off, and it required some effort to get it; she would not normally give it away. So Nasir laid his walking staff upon the rock and the spring came gushing forth. He arranged a ceremony called *khudoi* ("godly") involving mountain goats and then planted two burnt branches adjacent to the spring; they grew into the two sacred willow trees (*darakht-i-bed*) that are now in the courtyard of the shrine (Shodmon Hojibekov, pers. comm.).

The Nasir-i-Khusraw Millennial Conference, which I attended from August 31 to September 3, 2003, while I was in residence in the town, was planned primarily by IIS (London) and ITREC (Dushanbe and Khorog) to celebrate the great man's one thousandth birthday. I argue that through this conference, he becomes a transregional or transnational rallying symbol, an emblem of shared historical experience between Isma'ilis from Iran, Afghanistan, Pakistan, Tajikistan, and farther afield.

The conference was a seriously global gathering, with scholars from Tajikistan, Pakistan, India, Malaysia, the United States, the United Kingdom, Russia, Afghanistan, Iran, Canada, France, and Israel. Scholars presented papers on many aspects of the life, work, and impact of Nasir-i-Khusraw. A central feature of the conference was the showing of a film by S. M., a prominent Badakhshani, on Nasir's legacy in the religious practice of the people of the Pamirs. On the eve of the conference, H. K., a Khoja Isma'ili who had grown up in Africa, once lived in Canada, and now resided in Paris, put on a stage interpretation of Nasir's life. H. K., who was affiliated with IIS, showed in his play the journey of Nasir from Khorasan to the Fatimid court in Cairo and his eventual arrival at and conversion of Badakhshan. Nasir becomes through H. K.'s work a fact of contemporary social life; the past is thus rendered relevant in the present.

The introduction in the conference program stresses that "Nasir Khusraw is not just a figure of the past or 'yesterday,' but of the present and the future." Papers from the conference stressed this immediacy; many sought to construct Nasir as a living element of contemporary local Isma'ili life. Among them were the following:

"Nasir Khusraw: The Light That Enlightens the Lives of the Peoples of Pamir" (Nadezhda Yemelianova, Institute for Oriental Studies, Russia)

"Popularity of Nasir Khusraw" (Mirgand Shobozov, Khorog State University, Tajikistan)

"Descriptions of Nasir Khusraw's Personality in Badakhshani Folklore: Nasir Khusraw and Major Elements of His Traditions among Badakhshani People" (Nisormamad Shakarmamadov, Khorog Institute for Humanities, Tajikistan)

"The Significance of the Tradition of Nasir Khusraw and the Reinvigoration of Its Intellectual Aspect in Northern Pakistan" (Shahnaz Salim-Hunzai, Khonai Hikmat, Pakistan)

"The Influence of Nasir Khusraw's Religio-Didactical Teachings on the Formation of the Identity of the Ismailis of the Pamiro-Indukush Ethno-Cultural Region" (Boghshoh Lashkarbekov, Institute of Linguistics, Russia)

"Nasir Khusraw and Iranian Ismailis" (Said Jalal Badakhshani, The Institute of Ismaili Studies, United Kingdom)

Some papers focused on Nasir's potential as a moral compass, a blueprint for contemporary behavior:

"Nasir Khusraw: A Man of Faith and Principles" (Mirbaiz Khan, ITREB Canada)

"Nasir Khusraw and Interfaith Relations" (Orifsho Nasreddinshoev, Institute of Languages, Tajikistan)

"Father's Advice as a Stock of Gold: Didactic and Ethical Advice of Nasir Khusraw" (Aliqul Dewonaqulov, Institute of Oriental Studies, Tajikistan)

"Ethical Values from Nasir Khusraw's Perspective" (Fida Ali Ithar Hunzai, ITREB, Pakistan)

Others focused on some aspect of the universality of Nasir-i-Khusraw by appealing to his connection to Europe or to basic truths held to be rooted in modern academic disciplines:

"Nasir Khusraw's Civilizational Status" (Muso Dinorshoev, Institute of Philosophy and Law, Tajikistan)

"Nasir Khusraw from Pythagoras to Shakespeare: Seeking Order in the Universe" (Shafiq Virani, Harvard University)

"Comparing Humanistic Ideas of Nasir Khusraw and Francesca

Petrarka" (Elbon Hojibekov, Khorog Institute of Humanities, Tajikistan)

"Nasir Khusraw on the Dialogue of Wisdoms and Ideas and Dialogue of Civilizations at Present" (Mamadsho Ilolov, Ministry of Labour and Social Protection, Tajikistan)

"Rationalist Tendencies in Nasir Khusraw's Thought" (Nozir Arabzoda, Tajik-Slavonic University, Tajikistan)

"Nasir Khusraw and Literary Criticism of the 20th Century" (Alice Hunsberger Asia Society, USA)

"Justice and Civil Society from Nasir Khusraw's Perspective" (Yusufbek Shodmonbekov, Khorog State University, Tajikistan)

"Nasir Khusraw's Contribution to the Plantology and Anthropology" (Yusuf Nuraliev, Iranian International Academy of Science, Tajikistan)

And still others mobilized Nasir-i-Khusraw as a figure central in modern projects of state-building and intercommunal dialogue:

"Nasir Khusraw the Flag Bearer of the Protection and Development of Mother Tongue" (Dodikhudo Karamshoev, Institute of Languages, Tajikistan)

"Nasir Khusraw's Role in the Development of the Intra-Islamic Dialogue: Historical and Anthropological Approach" (Lola Dodikhudoeva, Institute of Oriental Studies, Tajikistan)

"Themes of Motherland and Patriotism from Nasir Khusraw's Perspective" (Shirin Bunyod, Badakhshan Sector of Tajikistan Writers' Union, Tajikistan)

The program also included a breakout session on "the encounter of this tradition with the forces of modernity, post-modernity, and globalization." The attempt here to construct Nasir-i-Khusraw as *modern* is telling, as it reveals something of the attempt at revival, at breathing life into him as a guide for contemporary Pamiri life.

The presence of Isma'ilis and non-Isma'ilis further legitimizes the status of Nasir-i-Khusraw as historically significant in an absolute, nonparochial sense; thus the historical Nasir is reified and becomes less partial. And the attendance of scholars like Yuri Rybakov, the director of the Institute for Oriental Studies in St. Petersburg, also enhances the international nature of the conference. On the other hand, the attendance of someone like G. H., a regionally prominent scholar of Isma'ilism from the Pakistan Himalaya, brings a sense of cross-border regional solidarity and commonality; his talk was received with great enthusiasm by the largely Pamiri audience, drawing nods, smiles, and applause upon the mention of ideas that are identified with Badakhshan.

As if to emphasize the eclectic syncretism of the moment, Hindi pop music was playing as the conference attendees, guided by ushers in traditional yellow dresses and Pamiri-style braids, took their seats in the auditorium of the Dompolit, the Soviet House of Political Education, at (the crumbling, Soviet-era) Khorog State University (KSU). Such a deployment of indigenous symbolism represents a certain reinvention and recontextualization of both locality and Soviet discourses of identity in a new, global context. H. K. opened the conference, explaining that such a celebration of Nasir-i-Khusraw represented, for him, a dream come true. H. M., a prominent representative of IIS, then went on to introduce the chairman of the Gorno-Badakhshan government. It is interesting that this was how the opening moment of the conference was planned; one could say that it reflects an Ismaʿili anxiety about themselves in the eyes of the state, or, perhaps, a governmental anxiety about the Ismaʿilis.

The chairman, introduced by IIS, began discussing "Tajik" heritage and pride, never mentioning "Pamiri," "Badakhshani," or "Ismaʿili." He discussed at length Nasir's relation to Firdausi, Rudaki, Omar Khayyam, and other literary figures. This had the effect of framing him as the property of the *legitimate* "Tajik" literary and cultural heritage approved by the Soviets. As mentioned above, "Tajik," as an institutionalized national ethnicity, is essentially a Soviet invention. However, "Pamir" and "Pamiri," as ethnonyms also Soviet inventions, become in this context, largely because of the civil war, charged, contested, and politicized sites and signs. The use of "Tajik" thus has complicated and strategic ramifications.

Sarfaroz Niyozov, a Pamiri intellectual from the remote Rushon valley and an important representative at the time of the IIS, then spoke. He thanked the government, the university (whose director also spoke later), AKDN, and, significantly (given the presence of many government representatives), President Imomali Rahmonov. These acknowledgements point, again, to a desire (or an anxiety) to show complicity and cooperation with the state, especially given a subject matter that is potentially subversive.

Niyozov's presentation, given in English, was significant in a number of ways, not least of which was its consciousness of the transnationality of the gathering. He told the audience that there were guests from thirteen countries and then listed them all. More interesting, however, was his mobilization of Nasir-i-Khusraw as a symbol embedded in the social and political context of the talk itself. He framed Nasir in the contemporary situation, in the relationship of people to states and historical events. Early in his talk, Niyozov said: "He was not the child of a mother and a father *but of a nation.*" Such a formulation recognizes explicitly that Nasir-i-Khusraw is being mobilized as a metacultural symbol (Urban 2001) in the present. Continuing, Niyozov proposed that "for many people in this hall the collapse of the Soviet Union might be seen as a tragedy," a controversial but immediately relevant statement, and one he seemed not to disagree with completely. Soon thereafter, he began to address a post-Soviet alternative to Communism — "neoliberalism" — claiming that it is imperative for subjects in a place like Tajikistan, "particularly in communities like ours," to understand its implications. He posed the question of how the idea of Nasir-i-Khusraw can help local people to shape the forces of a neoliberal economy so that they don't become victims of such forces. In the introduction to a volume based on the conference proceedings, Niyozov further elaborates upon these propositions:

> As a post Soviet country, Tajikistan struggles to establish its new and independent identity. In doing so, it largely reflects the fundamental challenges that confront Muslim societies passing through radical transition. The presumed triumphant march of Western modernity and neo-liberal ideology through globalisation and the free market have given a new boost to competition, individualism and technical rationality across the vast terrain of a defeated communist ideology. Tajikistan, like the other Central Asian states, has become a meeting point where the heterogeneous and diverse forces of the Muslim heritage, an incumbent socialism, Western democracy, and nationalism have converged. The enormous paradoxical challenge of building a nation and maintaining social cohesion at a time of penetrating globalisation has been further compounded by an increasingly intense encounter with the ongoing dramatic changes experienced in various parts of the Muslim world. (Niyozov 2006)

I believe that the entailment, at least at the moment of the conference, was meant to be: in such a conundrum, what does Nasir-i-Khusraw (as a symbol and an idea) offer us now? Niyozov, in his presentation, pointed out Nasir's universal appeal, calling him "Muslim *and* an asset of humanity in general."

Niyozov's comments were clearly directed in part at the governmental representatives in attendance. It is such moments that begin to hint at the role of the Nasir hero in articulating a critique both of the totalitarian state and of neoliberalism.

Niyozov suggested that despite the thousand years that separate the audience and Nasir-i-Khusraw, "one sees that the fundamental issues of human experience are the same," again making the past relevant to the present. He related the hardships of Badakhshan to those of Nasir, who himself faced many difficulties in the country. Despite them, according to Niyozov, Nasir was still "sitting in Yumgan like a king." The message seemed to be that the people of Badakhshan, despite the civil war, are still noble and can prevail.

Perhaps even more important in a global context is the way that the conference reflected, produced, and reinforced certain discourses of locality (Raffles 1999). Along with other speakers, Niyozov emphasized that Nasir-i-Khusraw wrote most of his books in *this* place. This emphasis, in my view, helped to frame the conference as a celebration of *this* Pamiri locality, with all of its historical specificity. Moreover, it is a component of the construction of a metadiscourse of identity in which Pamiri Isma'ili subjects are developing a new definition and image of self in the post-Soviet context. In such a context, Niyozov's presentation was quite radical, even daring, in its challenge to certain notions widely held in the region about the positive aspects both of the Soviet era and of the introduction of capitalism. At the same time, it pointed to the delicate relationship between the Isma'ili global structure and the nation-state.

Other moments of the conference, some of them embedded in fleeting discursive exchanges and hidden from public view, also revealed the dynamics of the relationship between the Pamiris and the post-Soviet Tajik state. One morning the entire conference audience sat suspended and waiting for hours for the prominent government representatives, who were having lunch elsewhere in town, to come. After an hour or so, resentment began to build in the audience, some of whom expressed in hushed voices that they were being snubbed. The whole event was suspended while the audience and the presenters waited for the representatives to arrive. Safdar Alibeko-vitch, an Isma'ili from the remote Roshorv valley, educated at Cambridge, and now living in Scandinavia, expressed great displeasure to me, saying how horrible it was, and that this system resembled other authoritarian ones. Later, he said that it represented the "worst form of slavery in Tajikistan," the way that Badakhshanis were expected to be at the government's beck and call, at their behest; he complained that Pamiris were the objects of condescension. He argued that as a result of the post–civil war "compromise," Pamiris were subordinated to the government's wishes. Sitting in the dining hall later with the conference attendees and the VIP's, S. A. pointed to the Pamiri dancers and said (in an amazing global moment, with academic metadiscourse informing social reality) that he couldn't look at this in the same way after studying the principles of Said's Orientalism.

Another major event of the conference was the screening of a documentary film about the sacred sites and shrines (*oston, mazar,* and *ziyarat*) of the Pamir, most of which are associated with Nasir-i-Khusraw. This film was directed by an important local Isma'ili woman, S. M.; I was hired for some time as a consultant on the film (in a moment where ethnographic observation transforms and influences its own object), in order to "bring an anthropological perspective to the film." The film explored the connection between contemporary practice and the history of Nasir-i-Khusraw in Badakhshan. The images focused predominantly on shrines and on rituals surrounding shrines, including the singing practices of the *Madoh Khon* singers. But much more than the content I was interested in the *form* and *life* of the film as a text of identity, locality, and religion. Rather than seeking to analyze the content of Isma'ilism or the history of local traditions, I hoped rather to explore the reality and perception of those elements as metadiscourses, as indices of citizenship and subjectivity and allegiance. I tried to ask what the effect was of the film on the audience, separate from its content, what the intended effect was, and in what ways it held significance as a social artifact and phenomenon itself. The film is interesting to our discussion here for the role it played in mediating, synthesizing, and actualizing a regional Isma'ili metacultural self-image.

The film was also interesting for what its screening revealed about the internal politics and dynamics of Isma'ilism in the region. I would argue that, in tune with other, similar Isma'ili social processes, the film helps to create a sense of simultaneity in the audience, a shared sense of locality and identity, and a common metadiscourse of self. All of these people came together from different areas and different experience and learned about the particular local Isma'ili culture of this place *together.* They have all shared that same, mediated experience, and such an experience provides key words or symbolic referents that subjects from disparate regions can share (see Spitulnik 1997). This film should also be seen as a contributor to the performative construction of a locality—the film conjures, produces, and creates a discourse of locality and a sense of connection among Tajikistan, Afghanistan, Pakistan, and even Iran (see Massey 1994; Raffles 1999).

The film itself was controversial and created quite a stir at the conference. ITREC, the primary Isma'ili regional religious authority in Gorno-Badakhshan, wanted to regulate the film because, according to them, it did not represent Isma'ili practice in the way that they would like to have it represented—in a much more standardized manner. Rather it showed very localized and indigenous forms of Isma'ilism, with a great deal of valley-to-valley variation and even more deviation from the form prescribed by ITREC. The critiques were about who was doing what right or wrong in the film in terms of proper practice. After the film, G. H., the regional director of ITREC, would not even shake S. M.'s hand; a sign of the degree to which he found her work antithetical to all of ITREC's efforts.

In many ways like the film, the *form* of the conference, and what that form indexes about the Isma'ili community, was more telling than its content. The conference delegates came from Iran, Pakistan, Canada, the United States, Russia, all over Tajikistan, and many other countries, and all came to share in a common (semi-academic) discourse on Nasir-i-Khusraw. What can we make of that in a post-Soviet context? In the mountains of Pakistan also, Nasir is important; but such a gathering, and such a conscious, institutionally sanctioned discussion of a cultural figure would be unusual and perhaps even out-of-character there. But such a formulation of history and culture is well-attested in Soviet discourse. Marx and Lenin, as well as secularized "national" figures (e.g., for the Tajiks, Sadruddin Ayni or Rudaki, or, for the Uzbeks, Alisher Navoi), were celebrated, studied, and widely discussed, often in the very type of forum in which Nasir was being commemorated in 2003. In the light of that tradition, perhaps figures like him are being mobilized as replacements in form *and* in content for Communist figures like Marx and Lenin. One could postulate that in a post-Soviet context in which the Soviets had created historical hero-leaders, a new figure was in demand as a central reference point of historical and present identity, a shared, post-Lenin and post-Marx common ground. Thus a personage like Nasir-i-Khusraw both fills the need for a system of meaning and provides a rallying point for public discussions of shared heritage. Why Nasir then? Perhaps because he could act as the most integral and commonly shared symbol available to Pamiri Isma'ilis. Nasir-i-Khusraw, then, would become a reconstructed element of the past, made relevant to the present, and used to engender a transnational sense of shared experience and identity, of simultaneity and commonality. Nasir thus becomes essential to a newfound ability to identify across post-Soviet borders.

Other elements of the context for this conference are also notable. First, there is a sense that it represented a rediscovery of *religious* heritage as a legitimate locus of identification. Perhaps even more important, however, the event cannot be seen as apolitical, especially in the post–civil war, post-Soviet context we have been discussing. The whole gathering can be seen as a reclamation of a *regional* symbol of identity by a community that has stood somewhat in opposition to the national society in which it is situated. In the context of the former Pamiri Isma'ili position of resistance, in which the group acted collectively against the ex-Communist forces, Nasir-i-Khusraw himself is not (and cannot be) seen as neutral but instead is re-contextualized, charged, and imbued with powerful meaning (see Comaroff 1985; Hebdige 1979). The conference is a statement about the value of *Pamiri* culture as an entity, in and of itself.

Another interesting sociohistorical reflection on the conference: Nasir-i-Khusraw's "millennium" brings to mind other uses of the ideas of millennium and millenarianism. In my interpretation, the conference and the new interest in Nasir-i-Khusraw in general can be seen as reflections of a particular type of post-Soviet revivalism that is emerging all over the former USSR. Throughout the lands of that disintegrated polity, ethnic and cultural groups, many of them created by the Soviets themselves (see Roy 2000), are rediscovering and reinterpreting heroic leaders of the past. Such figures are becoming, for these groups, new emblematic symbols of identity. They are in fact being deployed both by new nation-states (e.g., Ismail Somoni for the Tajiks, or Timur for the Uzbeks) and by smaller groups, and many of them seem to emerge from the official and approved secular folk cultures created for each ethnic group and nationality by the Soviets. Even in cases where these particular figures were not sanctioned by the Soviets, the idea that every group should have such a figure, and the process by which they became part of an institutional structure surrounding ethnicity, comes from the Soviets.

Thus, recently Cossacks gathered en masse in Novocherkassk, Russia, to celebrate the 250th birthday of their hero Matvei Platov in a festival lasting several days. They came from the immediate region and from the Cossack diaspora all over the world (including North America and Europe), just like the conference in Badakhshan. In Daghestan, in the Caucasus, Avars and other groups gathered in 1997 to celebrate the 200th birthday of the Naqshbandi "Imam Shamil," who fiercely resisted Russian invasion. There was a conference in Makhachkala, in Daghestan, entitled "North Caucasian Peoples' War of Liberation under the Leadership of Shamil: Its International Importance." It was also referred to as an "International Scientific

Conference Dedicated to the 200th Anniversary of Imam Shamil" (Henze 1998). Statues of such figures are being built in place of the old busts of Lenin. The pattern of the conference and celebration of Nasir-i-Khusraw in the Pamir does not sound entirely dissimilar: In the village of Porshnev, near Khorog, at the Nasir-i-Khusraw Chashma (spring), a Georgian artist unveiled a new bust of the hero. Thus, in the post-Soviet context Nasir-i-Khusraw can be understood as an *Isma'ili* hero whose role is analogous to Shamil for the Avars or Platov for the Cossacks. The conference, a truly transnational forum, thus contributes to a construction of Nasir as an emblem of Isma'ili identity, a banner to rally around as a marker of Isma'ilism, and a rediscovery and celebration of a previously forbidden iconic index of Himalayan Isma'ilism. Here the revival and globalization of identity takes on a very post-Soviet form.

New heroes are in many ways an extension or replacement of the Soviet nationalities policy but adapted to more recent compartmentalizations and negotiations of national identity, combined with emergent capitalist norms of choice. The heroes remain emblems of Soviet-created nationalities, or societies reformulated in the manner of Soviet-created nationalities, and not of new formations. The semiotic structure remains the same but the content is changed. We see in the adaptation a modern mythos filled with medieval characters. But the limitations of old languages do not prevent the construction of new meanings; in that adaptation lies an opportunity for a refashioning of cultural selves.

It was once the case that heroic images, murals, and sculptural likenesses of Lenin punctuated the public spaces of Soviet towns, directed the flow of movement, pointed to the inevitable revolutionary future, the End of History (or, according to a favorite Russian joke, to the public toilets). Everywhere in the former Soviet Union new heroes are emerging. Or perhaps it is more accurate to say that old heroes are reemerging. The streets of Dushanbe, Tajikistan's capital, once crowded with Lenins, Stalins, and Marxes, are now populated by the likes of Rudaki, Ayni, and Somoni in stone and bronze. The hero of the post-Soviet realm, I argue, though new in content, is cast in the morphological mold of Lenin and narrated in the lexicon of the Soviet nationalities policy.[3]

But this does not preclude the agentive articulation of identity. In fact the available Soviet forms provide a lexicon with which people on the margins of the Soviet realm can conjure and construct an image of who they would like to be in the new epoch, the post-Lenin age. In the wake of social crisis and the disintegration of both coherent political forms, commonly shared semiotic signs of belonging, and actual loci of affiliation, the newly selected, rediscovered, and refashioned hero creates a new shared narrative of identity and anchors it in certain shared symbols around which a redefined, post-Soviet community can rally. An excavation of the discourse surrounding Nasir-i-Khusraw belies an ambivalence among Pamiri Isma'ilis toward the abrupt arrival of neoliberal "millennial" capitalism and a search for some alternative organizing paradigmatic (and millennial) principle, motif, idiom. It provides an anchor of intersubjective experience for transnational polity-building. It suggests an active and ongoing bricolage (Comaroff 1985) of available emblems of identity and embodiments of meaning in the face of rupture, crisis, and the disappearance of a social fabric.

Inculcating the Young: The Camp as Mechanism for Socialization

The Isma'ili socioreligious institutions are actively involved in a number of ways in inculcating in Isma'ili children and adolescents both the community's religious ideology and an enthusiasm for participation in its social and political life. This is a crucial aspect of global community-building, of binding scattered communities to the imamate, and of maintaining ideological and material connections between subjects across territory. Engaging the young is central to maintaining, consolidating, and developing a loyal and active transnational populace and to fostering allegiance.

A key method by which Isma'ili religious institutions work to engage the young is the development of a centrally prescribed and globally uniform curriculum for Isma'ili religious schools. As we saw with *The Murids of Imam az-Zaman*, this is in fact one of the key functions of ITREB and IIS worldwide — to homogenize and standardize across the planet what children learn and think about Isma'ilism. It also stands in contrast to the curriculum development pursued by AKDN through institutions such as the Aga Khan Humanities Project (Tajikistan), Aga Khan Education Services (worldwide), the Aga Khan University (Pakistan), and the University of Central Asia (Tajikistan, Kyrgyzstan, and Kazakhstan) that are not explicitly oriented toward Isma'ili subjectivity or religion in particular, and that tend to privilege the liberal arts, pluralism, and the Enlightenment or modernist discourses of education.

An interesting activity of ITREB (and ITREC) in the ideological inculcation of the young is the operation of youth camps for religious education. The camps are not entirely religious in content, nor are they necessarily revivalist in tone. There are ways that they do resemble evangelical religious (e.g., "Young Life") camps in the United States with their all-encompassing religious focus, but the comparison is not entirely appropriate. They resemble more closely camps for Jewish youth (e.g., the National Foundation of Temple Youth, or NFTY) that are not entirely focused on Judaism, but that associate Jewish youth with others from their own community and that expose them, to some degree, to the polity of Israel. And there is a third parallel: these camps in form and even content are not altogether unlike the Communist "Pioneer Youth" organizations established under the Soviet state. This comes out to a degree in the effort visible in these Isma'ili camps to bring together Isma'ili youth from across a region to develop a sense of commonality and in the focus on ideological inculcation. The camps are designed to contain both religiously focused and nonreligious activities; an important purpose seems to be to associate Isma'ilism with having fun among one's peers and thus to foster a positive image of Isma'ilism as exciting and peer-sanctioned. Isma'ili camps, in their resonance with young people, play a small but important role in both the construction of the non-national "imagined community," as I have referred to it, and in the cohesion of a transnational community through the connection of widely dispersed localities. Like Village Organizations, these camps act as channels or forums for local participation in a global public sphere.

These dynamics can be discussed in more detail through a description of the closing ceremonies of an ITREC-organized Isma'ili summer camp in Porshnev, in the Shughnan district of Tajikistan's Gorno-Badakhshan (August 15, 2003). These ceremonies reflected many of the features and processes that characterize global Isma'ilism in general. This emerges in particular in their cultural syncretism, their promotion of a sense of trans-Isma'ili commonality, and their integration of religious and sociopolitical ideas. Deciphering the complex layers of cultural meaning and intertextuality at the ceremonies presented (even with the help of Safdar Alibeko-vitch, my guide and informant) a number of challenges.

The week-long camp was free and officially open to members of all religious groups (but largely catered to Isma'ilis). Its global eclecticism was emphasized by the Nivea advertising balloons scattered around the scene. Stretching across the top of the stage was a banner reading: "Boyad umed-vor bud ki ruze ham axloqu insoniyat misli ilmu san'at moro ba osmon bira-sonad" [We must be hopeful that someday humanity and proper behavior (Ar., *akhlaq*, or ethics, right disposition), such as knowledge and art, will deliver us to heaven], a sentiment that reflects the Isma'ili emphasis on learning and proper personal conduct. The camp's closing ceremonies began with an enactment of the traditional Badakhshani "Bull, Lion, and Fox" folk story; the story, however, was recontextualized and reinterpreted with modern elements—for example, one of the key animal characters travels on a journey to Switzerland (which, importantly, is the Aga Khan's place of birth and education and the location of the headquarters of AKDN). This was followed by the performance of traditional lamentation songs and "ethical stories" lamenting the troubles of the world, and by an invocation thanking Allah for the good things of the world. Soon after this, a small group of children danced to the music of a traditional Pamiri band playing modern electronic and electric instruments.

The centerpiece of the ceremonies, however, was a play based on Farid-ud-Din Attar's (1177) *Conference of the Birds*, a famous Sufi text. The campers presented the play as a modern reinterpretation of the text, a Saussurean recontextualization of its widely circulated signs and meanings.[4] The play (whose plot is a bit unclear) begins with a scene of a family lamenting the civil war while watching television, which then transitions into a scene of the war itself. In this scene, combatants abduct someone's son, and a daughter cries over her mother's death in a symbolic unraveling of contemporary social tensions. This daughter is the sole survivor in a family that has been slaughtered by soldiers dressed as Russians. She tries to escape but her bus is stopped by the *militsia* (i.e., police or military police) and she is barred from leaving her town because she lacks the proper documents. An argument over the documents ensues, and the guard asks for the girl's gold ring as a bribe to secure her passage.

The girl is now in the city, a space fraught with peril. She is wet and cold with nothing to eat and begs on the street. At this point she meets another girl who asks, "why are you living like this?" The heroine replies that she has no one, and the new friend says that she can help by providing documents. Eventually she is framed and accused of drug use, and she is put in jail. In jail, while some of the girl's fellow prisoners are cruel, others tell her that she is innocent, "an infallible bird." Soon after this scene she is able to recount her troubles to a policewoman, who helps her escape from jail and find documents, and her situation begins to improve. Here a narrator explains that "like birds [such as those in *Conference of the Birds*] the girls face difficulties," and the prisoners come together to thank God. The girl comes to the stage to explain that she used to hate people, and now she loves them. At the end a metanarrative is delivered that explains the meaning of the play: that "even in the face of desperation one gains freedom." The central theme of the play was an odyssey or journey—the heroine's odyssey across Badakhshani collective memory and through a series of difficult trials to a place of greater understanding (a place potentially made possible by Ismaʿilism). My guide elaborated further for me that the relationship to *Conference of the Birds* is in that message, in the idea that it is only after adversity that one finds one's (divinely ordained) purpose. Another connection can be found in the text's emphasis on the collectivity over the individual; the camp's organizers claim that they wish to emphasize this theme as well.

A number of other observations can be made about the play, which was clearly meant to be a statement about current social conditions and realities in Tajikistan. One is that the policewoman's role seems to emphasize and reinscribe the moral value of authority (or the value of moral authority), a point that gains importance in the context of the recent Tajik civil war and the arrival of the Aga Khan's institutions. A second is that it seems to be a rather explicit effort to disentangle and make sense of recent collective experience, especially of the civil war, and thus ultimately to produce a further sense of collective identity. Third, this play is also interesting for its symbolic eclecticism, which may be an attempt to reconcile and synthesize the many new elements of local social life into a newly fashioned culture; it is a bricolage that expresses, as Comaroff (1985) describes for the Tswana, a *shared* structural predicament.

As the campers in the audience passed around notebooks in order to write farewell messages to each other, the camp's closing ceremonies continued with a series of speeches and presentations focused on building a sense of collective experience and cooperation. The master of ceremonies made a number of statements along these lines (e.g., "nothing is better than being with friends"). He also expressed a variety of religious sentiments ("life is tested with dreams; with God's help you can do whatever you want") and quoted a Hadith ("like water, only knowledge can satisfy your thirst and provide you with a good life"). The ITREC youth chief expressed similar sentiments of collectivity-building: "We adapted to each other and learned from each other; it is difficult to separate. We did everything we could for you. Seven days is not a lot. I hope it was useful. I hope you will do and act according to what you learned here. Whatever you learned here— teach it to others. You will always be in our memories." In between and after these speeches, there were a number of other things happening, including the awarding of sports prizes and trophy cups, dancing, and the singing of songs with broadly Ismaʿili and Sufi themes (e.g., "O ʿAli assist us / hope for a brighter future / one day our life will be better"). Adding to the syncretism of the moment, organizers also played American rock songs (e.g., "Up Where We Belong").

What can we make of this? How can we begin to unravel the manifold layers of meaning visible in this moment? The camp is created by the Isma'ili Tariqah and probably initially authorized by the IIS in London, with the purpose of teaching "morals and ethics" (in this case, particularly through sports). The camp is also further legitimized through its self-presentation as nondenominational and ethnically universal. The organizers were keen to emphasize the fact that the camp included (Hanafi, "Imom-i-Azam" Sunni) Vanchis and Yazghulamis, as well as members of both the less well represented (Isma'ili) ethnic groups of upper Ishakshim district and the Wakhan, and Pamiri Isma'ili migrant children from Moscow and Dushanbe, in order to show that it was not meant to be exclusive in any way, or to favor either Isma'ilis or the powerful Shughni ethnic group. Staff members estimated that some 80 percent of the campers were Isma'ili. In past years Sunni Vanchis had complained that the camp was too homogeneously Isma'ili, a critique that may reflect a desire not to be excluded from the coveted resources and services of the Isma'ili community.

My reaction to the camp itself and its public representation is that it is meant to and does in fact create a sense of translocal commonality and connection. But commonality on what level and in what sense? It seems that the commonality that is developed is primarily among youth defined as *Pamiri* more than by any other criterion. This gains particular importance in the post–civil war context, in which multiple ethnic groups from Badakhshan share a single regionally defined political identity. It also points to the status of Gorno-Badakhshan as an anomalous territory with little connection to any nation-state or its discourses of citizenship. In light of this thought, though, what analysis can we make of the relationship of ITREC camps like these and Isma'ilism itself? In general, the camps can be seen as geared towards inculcating in Isma'ili youth an enthusiasm for participation in the local processes of the global Isma'ili community. My guide also connects the camp to Isma'ilism through its function in "helping the younger generation adapt to the *modern world*." Isma'ilism is commonly imputed with this purportedly adaptive social function, especially in the Tajik context where the new absence of the Soviet Union has created a perceived need for such an adaptation.

But it is not only in settings like this that ITREC/ITREB has implemented camps. Aliya Walji, a Khoja Isma'ili of Canadian and Indo-African origin, described to me the *'Ilm* (knowledge) camps of North America, which are only for Ismaʿilis and are perhaps again similar in their social form and inter-group relationships to Jewish NFTY camps. They are meant to generate in young, urban Ismaʿilis a sense of connection to other Ismaʿilis. Here again we have a forum for the creation of a common identity between people from different places.

Such activities taken together can clearly be considered as important processes in the project of global community-building. A second important aspect about such activities and institutions is their focus on "ethics and morals." This in fact amounts to a focus on culturally specific *Ismaʿili* values, morals, and ethics (presented as universal and absolute morals and ethics). In this way, Ismaʿili beliefs, in a program of "moral education," are natu-ralized as truth. But most important is what these moments reveal about the Ismaʿili emphasis on socializing borderland societies to basic principles associated with modernity and about the process by which this effort trick-les out from Ismaʿili metropolitan centers of symbolic production to such peripheries. The camp and the conference (and the children's book dis-cussed above) represent well, I think, the enactment of that semiotic trans-fer and transitivity.

Rural Reconfigurations: The Village Organization and the Reinvention of Social Life

I now focus on a different type of locally relevant Ismaʿili structure in the Pamir and Karakoram: the Village Organization. This represents a shift in emphasis back to the *imamati* institutions and to the Ismaʿili mechanisms intertwined with discourses of "development." It is of particular interest for its establishment of a shared form connecting villagers in Himalayan Pakistan, Tajikistan, and now Afghanistan, and for the directionality of its dissemination from Pakistan to Tajikistan. While the Village Organization is not explicitly tied to religious practice, its connection to sentiments and structures of devotion is not as distant as it might first appear. It is also of great significance, as we will see, in providing a channel (and a bureaucratic infrastructure) for Khoja interaction with Himalayan Nizaris and in incul-cating those borderland societies with an enthusiasm for modernity, capital, and "progress."

There are few intersections between Himalayan societies and the Ismaʿili global institutional complex more important than that embodied in the for-mation of Village Organizations (VOs). And few forms better demonstrate the ethnographic significance of the global proliferation of Ismaʿili institutions than the VO. It represents one of the most critical mechanisms by which the imamate's institutions have transformed rural lives and localities, and it reveals much about the dynamics of Isma'ili globalization in local settings. It also forms a context for critique of centralized Isma'ili institutions, and a site of local resistance to global forms.

The VO is at the foundation of the relationship between AKF (through its various regional institutions) and the local people with whom it works.[5] It is essentially meant to be a democratic governing council on the village level. It is not an indigenous form but a modern invention initiated and established by AKF, beginning in northern Pakistan in the early 1980s. While in some areas it may have superficial continuity with existing indigenous village council structures, I argue that in general it represents a completely new entity and an alternative conceptualization of citizenship and political decision-making. AKRSP in Pakistan established the VO as a replicable model that AKRSP India, MSDSP in Tajikistan, and other AKF subsidiaries have used, in modified form, as the basis of their rural development work.

The VO, as created by AKRSP, is presented as a means by which villagers are put in charge of their own "development," which is intended to circumvent the imposition of models from institutions disconnected with local contexts: "The beneficiaries are treated as active partners rather than merely passive recipients" (Aga Khan Rural Support Programme 1994: 1). AKRSP, furthermore, is eager to show that it "emphasizes that the villagers themselves have to undertake activities to improve their own lives. AKRSP is merely a facilitator and supervisor in this sense" (1). The perceived success of the process in helping to raise standards of living among rural villagers has won AKRSP and AKF, like the Grameen Bank, great prestige in the development world. Because the VO model has become influential outside of Pakistan, as well as outside of the Aga Khan's institutions, its underlying assumptions and ideologies deserve close examination. As we will see, this model emerges from naturalized and now widely distributed notions of development firmly rooted in metadiscourses of modernity.

When AKRSP moves into a new area, they establish a dialogue with villagers in that area: AKRSP offers extensive assistance, support, and abundant resources, provided that the villagers form a VO through which all development is to pass from that point on. The VO is meant to be the locus of all decision making and the conduit for all donated resources. A prerequisite for VO formation is the involvement of at least 75 percent of the domiciles of a given settlement (Aga Khan Rural Support Programme, 1994: 1). AKRSP itself defines the VO process as follows:

Social Organization is a process initiated by the villagers when they accept the terms of development partnership offered by AKRSP and form a broad based, participatory Village Organization (VO). As an incentive to organize, AKRSP provides investment in social organization in the form of a grant for village infrastructure. The project is identified, undertaken, and maintained by the villagers. The process of project identification, as well as follow-on activities in other sectors, is done by holding three dialogues with the villagers. Once the villagers have organized themselves into VOS, AKRSP provides support in the form of credit, training, inputs for agriculture, livestock, and forestry. Rural women are provided support in those activities in which they have traditional roles, e.g., vegetable cultivation and poultry rearing. AKRSP always felt that the VO/WOS will only function if they continue to meet the varying needs of their members. (xi)

The VO, moreover, is intended to function not only as a council to manage relations with and decisions concerning AKRSP, but to be a general council for the village and to meet regularly to discuss village matters. Thus, AKRSP creates a form — neither entirely exogenous nor entirely indigenous — that is not simply specialized and oriented toward "development" but is also a generalized, new, and enduring element of local society. AKRSP and World Bank materials refer to the relative "maturity" of a VO, or its ability to persist without external support. It is essentially a new type of village government and forum for popular representation.

Wherever AKRSP creates a VO in Pakistan, they also coordinate the creation of a parallel Women's Organization (WO), which is supposed to handle decisions and matters concerning the often separate socioeconomic sphere of women. VOS and WOS meet at least weekly to discuss matters concerning village resources and social issues. Members are expected to make regular financial contributions at weekly meetings to the VO; these funds are pooled and used for later projects. In this way, the VO also serves as a local bank of sorts, holding funds meant to be available for future village initiatives or for lending to enterprising individual members.

VO coverage is remarkably widespread. Almost every village I visited in the Pamir and Karakoram ranges had a VO and a WO. In northern Pakistan, there are reportedly 3,900 AKRSP-initiated VOS, covering a population of 1.3 million across most of the Northern Areas, Baltistan, and Chitral (Aga Khan Foundation 2003: 25). Coverage in Tajik Badakhshan by VOS established with the help of the MSDSP is said to be 100 percent: there are over 700 VOs in that region (MSDSP's Khaleel Tetlay, pers. comm., 2003). AKF is now active in 850 villages of Afghanistan, where it is working closely with existing indigenous village councils (Aga Khan Foundation 2003: 17); a major expansion is currently under way in that region. In all these places, the VO model seeks to profoundly transform the nature of social relations and political life. Moreover, the presence of the VO in alpine regions of Afghanistan, Pakistan, and Tajikistan creates a vast, contiguous area in which villagers are participating in the same process. It holds the potential to create a new sense of shared experience across these borders and to reconnect societies once they are bound together in a single sphere of communication. All of these areas, by virtue of the VO, are participating in a common system of local sociopolitical organization for the first time in at least a century.

As described, the VO model was pioneered in northern Pakistan in the early 1980s by AKRSP, and it has enjoyed enormous popularity and "success" in that region. A brief look at the institutional landscape of northern Pakistan prior to the arrival of AKRSP underlines how new and unprecedented the VO model really was. Until the early 1970s, northern Pakistan (including the Northern Areas and Chitral) was divided into a number of clan-based princely states. The feudal economy featured the exchange of cash rent or infrastructure labor for cultivable land rights, security, and access to common property. Upon the dissolution of these princely states, the Northern Areas (due to its proximity to Kashmir) became a federally administered territory of Pakistan without direct representation in federal structures, while Chitral was incorporated into the Northwest Frontier Province. However, government presence at the local level was quite minimal and "the formal liberation of peasant-pastoralist clans from labour and rental obligations to their lords did not place them under the development authority of an effective alternative government" (Wood, Malik, and Sagheer 2006: 40). AKRSP documents often refer to this period as featuring an "institutional vacuum." More explicitly, the entire region was uniformly poor, engaged in subsistence agriculture, while much public infrastructure declined. Wood et al. mentions that *mohallas* (neighborhoods, or more accurately in the rural context, regional divisions and associations) continued to perform limited localized maintenance, but much fell into disrepair (41).

It was at this juncture in 1982 that AKRSP introduced the Village Organization, novel in its relative inclusivity, its standardized operating procedures, and its promise of investment capital. So although some have argued that isolated rural poor typically have a "long and well-established tradition of cooperative or collective behavior for survival" (Khan and Khan 1992: 29), AKRSP certainly offered an exogenous form for the distribution of newly available resources. The people of the Northern Areas and Chitral were gradually socialized to a culture not only of the VO but of AKRSP itself and thus of its values. Villagers in Hunza viewed leadership positions in the VO as stepping stones, with the express goal of advancing into the ranks of locals employed by AKRSP and ultimately moving to the Gilgit regional offices or beyond. Both the VO and AKRSP are now deeply, even inextricably woven into the regional social fabric.

The context in which the concept of the VO has been applied in Tajikistan is radically different from that in which it was developed in Pakistan. Nonetheless, the same model has been used in both places. In fact, VO experts with years of experience with AKRSP in Pakistan were transferred to Badakhshan in order to implement the VO structure in this new region. Few adaptations were made, however, and the VO of Tajikistan, according both to NGO administrators and locals, was one that was adapted to a social configuration from Pakistan. Perhaps for this reason, the VO structure in the Pamir has taken on a different character from that in the Karakoram and Hindu Kush. It has not been embraced with the same level of enthusiasm, nor has it enjoyed the same level of participation. One villager in Khuf explained that there was 100 percent membership in the local VO, but "we never have meetings." The complete VO coverage of localities in Badakhshan gives the impression of success, but a closer look reveals that feelings toward the VO structure are highly ambivalent and sometimes critical. Often VO members complained that the services were not as extensive as those offered by the Soviet infrastructure, which offered them a complete system of social welfare. Some Pamiris are, furthermore, conscious that the VO is a form adapted to Pakistan in a context that they themselves define as very different. It seems to them out of place, involving decision-making norms and processes that they believe emerged out of a different cultural milieu.

On top of that, the success of MSDSP[6] and its associated VOs is inevitably compared with the services provided by the Soviet Union, which dealt with every imaginable aspect of social, economic, and political life. Many Pamiris find that NGO activity plays second fiddle to the efforts of that totalizing polity. In the eyes of many people in Tajikistan, especially in poorer areas, the Soviet era was a utopian one and it is remembered with nostalgia. Many Badakhshanis are expressing some doubt about the efficacy of VOs in and of themselves; they complain of corrupt VO leaders, misuse of funds, and non-implementation of projects. Some feel that the system has worked poorly in Gorno-Badakhshan.

The VO does have some superficial continuity with Soviet forms, in particular that of the *kolkhoz*, or collective farm community, with its accompanying local council (see Humphrey 1983). However, in the 1970s these cooperative farms in Badakhshan were amalgamated into the *sovkhoz*, or large, state-run farms, whose leaders were appointed by the party central committee in Dushanbe without significant local input. Smaller village *soviets* (administrative units) lacked any real authority because the *sovkhoz* leader controlled the distribution of nearly all resources, including water, energy, goods, and raw materials. And although the notion of collective work (such as house building) through the *amtabaq* system was not unfamiliar to Pamiris, when the Soviet Union broke down, even these kinds of activities declined due to severe resource constraints (Bliss 2006).[7]

AKF in the form of the Pamir Relief and Development Programme, or PRDP (subsequently MSDSP), became involved in the Pamirs in 1993 in response to the civil war, at first providing emergency food aid. The *sovkhoz* were in a process of collapse, and the land that they owned was eventually released for distribution by MSDSP (Bliss 2006: 308). It was in this context that VOs were introduced in Badakhshan, with leaders "elected for the first time by the population" (319).

Some Pamiris interpret the VO as a variant of the *kolkhoz* concept. Research revealed that VO leaders are often the very same individuals who were prominent and powerful in the Soviet era, much to the frustration of some villagers, who feel permanently disenfranchised (see Salmaan Keshavjee 1998). Fundamentally, however, the ideology underlying the VO is markedly different from the collective systems of Soviet Tajikistan. The goal of the VO, as I see it, is to provide a localized social form to mediate between individuals and larger market processes. And it expresses the emphasis on "collective capitalism" developed under Aga Khan III (see Boivin 2003).

According to Bliss (2006), "in the Pamirs there is no tradition of public discussion in which everyone takes part, including younger people, women, and girls, workers as well as management . . . only 15 years ago it would have been extremely risky to voice one's opinion publicly" (326). We can thus conclude that the VO was as new a form of social organization in Tajikistan as it was in Pakistan, though the prior contexts and historical conditions were drastically different.

It is crucial to distinguish the "participatory" model of the VO from the characteristic structures of "collective organization." AKDN institutions are themselves at pains to make this distinction clear, declaring that collectivist systems lack autonomy for the individual and sufficient incentive for individual effort (see Khan and Khan 1992). They instead view the VO as a local social institution providing means to "self-reliance" in a wider market system, offering supportive infrastructure above the level of the individual or household. The claim here is that the model of development advanced by the Aga Khan's institutions would never take such a form because belief in "democracy . . . private institutions, liberal economics, and a recognition of fundamental human rights" (Aga Khan IV, quoted in Salmaan Keshavjee 1998: 56) is at the heart of the mission of the religious leaders behind AKDN. In this way, AKDN intentionally promotes participation in wider capitalist systems and thus socializes its participants to capitalist ideologies, aiding the entry of those members of the Isma'ili community previously isolated in feudal or Communist polities into the global economic sphere. The observation by Morris (1968) that early modern institutional structures established by Aga Khan III in Africa were mechanisms for "economic education" among local Isma'ilis is certainly also true.

In some cases, Pamiris in Tajikistan consider the system offered by AKF through MSDSP a transitional form between socialism and what they see as unbridled market capitalism.[8] This brings us to some common features of and general observations about VOs across the two regions under consideration. In both Tajik Badakhshan and Pakistan's Northern Areas, AKF and the VOs arrived at the very moment that those areas opened up to capitalist market economies. In northern Pakistan, AKRSP first arrived when an enhanced connection to the outside world and entry into larger exchange systems was facilitated by the construction of roads, particularly the Karakoram Highway. In Tajikistan, the VO was introduced through AKF efforts as the Tajik civil war came to an end in the wake of the collapse of the USSR. AKF made a transition from relief work through PRDP to development work through its successor, MSDSP. Again, the VO arrived at the first (very tentative) contact with larger market systems, and in fact it helped facilitate early and small-scale attempts at capitalist activity. And more recently, AKF began its work in Afghan villages, at the moment that businesses and contractors began attempting to carry out their work throughout the country.

Perhaps, then, we might hypothesize that the villagers may associate the establishment and entrenchment of VOs with their communities' general entry into a market system and their integration or reintegration into a changing national polity, or as Salmaan Keshavjee (1998) puts it, the "penetration of global economic forces" (23). Using the same terms as are used to describe religious conversion, one villager in the Ishkashim region explained to me that it was through the MSDSP of AKF that they "*accepted the market* economy." The verb used (*qabul kardan*) was the same as that normally used to describe the acceptance of Islam. This is an apt reflection of the argument that the VO can function to encourage a sort of socialization to capitalism.

The VO is usually rationalized and described as a democratic and representative institution and a grassroots activist one, disseminated in the name of fostering social equality and enhanced standard of living. At the same time, because it so radically transforms social life, the VO becomes its own context for power relations and can itself create new forms of inequality and exclusion just as it creates new forms of equality and inclusion (Escobar 1994; Kamat 2002). There is certainly hierarchical prestige associated with the VO, and the ranking of VO managers, accountants, treasurers, and other representatives creates almost a new form of social stratification or class. The VO manager is a well-known figure in any village in Chitral or the Northern Areas. Salmaan Keshavjee (1998) notes more broadly, in his analysis of AKF in the Pamirs, that "because NGOs like the AKDN are often transnational enterprises that are products of transnational flows of capital and resources and certain dominant forms of organization, they often foster the emergence, or in the case of post-Soviet Badakhshan the continued existence, of a 'managerial bourgoisie,' who share a situation of socioeconomic privilege" (52). Both Wood, Malik, and Sagheer (2006) and Bliss (2006) observe that villagers in both regions are critical of emergent imbalances in wealth and status following the establishment of VOs.

AKF has in the past considered the VO as more or less a proprietary model. In Tajikistan, an incident occurred when representatives of AKF found that another global NGO was implementing VO-like structures in its project region. AKF approached this as essentially a trespass on their process and allegedly confronted the other NGO. An expatriate working for AKF commented, "they are trying to copy our model." The VO thus becomes a unique and highly marketable product in the context of competition over human loyalty, an innovation that may provide a significant advantage in winning over enthusiastic participants.

It is also telling (and obvious) that the VO has had greater relevance in Isma'ili areas in Pakistan than in Sunni or Shi'a regions (Nelson 2002; Wood, Malik, and Sagheer 2006), which says much about the institution's role as a constituent form in specific social contexts. The implication is that vos are intimately engaged with Isma'ili identity and participation and are particularly important loci of interaction between Isma'ilis and the global (but nominally secular) AKDN. For Isma'ilis it also involves interaction with a project of the imam to whom they devote their allegiance and often becomes connected with religious benefit and duty. As Bliss (2006) points out, the majority of the employees of the local Aga Khan institutions are themselves Isma'ilis and since "the project is directly supported by the imamate [this is] strongly motivating for the individual employee" (305). In this sense, there is little significant tension between the social organization projects of the development institutions of AKDN and the religious goals of the imamate. The development activities of AKDN socialize more isolated members of the polity to the values of the wider community, at whose center are diasporic Khoja elites. Further, young Isma'ili citizens from affluent nations are encouraged to spend time working in the Aga Khan development institutions as a sort of rite of passage, explicitly linking religious participation, this type of development work, and the ideologies underlying the model. The vo model also serves as a means by which local villages are socialized to capitalism. As I argue in the paragraphs below, the institutional language on vos echoes the discourses and ideologies of liberal humanism, citizenship, and rational individualism promoted by nation-states (cf. Mamdani 1996; Chatterjee 1986). At the same time, the published materials surveyed also establish a dialectic between the AKRSP model and the nation-state, only gradually bridged by an increase in the involvement of government in the project areas.

All this points to the role of the Enlightenment metadiscourses of political participation and rational consensus, as well as later discourses of capitalism and democracy, embodied and legitimized in a more modern lexicon of "development," in the production of the vos. Consider the following passage from an AKRSP report:

> What Makes a vo/wo Click?
> - *The vos/wos address a felt need and a common interest.* When the villagers share a common problem that can be best addressed by *collective* action they are likely to mobilize internal resources and work with support agencies to change the situation.
> - *The benefits of collective action outweigh the costs.* Benefits may be economic (savings, income generation, increased production); social capital formation (increased ability to collectively solve vil-

lage problems); increased individual capacity (Knowledge and skills); and or Psychological (sense of belonging, confidence).

- *Grafting of the new on the traditional.* VOs/WOs are most successful when based on existing/traditional social and economic structures.
- *Village level motivator/activists.* Honest/hardworking, informed and respected individuals occupying positions as VO/WO managers.
- *Rules and sanctions.* All successful VOs/WOs are characterized by internalized rules and regulations that are known and abided by all their members. VO/WO members have participated in the formulation of rules and enforcement mechanisms.
- *Management Structure.* Specialized committees are set-up to deal with credit, conflict management, education, water supply and sanitation, etc. (Aga Khan Rural Support Programme 1994: 4)

This discourse is replete with the global (and largely Euro-American) vocabulary of the Enlightenment, with the values and virtues of capital and democracy, and with the language of the modern: individualism, progress and tradition, rational decision-making, industriousness, thrift and capitalism, law and democracy.

In AKRSP texts, the VO model, and the VO itself are linked with notions of *progress* and *modernity.* This serves to establish the positive value of newness and change and disparage both the *feudal* political processes that predated the nation-state as well as the equivalent forms established by national governmental policies. The contrast is made most explicit in this statement about northern Pakistan from the AKF 1996 Annual Report: "Where once mountain tribes warred over control of the caravan routes between 8,000 metre peaks, they now meet regularly to plan the best use of village savings over $7.5 million" (Aga Khan Foundation 1996: 22). Interestingly, women's roles before and after the formation of WOs are often described in terms of their participation in economic spheres. While before the WO women had "little exposure to market forces," afterward they are "productive" and have been empowered through "economic change." The NGO is not only valuing the wider participation of villages in the market economy but even encouraging the production of useful subjects (particularly those previously excluded from market processes).[9]

We must keep in mind the primary audience for these reports. They serve in part to communicate and celebrate the NGO's perceived successes to a wider Isma'ili community across the globe, working both within and outside development contexts. That is, the reports themselves establish common ground, demonstrating to the Isma'ilis outside the developing world that the Isma'ilis of Pakistan and Tajikistan can now share in their metadiscourse of modernity. They may better identify with "farmers meeting each other on the way to the newly vibrant bazaars" who "now stop to talk about investment opportunities" (Aga Khan Foundation 1996: 23). The basis for the common ground is rooted in the language of capital and corporate entrepreneurialism.

It is likely that the decision-makers who devised and established the VO system had liberal humanist notions in mind when developing the program and that these ideas meshed well with their perception and image of those distant, exotic, autochthonous Isma'ilis' lives and needs. The idea of the VO may be the result of an orientalized imaginary by the Khoja elite of distant localities, of the romantic and organic life of a village.[10] Consider the following passage from an AKDN publication, which describes the advent of VOs almost as part of a transition from barbarism to civilization, from irrational tribalism to sensible capitalism:

When institutions of the Aga Khan Development Network (AKDN) first began working in northern Pakistan more than twenty years ago, it was one of the poorest areas on earth. Rural communities of different ethnic and religious backgrounds—Shia, Sunni and non-Muslim—struggled to eke out a meagre living, farming small holdings in the harsh environment of the mountain desert ecosystem. Relations among the communities were often hostile.

Since that time, over 3,900 village-based Organizations, comprising a mix of broad-based and interest-specific groups in such fields as women's initiatives, water use and savings and credit, were established by the Aga Khan Foundation (AKF). The quality of life of 1.3 million people living in the rural environment, that in many ways was representative of the majority of the population of Asia and Africa, has been dramatically improved. Per capita income has increased by 300 percent, savings have soared and there have been marked improvements in male and female education, life expectancy, primary health, housing, sanitation and cultural awareness. Former antagonists have worked together to create new programmes and social structures. Consensus around hope in the future has replaced conflict born of despair and memories of the past. (Aga Khan Foundation 2003: 2)

In such an imagining, a VO becomes a heroic concept, one that fits that mythic image of the distant yet connected other. That exotic and primitive "other" is not only spatially distant from the reader, but also temporally distant, associated with a different "chronotopic" moment in history (Fabian 1983; Bakhtin 1981). Such images of the heroic and locally rooted other fill the pages and the images of AKDN publications.

For the villagers, however, the VO is something altogether different, though it is not entirely disconnected from these imaginaries and processes. The VO is not only focused inward, on the community itself, but is also a forum for local participation in a transnational network. It mediates between the polity and the individual. It is a channel through which subjects are involved and incorporated into this polity by Isma'ili institutions; it inculcates in them an awareness of their connection to that macrostructural formation and is thus a central link between subject and structure.

Insofar as it represents a forum for discourse on locality itself, we might say that the village organization is a potential source for something we might call *metalocality*, a redefined, reflexive cultural construction of place that emerges out of a globalized situation (see Urban 2001). The globalization of community enhances communal self-awareness, encourages metadiscourses of community, new and conscious formulations of locality *as* locality. These metadiscursive self-formulations are in part informed and conditioned by others' (particularly Khojas') *imaginaries* of the localities in question. They are in a sense internalizations of those exogenous imaginaries, which, as I mentioned, are rooted in part in orientalist conceptions of the exotic other. These conceptions may be rooted in romantic visions produced by the global Khoja Isma'ili elite, some of whom valorize and idealize the far-flung Isma'ili villagers. Such orientalisms and imaginaries are recontextualized by the villagers themselves. Thus, a metadiscourse of locality that emerges out of the VO can be seen as having its origins in a kind of recycled or reappropriated orientalist imaginary of itself (Said 1979).

The VO is something else besides: it is a forum for local participation in the transnational Isma'ili assemblage, an interstitial point of connection par excellence between the local subject and the global network — and between Khojas and Himalayan Nizaris. Rural development is one of the sites where

Making yogurt in a traditional hide, Altit, Hunza, Pakistan, 1993. The boy later migrated to one of Pakistan's cities. His father still lives in the village and operates a small farm. AKRSP *Village Organization activity is intensive here.*

the imamate and the global elite come into contact with subjects. But these forms are neither simply introduced nor passively accepted. Negotiation and contestation are certainly also not absent from the histories of the VO, and those who participate in it succeed in molding it to their own vision and in critiquing it. Indeed, inherent in its structure are mechanisms allowing for such indigenization.

I suggest that through the VO model, AKDN has worked to radically change the very fabric of those localities where it has been established and to create new forms of civil society, social prestige, political participation, and citizenship. This effort at the transformation of the social fabric is certainly not without intentionality. It is telling that the division of Pakistan's AKRSP that deals with VOs is entitled "Social Organization." It is nothing less than human social organization itself that the AKF's VO has managed to reconfigure and reinvent in the Isma'ili Himalaya.

Bridging the Gap: Differential Experiences in the Divided Himalaya

A comparison between the two areas of the Himalaya under consideration sheds light on the progressive incorporation of remote Isma'ili communities. It draws attention to the influence of historical conditions on Isma'ili institutional activity in each area, which in turn has meant that the iterations of Isma'ilism generated in the interaction between the institutions and local people have been radically different. At the same time, the comparison reveals certain processes now common to both areas, including elements of the Khoja relationship with non-Khojas that seem to replicate themselves broadly and aspects of the interaction between Isma'ili institutions and local politics of identity.

In Tajikistan local social relationships and realities emerge as critical in global interactions; the significance of transnational Isma'ili institutions is determined and mediated by those intergroup relationships. The Tajik civil war is of particular importance in this regard, for it effected and cemented the exclusion of Pamiri Isma'ilis that, according to my hypothesis, motivated them to seek resources and membership in a new formation that accorded them higher status. For the first time, they were placed at the center, rather than the edge, and they were allocated material and symbolic resources that gave them a comparative advantage over the neighbors and competitors who had disenfranchised them. This history was itself determined by the inclusion—and marginalization—of this region in the Soviet Union, which was, in turn, determined by the intrigues of world empire in these mountains. The historical status of the area as a borderland thus forms a key element of its current situation.

Perhaps most significant in the contemporary context is the process by which, after the collapse of the USSR, the Pamiri Isma'ilis, in part because of their particular status under Soviet politics that favored ethnic apparatchiks from another region, became isolated from any political system or macrosocial formation. Locality, and at most region, became the context for social interaction, an important fact for a population that had for many decades been closely tied to the intensive circulation of the Soviet sphere. This isolation set in motion a search for some *new* locus for participation and organization, a search for a new site for allegiance and participation (and drew the interest of the Isma'ili institutions). The appeal of transnational affiliation and participation parallels similar dynamics of exclusion and dispossession in Pakistan, where Isma'ilis marginalized at the hands of both the state and Islamist groups have also sought a comparative material and symbolic advantage over their neighbors.

But participation in an Isma'ili transnational social structure is also tied to market processes, and in the case of Tajikistan, to entry into a global capitalist system. For some perspective on the degree of intentionality in this effort, consider the words of the Aga Khan on his first visit to Tajikistan:

> The inventiveness of human beings is a resource given by Allah,
> and it flourishes where the environment nurtures it, and is wasted
> where diktats deny its importance and fetter its practice. . . . Plural-
> ism draws its productivity not just from variety but also from com-
> petition. Some ideas turn out to be more persuasive than others,
> and gain acceptance. Some people are more inventive than others,
> and harvest the fruits of their accomplishments. The world is rapidly
> being pervaded by a spirit of meritocracy. The world that is opening
> up to Tajikistan is one in which merit will be rewarded.[11]

Not only in this setting but in multiple settings around the world, and not only in this moment of history but also in the recent past, we see that interaction with the central institutions of Isma'ilism is connected to economic systems and exigencies. We have seen that the formation of an Isma'ili transterritorial sphere, with populations around the Indian Ocean rim and in Europe, was intimately linked to the markets of the British Empire. We also observed that earlier Isma'ili translocal systems of circulation and movement were determined largely by the imperative of the collection of the tithe from across the Ismaʿili world. In a similar way, the arrival of transnational Ismaʿili institutions as a major component of local life in Tajikistan is associated with new channels and corporate models made available through new connections with global markets.

Ethnographic observations from Pakistan when compared with more pointed observations from Tajikistan are essential in isolating what aspects of Ismaʿili social process are rooted in local conditions and what can be hypothesized to be systemwide. Moreover, the comparison provides some insight into what aspects of transnational Ismaʿili participation and organization transect local realities as manifestations of more universal sociohistorical conditions shared across the planet. Local participation in transnational Ismaʿili institutions and processes in the areas of the Pakistan Himalaya adjacent to the areas of Tajikistan under consideration displays a number of features that parallel observations in Pakistan. However, the Ismaʿili areas of Pakistan have had a longer connection to the central Ismaʿili leadership, though from the historical point of view it is nonetheless recent. Their contact with the imamate has been particularly intensive since the first Aga Khan moved to Bombay in the 1840s. The sphere of circulation facilitated by the British Empire in India, more than anything else, made this possible; the British Empire provided a context for interaction that served as an essential precondition for more recent global forms. In particular, it allowed for the interaction between the diasporic component of the Ismaʿili community, originating in the region of Gujarat in India and now located in East Africa and Europe, and the long-settled Ismaʿili areas of the Himalaya.

In Pakistan's Northern Areas, even more than in Tajikistan, the AKF-initiated VOs have altered the very organization of the remote villages of the Ismaʿili areas of the Himalaya. They have become the central decision-making councils for those villages and the primary body for the allocation and the distribution of resources. They both perpetuate and enact status distinctions within the villages. These VOs, now a trademark of Ismaʿili social service initiatives around the world, are a key forum for local participation in a transnational social sphere. They allow for daily contact, albeit indirect, with the central organizational structures of the Ismaʿili network.

In Pakistan too, like in Tajikistan, local social relationships, especially ones of conflict and exclusion, show themselves to be significant in the development of local affiliation in and participation with transnational Ismaʿili formations. In Pakistan's Northern Areas local people for some time felt alienated from the regional administration. Because of the Kashmir situation, the Northern Areas were not made into a province; they were thus administered directly from the Pakistani capital. The administrators of the region were not elected and not local, and they garnered resentment from the region's people. This situation, moreover, was affected by sectarian conflict, which made the local people even more dissatisfied with their control by outsiders and generated suspicion about the state's role in these conflicts. In light of the tenuous condition of relations between locality and state here, villagers in the region were not always favorable toward Pakistan and were open to alternative loci for identification and affiliation.

Here my observations suggest that the low status accorded to Isma'ilis by locally dominant Sunni societies and organizations motivates, at least in part, an interest in finding a locus for membership in which Isma'ilis would be fully enfranchised and embraced. Other dynamics observed in Pakistan that seem to encourage enthusiastic affiliation with the Isma'ili transnational structure are the perpetual flow of Isma'ilis from around the world as personnel through the AKDN system, a process that inculcates in those subjects a sense of their connection to each other; the ubiquity of AKDN signs and symbols in the landscape and in the daily social fabric; the importance of migration in putting Isma'ilis from different areas in touch with each other; and, of particular note, the primacy of "Isma'ili" as local emblem of identity in an area where such labels are key.

But most important in considering the differential experiences of the two nationally circumscribed areas is the role of divergent interactions with European empires. The discussion of "differential experiences" of the "two regions" only makes sense through this lens; before the interaction of the areas now in Tajikistan with the Soviet Union by way of Russia and the Emirate of Bukhara, and of the areas now in Pakistan with the British Empire, culture and difference in the region were organized along other (more fluid and complex) lines. It was in particular the access to larger markets made possible by incorporation into the two polities that has caused contemporary configurations of transnational participation to be so radically different. In the Soviet Union, Isma'ilis had little access to Isma'ili institutions as they developed over the past two centuries. The introduction was abrupt and associated with crisis, whereas in Pakistan, the introduction was gradual and involved intensive missionary activity. Even the available categories of identity in each region were directed by the colonial context; northern Pakistani adherents have long been "Isma'ili" at this point, whereas Pamiri identity is in flux. The variant experience of empire, moreover, corresponds to a markedly different set of interactions with Khojas. Where northern Pakistan has been well established within the Khoja fold for much longer, southern Tajikistan (and Afghanistan) reveal an uncertain relationship with Khoja elites whose status was determined by the British Empire. That relationship is the object of continued negotiation.

Villages: Pamir

Some of this book's claims are best put to the test through a more detailed picture of villages themselves. Here what I call the "messy" complexity of real life illuminates many of the realities of Isma'ili institutional globalization. I start with Khushk Hamlet, a village not far from Khorog, the capital of Gorno-Badakhshan, and up the mountainside from Porshnev, which is where the old capital of the region was situated. In the village is an old and important Isma'ili mausoleum, or *gumbaz*, to which pilgrimage in Soviet times was forbidden. The older generation feels that despite that fact, people don't respect the shrine as much as they used to; shrines here — and even rumors about the imam's prescriptions on them — seem a flashpoint of contestation. The village has faced very difficult times in the past ten years, but things have improved since the Tajik civil war. Before the Soviet Union, the villagers say, the area was administered by local rulers, the tsarist regime under Nicholas, the emirate of Bukhara, and the emirs of Afghanistan. Before the Soviet period, a strong translocal connection was maintained between the area and the imam in Bombay. "Hajjis" would travel to Bombay from the area bearing their monetary tithe payments from villagers, and the imam would send them back with *farman* edicts on paper. It was a central ceremony of the past. Nowadays, say the villagers, *farmans* come by fax and copy machines, and people trust the papers less as they are suspicious of their authenticity. Moreover, they say that during the reign of Sultan Muhammad Shah the imam was clearly in control of everything; now they see the institutional control of everything as an inferior alternative.

It is the imam's face-to-face communication that the people see as most compelling. A village schoolteacher here, Jafar, twice experienced the formal *didar* audience with the Aga Khan, and once saw him on an informal visit. "If you travel all the world," he says, "nothing is so great as the *didar*. It is inexplicable." AKF's MSDSP has a strong presence here — they repaired the school, built water channels, and formed a VO. Of the future Jafar says, "no one knows except the imam." But in Badakhshan, he says, "plans are dreams."

A visit to the village of Khuf reveals some notably different dynamics. A tributary of the Panj in Rushan district, the small valley is remarkable for the distinct dialect it features (see Andreev 1953). The area is hardly accessible by car, and there is little habitation along the walking path, requiring some three hours each way, between the lower village and the upper village.[12] Part of the ascent circumvents a waterfall. The settled area of Khuf is hidden in a wide, fertile bowl behind the lip of the waterfall. One climbs up into the niche and the valley opens out to green fields with snowy mountains behind. The central village is very poor and remote, and the houses are primarily mud. Villagers seemed surprised by my arrival; outsiders are apparently rare here. Some of the houses have ornate mud and window work. There are a few skeletons of old Soviet trucks scattered about.

Nafar Shah, a Khufi who lives in Bishkek, brought me upon my arrival into a village wedding. While I saw AKF t-shirts, Nafar Shah claimed there was no AKF presence in the village, which during the Soviet era had been a *kolkhoz*. From the villagers' perspective, *kolkhoz* structure and VO structure seemed connected. There had formerly been a VO that carried out a channel-building project, which has seemingly dissolved. There is no AKF representation in the village otherwise. Participation is on the level of the *rayon*, or region, an official Soviet administrative unit. Shah says that life in the village would be much better if there were an Aga Khan school there. AKF provides highly desired services. Migration from these areas is heavy, and guests at the wedding were to include Pamiris resident in Russia.

Ryn village, the next stop, is located in the only area of Tajikistan where the Ishkashmi-Sanglechi language, locally called Ryndagi, is spoken. The village has undergone a lot of changes lately: ten years ago, there were only ten families, and now there are thirty-five. Recently a new school was built, and now there is also an AKDN medical center. AKDN is also working on water supply in the village. There are a number of migrants: 10–12 of the 190 villagers work in Russia. During Soviet times, villagers say, life was much better: "Moscow provided." But now, they say, due to the "creativity" of AKF, "lots of good things are being planned." The villagers describe two *didars* here, in which the Aga Khan said "the best words for our people." They were able to listen to the Aga Khan's *didar* in Afghanistan as well, as they are situated right on the border. A *khalifa* (lit., successor or lieutenant, referring to an Isma'ili community leader) functionary now provides a major connection with the Aga Khan when he delivers *farmans* from Khorog.

During the Soviet times, they say, "no one thought about the imam," and "people would swear by the name of the Aga Khan Sultan Mohammed Shah," an earlier imam. At the *didar*, the Aga Khan said there will be an international airport at Ishkashim with flights "from Pakistan, from Iran," and maybe from "Africa or America." Of this *didar* the villagers say, "it is difficult to imagine — it was so touching." And the villagers say that the difference between here and Afghanistan is the "difference between earth and heaven." My main informant in this village was a member of the AKDN VO and says that everyone else is also a member. The VO takes seeds from AKF and distributes them to people; they find donors for their projects. The current VO leader is the school headmaster. They gather fifteen *dirhams* as a contribution to the VO's budget and then they assist small entrepreneurs in a sort of credit system. A prominent religious leader in the community says that local people have a great deal of contact with other Isma'ilis from elsewhere through MSDSP and the ITREC. Another religious leader I spoke to in Ryn claimed to have seen the imam in a *didar* ceremony six times and that that these experiences gave him great hope. People didn't even imagine the imam during the Soviet period, he said. Only older people knew about him. After 1995 people understood that they "had a guide." He explained that he feels brotherhood with other Isma'ilis and Hazir Imam, the current imam, has been mentioning this in his *farmans*. In his village, MSDSP provides people with credit, forestry, vegetables, schools, and a health clinic. Even a very poor house I visited in this village was filled with AKDN materials.

Jelandy is a Shughni-speaking village clustered by the road between Khorog and Murghab. It is among the highest-altitude villages in Gorno-Badakhshan. It only became a village during the Soviet period. MSDSP and AKDN have a strong presence here, as does the ITREB, which delivers messages weekly; a *khalifa* missionary brings *farmans* on paper. The *didar* he received at Shikht was, according to him, beyond words.

A nearby village, Murch, is very poor, and has a population of ninety-eight people. The main crop is *chush*, a small potato, and the herds are very small. The family I spoke to exchanged most of their goats for flour at the rate of one goat per one sack of flour. They equate the AKDN VO with the earlier Soviet *kolkhoz*, the collective farm council. In the village MSDSP is building a medical center, and like in Jelandy, a *khalifa* brings *farmans* from

The village of Ryn, Ishkashim, Tajikistan. The mountains are in the Isma'ili areas of Afghanistan, visible just beyond the Panj River, at center.

the main ITREC office. While these people express very little awareness of Ismaʿilis from elsewhere, on their wall is a poster from the AKRSP across two borders in Pakistan.

"Uncontacted Outsider" to "Institutional Insider": Globality in the Life History of a Chinese Ismaʿili

The life history of a Chinese Ismaʿili, because of its location largely outside of the imperial contexts of either British India or Soviet Central Asia, reveals much about the centrality of those historical contexts in the production of identity. Of particular note in the story of this subject is the absence of well-worn pathways of interaction with Khojas and the consequent room for creativity in his use of globally prescribed framings of self (in relation to locally relevant ones). As we will see, this subject points to interesting possibilities both for self-fashioning of new modalities of selfhood within an Ismaʿili framework and sheds light on the socialization to dominant Ismaʿili institutional ways of representing cultural affiliation.

Amanullah is an Ismaʿili from Kashghar in China's Xinjiang province, sometimes referred to as Chinese Turkestan. His father was from the Pamiri town of Tashkurghan and came from a family of Persian-speaking Tajiks from the Mashhad region of Iran who then adopted the Pamiri language of Wakhi as their language of communication. His ancestors seem to have fled three generations ago in a feud over land or resources. His father was born on the way from Iran to China in Afghanistan and was named for the pastureland in which he was born, in Wakhan. His father settled first in the Chinese Pamiri village of Tiznef and then in Watcha and was educated in the Uyghur language in Ürümchi. His father then became a local politician of some note, heading the "local parliament," a kind of "national council." Amanullah's mother is an Uyghur, so he identifies himself as having "half Turkish blood, half Tajiki." His first language is Uyghur.

As a child in 1977, Amanullah was sent back from the city of Kashghar to the mountain town of Tashkurghan, where there were more Ismaʿilis, because his mother was experiencing financial stress, but also seemingly because of a rift between China and the Soviet Union that necessitated resettlement in a rural area. It was at that time that Amanullah learned Wakhi and Sariquli. In recent years he has become essentially the first transnational Chinese Ismaʿili subject able to mediate between his own society and global Ismaʿilism. He has become an expert on the Ismaʿilis of the region, conducting many studies on them and thus developing a connection with them. He claims that the Isma'ili Wakhis of the Guma and Pishan oases migrated in the seventeenth century from Afghanistan. Their isolation, he says, has decreased in recent years through heightened contact with the government and "Tajik" Isma'ili representatives. He is interested in doing more research on the local people and in their Saka and Tocharian past.[13]

Amanullah suggests that the last *farman* was received from Imam Sultan Muhammad Shah in Bombay in 1947. Since that time there has been no contact between Chinese Isma'ilis and the imamate. In 1949 the very open border was closed. Our conversation about the text of the *farman* is indicative of the state of Isma'ilism in China:

J: So did people keep that last *farman* and, and sort of, I mean they must have felt that that last *farman* was very important, they must have remembered it or told stories about the last communication.

A: The *farman* is still in the hands of the people; I have seen some of the *farman* but I can't make a copy because it's in Arabic script, and if you make, try to xerox it, the people will become very suspicious. The old Arabic script became a kind of no matter what it's religious literature or whatever and the government became very suspicious of its nature. They think it may have something to do with some kind of subversive religious activity. This is very sensitive so I did not want to place people in any kind of jeopardy by making a photocopy which might indicate where I got the original papers from. Those people try to keep such things by hiding it in their families, because during the Cultural Revolution in all the regions there were a lot of political activities and they destroyed the old manuscripts and religious documents and everything related with that past, that community's past. So these are the things which survived that onslaught, so if I do anything to that then I will be blamed for the rest of my . . .

Before 1917, says Amanullah, the region was loosely under Chinese administration; there was a garrison town nearby since the time of the Qing dynasty's rule in eastern Turkestan. Amanullah indicated that the first Khoja-style *jama'at khana* was established in Chinese Turkestan between the years 1917 and 1921, in the village of Toghlanshahr, through the efforts of a member of the imam's family from Bombay. In fact, Amanullah points to a *jama'at khana* of even earlier provenance than this one, in Tiznef, that has no written history. In the newer one, the religious leadership used to open and read *farmans* from the imam to the followers in a special ceremony for which an edifice that the local people called *bangalow* was built.[14] This translocal contact between Chinese Turkestan and the imamate was more extensive at this time even than in Tajikistan.

More recently, contact, though still limited, between the imamate and the local Isma'ilis has increased. Consider the next part of Amanullah's dialogue about the first contact between the area's people and the imam in over sixty years:

J: So when did you guys start to have information about the Hazir Imam? Was it when the border opened up, like you said?

A: That was one point but actually we started to have access to such information in 1982 when Hazir Imam visited Kashghar.

J: Really?

A: Yeah. He comes to Kashghar. The Kashghar Id Gah Mosque was selected for the Aga Khan Architecture Award or something like that. It was a part of that. And he comes to Kashghar, and I was in secondary school at that time. My mom was one of the government delegates that was allowed to participate in that concert given in honor of the imam. And she comes back and says . . . And the Uyghurs all started, you know, from that point they all said that "oh your god came" [laughs] . . . and she comes to home and says "don't tell anyone our imam is here." I say, "why not?" And she says, "our imam is the Aga Khan," but we knew of the Aga Khan but we didn't refer to him as "imam." We thought he was a god, not . . . the idea of "imam" was very new to have. We regarded him, the Aga Khan himself, as a supreme being, a god himself. He comes with Aga Khan the title. And the imam was kind of new concept. It started from that time I think.

J: But he didn't actually address the jama'at, he —

A: No no no.

J: He didn't, he didn't actually give *didar*, did he?

A: He didn't come as the imam, he came as a philanthropist.

J: He has not yet come as an imam?

A: No, no.

J: So there's not official contact.

A: Nah.

J: But does he send *farmans* to the . . .

A: No, it's very dangerous to send any *farman*. The Chinese constitution makes it very clear every Chinese citizen has a right
to believe in their religion, any religion they want, or not to believe, but their religion must not be subject to foreign domination, which means that any foreign power cannot intervene in the
citizens' religious practice in China. So we are also not excluded
from that.

Later he told me, "I want to see my imam . . . As a child I said, 'I have to
see my God someday, I have to try to find a way to see my God and which
kind of God do I have.'" Nowadays, he says, the imam, at least in the cities,
is no longer regarded as a superhuman being and access to information
about Isma'ilism is increasing. But in the countryside, where Amanullah
has spoken to people about the imam, they still believe in his superhuman
nature. Amanullah said that when the border opened up local people were
quite disillusioned with the moral laxity of the Isma'ilis from Pakistan, but
that all the same they brought across the boundary at the Khunjerab Pass a
kind of "new wave of awakening of the consciousness about the imam. They
brought some literatures, pictures, videocassettes, things like that, about the
activities of the imam and all these things. They showed them in secret to
some people. It's forbidden by law but they still . . . but they didn't introduce
the practice, because they weren't very good people themselves." Amanullah also expresses a strong sense of connection with post-Soviet Central
Asians, across the border. He says that they will say that the culture in Xinjiang is an extension of theirs, and that the Isma'ilis of Xinjiang will say the
opposite, but that either way "it's almost to just find yourself at home. . . . I
don't think it's a very foreign country."

I asked Amanullah how he ended up at the IIS in London. He traces
the desire back to 1982 when he began to entertain thoughts of someday
"getting in touch with the imam." When he graduated from university in
Xi'an in 1993 he went back to Ürümchi, which he fundamentally thinks of as
his home. Amanullah became a prosecutor and eventually was in charge of
the "international department" in Ürümchi. In summer of 1993 he went to
Kashghar and by chance met three Canadian Isma'ilis (according to other
versions of Amanullah's story, these were Isma'ili missionaries). These
Canadian Isma'ilis gave Amanullah a picture of the vast complex of Isma'ili
institutions, a picture by which he was deeply impressed. He started circulating his résumé and making applications every year. In 1996 he went to
Pakistan and asked around; he said that ultimately the Pakistani Isma'ilis

didn't pay much attention to him. He stayed three months in Karachi and found no employment in or affiliation with Isma'ili institutions. In 1999 he met three Isma'ili dignitaries, one of whom carried his materials from Ürümchi to Moscow to London. The IIS, in turn, sent a letter back from London via Moscow to Ürümchi.

After seven years of trying, and seven years of working for the Chinese government Amanullah reports that he gained admission to IIS. He faced four months of harassment while his visa application was being processed. He received a letter from IIS, a fact that put him at some risk, especially since, as he said, "we never *admitted* that we had any contact with the imam." Religion, moreover, was seen as "backwards" and to admit affiliation with it could be seen as "degrading yourself." Instead, he showed an older letter from Edinburgh University and got permission to attend a three-month language course there.[15]

Amanullah says that being in London called everything into question for him and created some confusion about how to present himself and his identity. In China, he said, you can't separate being Isma'ili from "your Tajikness." Ethnicity and religion are the same. In London he met Isma'ilis who are not Tajik. He says, laughing, that somewhere in the back of his mind he still thinks that proper Isma'ilis should be Tajik. As for being part of a global community, he says,

> I also feel that this is a hope, this kind of being a part of this kind of big community is a hope for my people there in the future to get some access for communication . . . because they haven't yet had much interaction with outsiders. Tajikistan . . . the Soviet government actually promised to educate our Tajiks in Tajikistan from primary school; actually they signed some contract with that Xinjiang Government, but that did not last that long, so everything is shattered, that dream is crushed now. The imamate and institutions opening and all that . . . and, my success actually opens a new hope for the new generation. They will think it could be possible for a, even for a Tajik from that part to study abroad and get a good career.

Amanullah thinks integration and cooperation with the Chinese system are the best path for Isma'ilis in the future. But he hopes that increased connection to the imamate's institutions will be part of that. And even of himself he says that "I think China offers me more opportunity than the West does." Of his own situation as one of the only Chinese Isma'ilis outside of China he says the following:

Actually, I am a pioneer, I am the first one who established that kind of contact with the institutions here—after seven years of perseverance it paid off. . . . I am the one who actually can think and to some extent understand the western perspective, ideology, and philosophy. I say this because this institution offered me that kind of opportunity, and how my mind changed, honestly! I was a different person, I am a different person now than I was before, because once I was a product of Communist-controlled indoctrination. I came with a kind of dogma to guide me and I thought I knew the truth, everything . . . but here they gave me the opportunity to reflect and think instead of reaching a judgment, start before reaching a conc-, in China we start from the conclusion and we work to build up, to prove this conclusion. That's the kind of education they taught us. . . . So here, yeah, I was kind of re-made in that sense.

Transnationality fundamentally emerges as an element of personal transformation in this narrative. The life history here also shows how *transnational* Isma'ili identity is intimately tied up with *local* discourses of ethnic identity, how it is in dialectic relationship with other Islamic sects, and how it changes in relation to national boundaries and globalization. It emphasizes the relationality and fluidity of this identity, and the strategic use of global connections. We see here, then, the way that the instantiation of transnational membership has much to do with local relationships. The narrative shows that in the greatest isolation, even in the mountains of Chinese Xinjiang, with no official contact with the imamate, subjects can have significant contact with the Isma'ili transnational structure. But it also shows the complex and continuous process of institutional induction and incorporation. In this case, the imam's institutions, unable to establish themselves in the subject's milieu, helped him instead enter into their institutional space.

What Amanullah's story suggests for discussion of Isma'ili modes of self-description is significant. Amanullah's trajectory is outside both of the colonial and institutional histories of Tajikistan's Pamir and Pakistan's Karakoram. Thus the lexicon that Amanullah possesses for self-description and affiliation shows important differences with those of subjects in the other settings under discussion. His sense of group relationality has consequently until recently been oriented toward the regional politics of southwestern Xinjiang. Nonetheless, he is now forging for himself a special place among Khojas and other Isma'ilis in Isma'ili global institutions, and they are in turn forging a special place for him, for he is surely an object of great interest to the experts and managers of these institutions, just as he was for the missionary Khojas who "taught him" about global Isma'ilism. From the institutional perspective, he is both "exotic" and "authentic," "uncontacted" in important and intriguing ways. He is to them the potential source of captivating information on Isma'ilis and their knowledge of Isma'ili globality. We thus see in the anomalous case of Amanullah, whose Isma'ili relatives and friends in China have little or no parallel experience, interesting elements of the process and imperative of incorporation into global Isma'ili space. This isolation in turn sheds light both on the role of larger imperial and national polities in creating important (and importantly different) contexts of unique *shared* experience in Tajikistan and Pakistan respectively. But it also sheds light on the effort of global Isma'ili institutions to create (and bring new subjects into) a *single* context of shared experience, inculcation, and inclusion despite these differential histories.

Decoding Globality

Modern Ismaʿilism and the Institutional Encounter

What is the form and meaning of the mosaic that begins now to come into resolution? Certainly something remarkable is embodied in Ismaʿili globality. But the evidence is scattered and fragmentary. It might help to return once again to the question of the subject. In large part because of the labors of the Ismaʿili global institutional complex, Sher Ali and Sultan Ali were born into a world radically different from the world of their parents' birth and with an identity radically different from that of their parents. And so on, for every generation of the past century and a half. Before that, before imperial channels and the ruptures of capital, we imagine and presuppose greater continuity from generation to generation. It also should be noted that these two men are conscious of their transformation by global processes: this historical change is part of their own self-image. Nothing less than the transformation of the lifeworld and experience of the Ismaʿili subject is at stake here. That a global assemblage with neither parallel nor precedent should impact so profoundly the formulation of self and the structure of locality is remarkable indeed. What I have attempted here is an interrogation of the institutional mediation of subjectivity, the interstices between history and locality, and the complex relationship between community and shifting frameworks of power and production.

At the heart of the historical narrative I recounted is the critical role of empire in the formation of a unitary and eventually global Ismaʿili community. At the dawn of empire, what has now turned into the integrated Ismaʿili ecumene consisted of a set of scattered populations (Himalayan, Hazarajat, Western Indian Khoja, Zanzibar Khoja, and Syrian among them), pelagic in their distribution and isolation, with widely variable, historical relationships to the formation called Ismaʿilism, many of them with little or no connection to the imam of the time. The intensive process of consolidation and incorporation of remote communities that has occurred in the intervening generations has fundamentally reconfigured the relationship of those communities to each other and to the imamate.[1] I propose that empire was critical to the construction of a centralized and eventually global community for three reasons: first, it opened up channels of movement, exchange, and labor that aided in the creation of an extensive Indian Ocean diaspora; second, the British saw in the Aga Khans and their adherents strategic allies for the perpetuation of their own objectives and the possibility, part of a well-established practice, that a third party would do their bidding; and third, the empire's orientalist legal discourses of community were essential in according a unitary status to its component populations. Indeed, the modern position of the imam is in large part a product of the negotiation and interaction between the influential Khojas and the representatives of empire, mediated by law and colonial scholarship. As we saw in the discussion of the 1866 Aga Khan case, the British High Court in Bombay legally decreed the authority of the Aga Khan over Isma'ili subjects, proclaimed him the official leader of all Isma'ilis, and produced through presupposition and "expertise" the aggregation of a single and unified Isma'ili community (see Shodhan 2001). It is certainly relevant, despite the radically different political setting, to draw parallels between this and the later Soviet production of "Pamiri" and "Badakhshani" identities that would come to articulate closely with the emergent post-Soviet "Isma'ili" identity in Tajikistan. Both represent the interaction between modern European politico-legal discourses on and classifications of culture, on the one hand, and ethnographic complexity, on the other.

The story of the globalization of the Isma'ili "community," then, is in part a story of historical conditions and forces—conditions and forces to which the community was already subject and that the Aga Khans mobilized and perpetuated to their own ends. Thus the image that emerges is one in which the inception of empire and the expansion of capital articulate and intertwine with existing sociocultural forms. The historical conditions and forces could be said to have operationalized and activated the potentialities of those sociocultural forms. This accounts for their rapid growth and expansion and the readiness with which their institutional proliferation was accepted by the community.

In the subsequent period of Isma'ili political development, the period of Aga Khan III, the roots of the Isma'ili zeal for modernity come into plain view. This imam, Sultan Muhammad Shah, would take advantage of the full potential of the imperial infrastructure to expand his institutional domain and to socialize all the populations now considered his subjects to norms associated with modernity, rational individualism, liberal humanism, political participation, and capitalist accumulation. Also among the innovations of Aga Khan III were his mobilization of diasporic networks in the service of institutional proliferation and his mobilization of institutional forms in creating a more unified diasporic sphere of communication. Much of the development of the Ismaʿili institutional complex can be attributed to forms (constitutions, councils, educational institutions) first established for the administration of Khoja communities in East Africa (see Morris 1968; Boivin 2003), their initial migration itself largely a product of colonial population movements. East Africa in fact became a major node in the production, refinement, and global dissemination of these institutions. Fifty years after the death of Sultan Muhammad Shah, under Aga Khan IV, the zeal for modernity, remolded according to corporate sensibilities, remains as it likely will a hundred years hence (see Salmaan Keshavjee 1998).

The process of socialization to modern norms also remains. Under the current Ismaʿili administration, "development" becomes a vehicle for the inculcation of remote Ismaʿili populations to modern models of personhood and citizenship, political participation, and corporate entrepreneurialism. The current Aga Khan's emphasis on business and commerce (some of it a result of his Harvard years) adds another ingredient to the institutional lexicon of contemporary Ismaʿilism. Indeed, there are many ways in which Ismaʿili institutional globality takes on a corporate character (see Kaiser 1996). Through such forms as the AKF's Village Organizations, subjects in isolated areas learn the principles of "proper" bureaucratic process, of Euro-American forms of "civil society," of institutional discipline and liberal education. But it is not only under the rubric of "development" that the continual consolidation, incorporation, and induction of far-flung Ismaʿili societies occur; a separate institutional infrastructure exists, the *jamaʿati* institutions, to ensure the standardization of Ismaʿili practice and to work toward the universalization of its doctrines. Thus a markedly active effort is made to construct and establish a common ground, a basis for shared experience, among distinct Ismaʿili subgroups.

This process, however, is far more complex and contentious than the simple description above reveals. The diasporic and generally affluent Khoja community, its roots in western India, with colonial migrations to Africa and later migrations to Europe and North America, forms the Ismaʿili elite. They are at the helm of many of the imam's institutions. They constitute the inner circles of the imam's advisers. Their practice determines the standard and the norm for other Isma'ilis. It is only recently that the imamate encouraged Khojas and non-Khojas to see each other as part of a single community; indeed these various groups are a single community largely by virtue of the imamate's encouragement itself and their common participation in its institutions. But the imbalance of power between Isma'ilis and the local populations with which they interact has generated some friction and resentment. The mediation of that relationship through Isma'ili institutions has drawn attention to the inequalities of power, influence, and semiotic production that the Khoja arrival introduces. In Tajikistan, for instance, the conflict surrounding the campaign to establish *jama'at khanas* in the Khoja style reveals the fraught politics of diversity inhering in the Khoja relationship with others. And yet, despite all this, an explicit discourse of radical equality is overlaid on the inequalities that pervade Isma'ili institutional interactions. Institutionally prescribed notions like "frontierless brotherhood" belie the intentionality behind Isma'ili community-building and polity-building projects.

The relationship between Khojas and others displays a number of other important features. Imbalances of wealth and influence are only one component of the complex relations of power and meaning that characterize their interactions with remote Isma'ili societies. The politics of representation are also at stake, and romanticization and exoticization figure into the calculation. The spatiality of Khoja diaspora corresponds to a certain chronotopic construction of Isma'ili temporality that emerges not only in the discourse of connections to the Fatimid past, but also in the real-time interaction between the various components of the now-centralized Isma'ili community. Remote Isma'ili subjects in places like Hunza or Chitral—and even the landscapes they inhabit—are for Khojas objects of desire, living embodiments of an authentic Isma'ili past (see Fabian 1983; hooks 1992) that contribute to a framing of Khoja selves as modern and powerful. This temporalization of culture can take two overlapping forms: one in which borderland Isma'ilis are framed as existing in a different time, needing to be brought up to date;[2] and one in which they constitute the most authentic, pure, pristine, exotic Isma'ilis, representatives of a Khoja self of earlier times. Such orientalized notions of the heroic and authentic Isma'ili navigating a mysterious and grand landscape are certainly not irrelevant to the motivation of policy and global institution-building. Throughout the imamates of Aga Khan III and IV alike, they have played a critical role in informing the construction of a well-connected sphere of circulation.

But why the intensive effort to incorporate these societies into a unitary structure? And why the fixation on their socialization to an institutional and corporate modernity? Much of Isma'ili institutional history has been driven by the imperative of ensuring the loyalty (and tithe)[3] of scattered subjects, of producing a universally loyal and obedient population of followers. It is this project of induction, incorporation, unification, and consolidation that is of greatest consequence in the story I tell, because it represents an intentional effort at modern polity-building, reveals interesting forms of conflict, negotiation, localization, and appropriation produced in the process, and it illuminates the intersection between historical change and social organization. But the scope of the outreach takes on an almost missionary character, and it is presented as an effort to bring long-separated, forgotten, forsaken, and isolated Isma'ilis *back* into the fold, as a *restoration* or *revival* of contact. It is framed not as "you're invited" but rather as "welcome back." Despite the fundamental modernity of this moment, it is represented as one that reactivates an objective reality of the past, now lost.[4] Presuppositions of historical unity are thus conjured and enacted here, and mobilized in the service of introducing those long-forsaken societies to the revelatory truth not only of the imamate but of modernity.

In this situation of "renewed" contact, the phenomenon of the cargo cult (see Christiansen 1969; Kaplan 1995) comes to mind. Writing on the Pamir, Salmaan Keshavjee (1998) observes: "In some ways, the reappearance of the imam in Badakhshan is reminiscent of Sahlin's description of the appearance of Captain Cook in the South Pacific" (87). Another classic example is represented by the worship of the messianic figure of "John Frum" in Vanuatu. The role of capital, empire, consumption, and commodification, in particular, draw anthropological attention to the parallel. There are of course important distinctions between the colonial encounter embodied in Cook's appearance (Sahlins 1987, 1995; Obeyesekere 1992) and the religious revival represented by the Aga Khan's reappearance, and between the indigenous populations of the Pacific Islands and the Muslim populations of the Himalaya. Certainly the *idea* of the Aga Khan was far more familiar to the "uncontacted" Isma'ilis than was the notion of a European explorer to the Hawaiians. But the charismatic position of the imam as an exclusive source of prestige, authority, and truth; his association with the (sudden and seemingly magical) arrival of commodities, markets, and consumption; and his prophetic reappearance during times perceived as millennial and apocalyptic, lend further weight to the comparison.

The "missionary modernity" enacted through the encounter between Khoja elites and the imamate's institutions becomes in the global community-building project a "root paradigm" (Turner 1975) a fundamental organizing principle of the utmost importance, and the basis of emergent shared norms. In such a context, the Khojas become the self-designated bearers of the civilizing mission. What motivates them? Certainly a sense of responsibility, a degree of paternalism, some self-interest, genuine benevolence, and the enactment of ideology are all in play here. There has developed a norm in Khoja circles of concern for the "forgotten" and exposed non-Khoja Isma'ili societies — and indeed concern is warranted. But the Khoja interest in these peoples has taken on a ritualized character; indeed, like diasporic Jewish journeys to Israel or Mormon missions abroad, a period working for the benefit of poor Isma'ilis abroad has become something of a rite of passage, a period of selfless service, a formative journey before embarking on a more established life in the metropolitan West. The routinization and normalization of these journeys through the institutional channels that enable them establishes in the process of modernizing the "backward" Isma'ili (and socializing him to market behaviors) a new (and exotic and exciting) common ground for shared experience among Khojas. And the encounter with Khojas, in turn, becomes a common ground for shared experience among other, non-Khoja Isma'ilis.

And in response, on the borderlands: complex and contradictory reactions, simultaneous enthusiasm and discontent, deeply ambivalent articulations of uncertainty and anxiety. Non-Khojas in Tajikistan, and even in Pakistan, at once express, in the face of this institutional proliferation, passionate gratitude and doubt, laudatory excitement and resistance. On the part of the institutions, the promotion of capital (in its moderated "collective" form) is clearly central. On the part of the "villager" audience, we see a cautious reaction to its arrival. In the sum of their voices, is there a unitary message? Does it amount to a critique of capital? In the exploration of Isma'ili institutions, the resonance of these voices is not given its due. The scope and scale itself of the institutions themselves make locating these voices more difficult, but they emerge nonetheless.

There are, then, at least two simultaneously occurring, overlapping, historically inflected Isma'ili globalities: one diasporic, embodied in the widely dispersed Khoja community, and one comprised of the interaction of remote and vulnerable Isma'ili societies, on the physical and conceptual margins of the states to which they belong, with the transnational Isma'ili institutional assemblage centered in Europe.[5] This initial proposal of a structural duality is lent weight by the differential meaning of "Isma'ili globalization" for Khojas and non-Khojas. To subjects in Chitral or Badakhshan, institutional participation is all-encompassing and may form, as I have observed, a site of identification and political organization. In metropolitan Canada or Britain, on the other hand, it provides few essential services and displays the features more of a (relatively secretive) network or association—one that is nonetheless central to subjects' identities. It is in the encounter and interaction, the points of contact, between these "two globalities" that the most interesting dynamics emerge.

On closer inspection, still more globalities come to mind than the two initially proposed here: new modes of transregionalism formed, for instance, by the opening of borders between Afghanistan, Pakistan, and Tajikistan and associated lateral flows of subjects, or by the reunions and associations of poor Isma'ilis formed in the process of labor migration.[6] The historical conditions under which Isma'ili institutions developed in the milieu of the diasporic (and Indian) Khojas was radically different from those in which Hunzakuts like Sher Ali and Sultan Ali are engaged by AKDN and ITREB. And the meaning of Isma'ili institutions is radically different even among their various Himalayan settings in Gorno-Badakhshan, the Northern Areas and Chitral, and Afghan Badakhshan. And yet, lines of connection can be discerned in these histories of institutionalization. The multiple globalizations of Isma'ili society, then, are deeply imbricated with each other and cannot fully be teased apart. Their historical development, however, is clearly distinct.

Thus power is certainly at work here. The egalitarian imaginaries of Isma'ili community-building, and even popular or scholarly constructions of heroic grandeur of the global moment broadly defined (see Tsing 2000), can mask the operation of governmentality in postnational assemblages—even if they circumvent or resist dominant structures of power. And there is more: alongside the institutional subjectification and Khoja hegemony discussed, there also exist multiple other nested status hierarchies, all of which have been evident in these pages: Shughnis to other Pamiris for instance; or the prestige of the Pakistani Himalayan Nizaris to Pamiris; or the Pamiris' self-image of modernity and advancement in relationship to Afghan Badakhshanis'; or Hunzakuts to Gojalis or Yasinis; and so on and so on. The Khoja elite, whose unitary homogeneity I have generally presupposed, features its own hierarchies: a select group of families enjoys a great deal of prestige and control. Moreover, the institutions themselves also produce new configurations of social class and status—even *within* groups—

and thus new configurations of inequality. Jobs in AKF's local bodies are the most desirable, and local directors, professionals, and functionaries come over time to form regional managerial and service elites.

And yet, despite all of these intricacies, the Isma'ili institutional complex and even new forms of identification are immensely important—and frequently cherished—by the inhabitants of these marginal spaces. What exactly *is* in it for them, then? More, perhaps, than can be enumerated here. The benefits are vast. Among them: material security; an advantage in the pursuit of prosperity; enhanced health; enhanced choice; tools for survival and subsistence; a sense of being cared for; paradigms and symbols of identity; frameworks and narratives for the interpretation of history and crisis; new forms of political participation; new forms of insurance, regulatory bodies, and mechanisms for personal protection; new forms of social solidarity; and much more besides.

I have described the role of Isma'ili institutions in socializing local societies to modernity and capitalism. But here I assert that global Isma'ilism is much more than that. It provides for adherents a deeply personal system of meaning and a totalizing space suffusing and circumscribing subjective experience. It is a site of affective expression and emotional production (see Marsden 2005). Isma'ili institutions and networks engage their subjects at the most intimate and personal levels. It is thus clear that the formation of the transnational complex is a partnership that serves the goals and objectives of *both* local subjects and the elite leadership of the community; individuals in both of these structural positions have interests, needs, and desires that motivate interaction with the other.

But something else is happening here—something on the level of group relationships and disparities of power and wealth. The Isma'ili global assemblage in the form of the imamate's institutions plays directly into local, social, and ethnic relationships. As I suggest in my introduction, Sassen's (2006) "exit options for the disadvantaged" (43) are certainly at play here. In the face of conflict, exclusion, and marginality, participation in and benefit from an Isma'ili transnational ecumene offers a comparative advantage, a chance to advance one's group and self in an inhospitable, violent, and unrelentingly antagonistic climate. Membership in such a global assemblage bypasses the state and regional power-holders alike and makes Isma'ilis the beneficiaries of privilege, protection, and profit from an entity that cares for them and prioritizes them. The pervasive presence of this benefactor and its enhancement of the status of Isma'ilis are plainly visible to all of the Isma'ilis' neighbors, and it bestows on them not only material advantages and an increased sense of safety but also a certain enviable status in wider arenas.

Thus the arrival of the Aga Khan's institutions in certain remote areas has the effect of reconfiguring regional relations of status and identity. What were previously the poorest, most marginalized, and least powerful members of state polities and ethnic hierarchies are now "upwardly mobile" beneficiaries of a vast institutional structure, much of it mounted over the course of just a few decades — or even a few years. The services they receive at the hands of those institutions are too diverse and too many to enumerate. But the important point here is that their status is turned around in the process. Suddenly Ismaʿilis find themselves relatively privileged.

In the context of friction, a global assemblage itself can be seen as a collective actor in conflict and interaction, embodied in local institutions and embedded in local societies. In conflict, Ismaʿilism becomes politicized and galvanized as a central idiom of identity. Violence and persecution, moreover, in effecting exclusion, alienation, and isolation, like migration and technologies of telecommunication, form yet other factors helping to produce the isolation that engenders collective desires to look further afield, beyond the state, the region, and the locality, for alternative modes of identification.

In Pakistan, Ismaʿilis find themselves exposed to sectarian conflict and local persecution at the hands of militant revivalist Sunni movements such as the Sipah-e-Sahaba of Pakistan (SSP); many of these movements are explicitly anti-Ismaʿili and seek to frame them as not even nominally Muslim.[7] Some, like the Tablighi Jamaʿat, target Ismaʿilis for conversion; others seek more violent agendas. Such movements, moreover, do not operate in isolation; they are engaged in complex relationships with ethnic hierarchies and the state that make the position of the Ismaʿilis even more precarious. All this has reinforced Ismaʿili interest and investment in their global institutions, pushing them to see the institutions as a sort of stable sanctuary in terms of membership benefits and protection. Second, it has highlighted the precarious status of the state in Pakistan's Northern Areas, presenting the transnational structure as a viable alternative for political participation and economic services. And third, it has entrenched and charged the Ismaʿilis' resolve to develop and present an antimilitant identity. The relationship between violence and Ismaʿili global institutions, however, is complex: Rieck (1995) underscores the role of AKRSP as an object of regional contestation and a source of tension. But ultimately, the nature of sectarian conflict in Pakistan has made Ismaʿili identity a charged site of contestation and has in part motivated the extensive investment of local constructions of self in global institutions (see Sökefeld 1997, 1998; Marsden 2005).

The Isma'ilis of Tajikistan have experienced a violent conflict on a much larger scale (Rubin 1998; Roy 2000). During the Tajik civil war they aligned themselves with the opposition Islamic-Democratic Party. In the war, regional groups formerly favored by the Soviets, mostly former power-holders who fought hard to retain their privileges and the rights to the profits of the highly lucrative drug trade, formed the pro-Communist bloc against the Islamic-Democratic alliance that included Pamiri Isma'ilis and Gharmis. The Islamic-Democratic alliance lost badly, and the government forces punished them by isolating their region from contact with the rest of the country and the world. The roads were allowed to decay, cutting them off even from their capital, Dushanbe.

Then aid started to flow in from AKDN via Osh in Kyrgyzstan, another state altogether, albeit also a post-Soviet one. The people of the Pamir began to receive their lifeline from their new transnational network and not from the nation-state. For some time, Tajikistan's Gorno-Badakhshan became a floating province that was more materially connected to a global socioreligious structure than to any territorial state at all. This points to the role of resources in the development of a transnational polity—it was only the Isma'ili global structure that offered them the benefits they needed not only to survive but also to gain a comparative advantage in the region. Moreover, the post–civil war situation reveals that Isma'ilism has become a politicized identity, and it has been heightened in local consciousness as a potential primary site of identification. The war galvanized the Soviet-created (but naturalized) cultural categories of "Badakshani" and "Pamiri" and reinforced the notion that such units of social organization are the true sites of recognition, the bearers of rights, and the loci of legal status in wider publics. The arrival of AKF as savior encouraged the conflation and fusion of these categories with "Isma'ili" and sealed its value as the preferred and most felicitous site of membership.

In sum, then: participation in these institutions and affiliation with the worldwide Isma'ili community is clearly at some level a political and economic fact. It offers local people, many of whom have historically been marginalized and spurned, leverage over their neighbors. This is a central component of its appeal; it can play the symbolic role of putting them at the center, not the edge, of a political structure, and it is associated with the provision of resources and even survival. Thus we see in the establishment of institutional Isma'ilism in Himalayan Tajikistan and Pakistan, especially in the context of violence, the chance for historically marginalized populations to gain power and prestige for themselves and advantage over their neighbors.

But considerations of the divergent experiences of these neighboring regions cannot be confined to these recent histories of conflict alone. Indeed much insight is gained by a comparison of the distinct and unique evolution of local interaction with Isma'ili institutions in each area. What do we see when we put the institutional globalization of Tajikistan and Pakistan side by side in comparison? Both the Tajik Pamir and the Pakistani Karakoram (and Hindu Kush) have come under the purview of the same metropolitan Isma'ili institutions, located in Europe; this has established a basic foundation for common experience between them. But because of profoundly divergent engagements with European empires and the national states that emerged in their wake, the manifestation and operationalization of institutional forms on the ground in each area has been radically different, and the impact on the local construction of Isma'ili identity and practice has been profound.

The obvious and simple explanation for the differential experience of the two areas is thus rooted in political history: what is now Himalayan Pakistan formed the northern limit of the British Empire in South Asia, and what is now the Tajik Pamir, the southern limit of the Russian domain. The two empires vied for the mountains in Kipling's "Great Game," but the boundaries that would produce such variable fates were at that point drawn and sealed, set in stone for the centuries to come. The fixity of those boundaries put one population in the hands of an internationalist, Communist regime and the other under the authority of a turbulent Islamic republic and determined drastically different living conditions in each area. In the former, Isma'ilis navigated a grand and totalizing project of social engineering. In the latter, they inherited the troublesome legacy of colonial communalism. In the two areas access to larger systems of exchange was vastly different. The tendrils of global markets had penetrated the Karakoram and Hindu Kush since the period of British administration, but with the construction of the Karakoram Highway (as well as other national roads) and the incorporation of autonomous princely states into Pakistan, the impact of capital was suddenly explosive and profoundly altered local society. Isma'ili institutional expansion in the far north of Pakistan cannot be separated from this historical development; as with the relationship of Isma'ilism to other systems (such as colonial labor diasporas or communal law) the two were intertwined in dialectic complementarity. This differential access to markets and the circulation of commodities correlate to differential access to media and the circulation of information and thus to different types of discourse on culture, modernity, truth, and identity. Lives in each setting, as we have seen, were governed by radically divergent master narratives. Within the respective epistemic regimes of truth and knowledge established by each state and its dominant classes, the place of religion in daily life was also profoundly different. Thus the stark contrast between the Isma'ili institutions' form and reception in each mountain area emerges largely from their divergent engagement with larger polities beginning with the arrival of European imperial structures.[8]

The status of global Isma'ilism *as* global Islam warrants careful consideration. Isma'ilism certainly bears very little resemblance to most other contemporary Islamic globalities, but that does not negate its interest for the study of Islam. The media fixates largely on (armed) Sunni revivalism: the Taliban, for instance, or the Swat Valley's Maulana Fazlullah, or the Lashkar-e-Taiba. But Isma'ilism is also a modern and transnational Islam. Where these movements claim authority through textual literalism and present vivid eschatological visions, Isma'ilism takes the external form (*zahir*) of religious text only as a starting point for interpretation, the imam's *ta'wil* of its inner (*batin*) and allegorical meaning. Doctrine is metaphor for the imam to elucidate. This provides a springboard for the development of the widely circulating notion that Isma'ilism is able to "adapt its message to modern times." This is of course true of many Islamic modernities, but the *notion* of adaptability and flexibility is particularly important to Isma'ilis as cultural ideology. The belief in a historical relationship of opposition between Isma'ilis and other Muslims manifests itself in the current global moment as a conscious rejection of the orthodoxy and radicalism that characterizes current dominant public images of the Muslim world, in a "militant-modernist" dialectic where Isma'ilis seek to establish themselves as the progressive, liberal, counter-radical Muslims. It is in this context then, that the Isma'ilis consciously work to frame themselves as the "antifundamentalists."

Thus an Isma'ili orientation toward liberal modernism, and sometimes toward postmodernism, emerges not only out of the colonial context but also in the contemporary relationship to other globally relevant Islamic formations; as we have seen, this is manifest in emphases on rationalism, expressed in social programs with the rational and benefit-maximizing individual at their center; science, along with discovery through observation and experimentation; education, as a cultural priority and a naturalized right; Euro-American values of cultural relativism, multiculturalism, inclusion, and syncretism; market capitalism and monetary profit; individualism and identity, as the bases for the political order and social activism; and academic liberal arts, with a focus on interpretation (for instance, through Tajikistan's Aga Khan Humanities Project for curriculum development). All this is rendered meaningful in part in the cultural politics of Islam. Religious practices and beliefs, and their secular by-products, now emerge as sites of contestation.

What is new about this? One of the questions I have explored is the relationship of contemporary Isma'ilism to the forms often represented as its historical antecedents (the early *da'wa*, for example, the Fatimid state, or the Iranian Nizari fortress network). My approach to this question has changed during the course of my research; in earlier iterations of this work I argued for a substantive connection in form and history between the Fatimid state and its structures and contemporary Isma'ilism, with the Aga Khan's institutions replacing *pirs* and *da'is*, fiber optic cable replacing horse-borne messengers, and so on. The representation of a close association between the mythical Isma'ili past and the present, however, is in part a project of Isma'ili institutions. IIS, along with various institutions of the imamate, has played a key role in constructing a direct and close linkage between those established territorial and semiterritorial polities of the past, in claiming ownership over those earlier forms designated as Isma'ili, but the historical evidence to support such a direct connection is inconclusive. However, the effort in itself is interesting, and these historical narratives have come to form an important part of the Isma'ilis' self-image. It is the Aga Khan Case, the formation of a colonial diaspora, the institution-building project, the construction of a corporate ethos, and the circulation of modern ideology that figure prominently here and that yield an Isma'ili community unrecognizably different from what came before. The answer then: from a historical perspective, most everything is "new" about the globality I observe. The shape of the community and the role of the Aga Khan emerge from a modern moment. Certainly there is a connection to prior forms, and older networks and systems have been activated. The geography of Isma'ili settlement is historically determined. But the relationship is orthogonal.

Fine, as far as it goes. But, one might counter, what if it is the other way around: does the persistence of large-scale Isma'ili transterritoriality not point to some basic and essential elements of the Isma'ili Muslim collectivity shared *across* all these historical eras despite the appearance of discontinuity? It is my sense that the ruptures of industrialization, urbanization, and nationalization have been too profound to sustain a sufficiently robust continuity to uphold such a claim. At the same time, it is true that Ismaʿilism has displayed a great deal of theological cohesion as it has evolved. This raises important questions about Ismaʿili globality: What can we make of the role of religion here? How much of what is observed in these pages can be attributed to the magnetic gravity of devotion, or to the charismatic leadership of the imam? How much of this is a historical exception produced by the unique features of Ismaʿili belief and practice, and how much of it is a product of more widely shared historical questions? Sassen (2006) observes that the mobilization "of religion and 'culture,' rather than citizenship, to construct membership may well be a function of the changed relationship of citizens to the state and the insecurities it produces. In this regard, use of religion is not an anachronism but a formation arising out of particular changes in the current age" (414). In the final analysis, religion and modernity are inextricably intertwined here in an intimate dialectic. I return again and again to the same conclusion: Ismaʿili globality cannot be fully explained by virtue of the special features inhering in Ismaʿilism itself, but must rather be theorized in light of historical conditions widely shared across the planet.

A preoccupation with the connections between the Ismaʿili assemblage and the nation-state permeates this analysis. I have raised the question both of their relationship in form and their real-time interaction. The comparison between the Ismaʿili transnational network and the nation-state is problematic in multiple ways, not the least of which are the questions of territoriality and force. Moreover, the historical conditions of their respective development — and their meaning for subjects — are radically different. This is not to say that there are not parallels — there are many indeed. But in the final analysis Ismaʿili globality is clearly not simply a modification of the national model, but something altogether different. Components of political process, claims Sassen (2006), are "becoming reassembled into novel denationalized configurations that may operate at the global, national, or subnational level. The disassembling, even if partial, denaturalizes what has often unwittingly become naturalized — the national constitution of territory, authority, and rights, and the global constitution of their undoing" (406). Perhaps, then, while what we observe in the Ismaʿili example embodies historically new possibilities, it is nonetheless inextricable from the ever-strong persistence of states.

Much is revealed in the real encounter between the Ismaʿili complex and the states with which it deals. That complicated relationship, characterized as it is by contradiction, conciliation, and confusion, reveals the status of the Isma'ili assemblage as an unclassifiable anomaly, an alien element, in a world of territorial states. The presence of a nonterritorial Isma'ili administration commanding subjects' loyalty disrupts the uniformity of that system and the stability of its operation; from the states themselves we see some anxiety and more than a little discomfort. Is this a competitor, they wonder? An ally? A threat? In reply, from the Isma'ili "administration" emerge various messages, proposals, and negotiations: efforts to assuage and assure, agreements written and signed, and occasionally insistent assertions of primacy and expertise over and above national entities. At the same time, the presence of Isma'ili institutions providing services that are conventionally the domain of government is unavoidable, undeniable, everywhere visible. The result, in many cases, appears to be a tacit and sometimes tense détente, an agreement to avoid explicitly addressing the issue in order to coexist.

What kind of social formation is this, then? To what can we attribute its intensive organization? Not only a diaspora, but the interaction of a diaspora, mediated by institutions, with long-settled indigenous Himalayan peoples. Not only a secular polity, but a devotional faith with a charismatic leader. Not only a religion, by the same token, but also a vast institutional network providing every imaginable secular service. Certainly neither a territorial state nor a nation, but nonetheless a site of citizenship, membership, administration, and political organization. The array of populations now classified as a single Isma'ili community is ethnically diverse, so ethnicity only classifies certain of its components. Some analogues to global Isma'ilism are found in NGOs, but a comparison to the International Committee for the Red Cross, for example, or Oxfam is deeply insufficient. The engagement of such formations with subjects is radically different; they lack the totalizing quality of global Isma'ilism. An effective parallel can, however, be drawn between the Isma'ili complex and corporate enterprise; the Aga Khan has clearly organized his organizations around this paradigm (see Kaiser 1996). But production and consumption, accumulation and profit, marketing and efficiency, while all ideological ingredients favored by the Aga Khan's networks, are also less than the whole story. The interplay of meanings and institutions embodied in Isma'ili global forms cannot be captured entirely by the corporate analogy. Simultaneously, then, many forms at once: a polity, a religion, a corporate structure, a bureaucratic network. This is why Sassen's (2006) "assemblage" seems so appropriate. In Isma'ili communality we see the intersection or aggregation of multiple overlapping social forms operating under an institutional infrastructure that endeavors to synthesize and integrate them.

The institutions, however, are not the whole story. A focus on the institutions alone, important as they are, would nonetheless obscure the Isma'ili subject. Though I try to account for it, even this work does not sufficiently address that obfuscation. This book is neither entirely about the institutions nor entirely about the person outside of the institutional context; rather it is about the *interaction* between institution and subject, the places and moments where the two come into contact, and the meaning of those moments for the construction of self and phenomenological experience. What kinds of emergent identities, I ask, do these encounters produce? What kinds of subjectivities do they build? How are the lives of localities reconfigured in the process? And are the institutions responsible, or are they the incidental products of larger historical processes? Finally, I ask, how do local subjects resist and alter the institutions?

Where to begin a synthesis, then, of what is important here? In the final analysis, what reveals itself as most worthy of attention? The historical questions, for their part, have been enlightening. We have seen that contemporary Isma'ilism is much less a product of the distant past its institutions focus on than of more recent developments. Modern Isma'ilism in fact emerges from the larger historical conditions and political economies that surrounded its subjects and leaders as empire and global markets transformed the planet. In its current institutional form it could be seen in fact as a reconfiguration of earlier translocal forms established by Soviet Communist and British Imperial polities, an iteration of the oceanic and Eurasian connections they established, surviving in their absence. The Isma'ili community represents a unique convergence of global political economies and socioreligious structures, and it sheds light on the role of colonial states in the production of subject and community.

Also worthy of attention are the implications of Isma'ili globality for sovereignty, territoriality, and citizenship. Certainly in a world of nation-states the Isma'ili formation embodies something anomalous and unique. Whether Isma'ili transnationality, emerging as it does from a set of widely shared historical conditions, might potentially constitute a token of a more universal type, a harbinger of things to come, cannot yet be answered. Whether it fills the role formerly or normally filled by the state is a question whose answer varies from setting to setting. That it draws attention to a possibility for allegiance and membership external to the system of states is undeniable, but the long-term implications even of this claim cannot yet be determined. Most important, global Isma'ilism calls into question long-held, naturalized, and widespread assumptions about the exclusivity of territorial power, the spatiality of social organization, and the universality of national citizenship. In defiance of a number of given categories, it also raises questions about the intimate relationship between *social* modes of globalization and capital, about the imbrication of *religious* globality and the promotion of discourses of modernity, rational individualism, and liberalism. Finally, it draws attention to global structures as disciplinary agents, in the Foucauldian sense, of standardization and normalization, as regimes of socialization. All this ultimately has serious implications, I believe, for the study of globalization and of global Islam.

There is much indeed in the story and structure of transnational Isma'ilism to capture scholarly and popular attention; its features raise compelling and captivating questions that provide serious theoretical challenges to long-held epistemological paradigms for the analysis of human political organization. The progressive and continual incorporation of widely distributed communities into the Isma'ili infrastructure reveals an intensive project of polity-building with ideologies of modernity at its center. This effort at consolidation, centralization, and homogenization requires the deployment of a vast institutional infrastructure whose operation involves intimate engagement with Isma'ili subjects and the localities they inhabit. The historical situation of which this institutional proliferation is a part has meant the profound transformation of the social fabric of these localities that, in turn, has important implications for the construction of self and the everyday experience of the world. In the process, then, it is subjectivity itself that emerges reconfigured.

Notes

Introduction

1 In addition to the tithe (*dassondh*), whose payment is generally not a flexible matter, Isma'ilis are expected to furnish to the imam a wide range of dues, fees, and gifts of other types. The giving of both public and private gifts to the imam is historically well attested. There is also some precedent for the imam to impose an exceptional levy on the income of a wealthy Isma'ili (Morris 1968: 82–83).

2 In a discussion on doctrine, a Canadian Khoja Isma'ili described the imam to me as a "walking, talking Qur'an." Magnus Marsden (2005) claims that Chitrali Isma'ilis, in northern Pakistan, view him as a "speaking Qur'an" (16).

3 Morris (1968), referring to the role established by the previous imam, Aga Khan III, uses the term "institutional prophet" (90).

4 In a *farman* issued September 1, 1885, Aga Khan III said: "*Jamats*, do not consider me small. I am the descendant of the Prophet and my grandfather is Hazrat 'Amir-ul-Mo'minim (Hazrat Ali) and my grandmother is Khatoon-e-Jannat (Lady of Paradise) Hazrat Bibi Fatima. I am the Light (*Noor*) of both Hazrat Ali and the Holy Prophet (Mohamed). Though young in age, I am exalted" (quoted in Boivin 2003: 196).

5 In another *farman*, September 8, 1885, Aga Khan III said: "We (imams) change the physical bodies in the world but our *Noor* (Light) is eternal and originates from the very beginning. You should therefore take it as one *Noor*. The (Light of God) is ever present, only the names are different. The throne (of the Imamate) of Mowla Murtaza Ali continues on and it will remain till the day of Judgment" (quoted in Boivin 2003: 196).

6 Morris (1968) attributes great significance to this adaptability to modern conditions. One of his East African Isma'ili informants explained: "We are not like other Muslims. They are tied to the Koran which was written for a different kind of world and they *must* follow it, they cannot change it. We follow our imam who can interpret it. So we find it easier to live in the modern world" (89).

7 But these AKDN officials, suggests reviewer Faisal Devji, enjoy such status only at the price required to purchase influence.

8 There exist, by virtue of various historical processes, rifts, and events, several populations of non-Isma'ili Khojas (including Sunni Khojas and Twelver Shi'i Khojas).

9 "Read our history," said Aga Khan III to his followers, "and know about the Imams who succeeded one after another. Study the whole history of Fatimid Ismaili Imâms—our forefathers who ruled in Egypt for 200 to 300 years" (quoted from *Precious Pearls: Farman Mubarak of Hazrat Imam Mowlana Sultan Mohammad Shah*, in Boivin 2003: 204–5).

10 Most names of local participants have been changed.

11 Official accounts and popular belief, however, posit an intimate and direct connection between the medieval past, particularly the "golden era" of the Fatimid dynasty, and the global present.

Chapter One

1 For more exhaustive discussions of Isma'ili medieval history, see Daftary (1998); Lewis (1967); and Hodgson (1955).

2 Isma'ilism is generally nonproselytizing. Nonetheless, occasional large conversions have occurred in the modern period under the last two Aga Khans, especially among various Hindu populations of the Indian subcontinent. See Boivin (2003): 284; and Aga Khan (1954): 7.

3 This was told to me by Bruno de Cordier in a private exchange in 2003, backed up and confirmed by several local sources.

4 The primary corpus of evidence for such claims comes from the history of British interaction with Isma'ilism, but a similar case can be made, drawing from more recent events, for Soviet manipulations of categories and classes of identity (e.g., "nationalities" policies) in Tajikistan. See Hirsch (2005); and Bliss (2005).

5 The collection of the tithe (*zakat* or *dassondh*) has long acted as a motivating force for the construction and maintenance of Isma'ili transterritorial spheres. The consolidation of a loyal and cohesive community ensures the regular payment of the tithe. Indeed, it was an essential element in the Bombay Aga Khan case and it is an essential element in the discourse of Isma'ili global "development": the tithe is seen as (and, to a degree, appears to be) benefiting the community through reinvestment in projects for its betterment.

6 *Darbar* literally means "court," usually royal; in contemporary Isma'ilism it refers to any occasion at which the imam addresses his followers in the company of his advisers and in full regalia.

7 See Dirks (2001) on similar processes in the colonial construction of caste; Chatterjee (1986); and the chapter "Census, Map, Museum" in Anderson (1991) on the colonial construction of categories of identity.

8 In the later Haji Bibi case of 1905, brought against Aga Khan III, though less important for our purposes, once again the British Court pronounced a definition of religious community, this time asserting that Isma'ilis were distinct from Twelver Shi'as (Boivin 2003: 289–91).

9 The style of modernization enacted by the Khojas was neither original nor unique: it followed a precedent set at the time by the Parsis (Zoroastrians) of Bombay. See Palsetia (2001) for more detail on Parsi modernization under the British Empire.

10 The sultan's alliance with the British Empire was in part a strategic response to a common enemy: the Wahhabis (Boivin 2003: 270).

11 The revised constitution of 1946 also created the "Diamond Jubilee Investment Trust Company" for the profit and welfare of Isma'ilis (Boivin 2003: 276).

12 I was shown by villagers in Shughnan a booklet containing a Gujarati version of the missionary's journey. At least one villager I met was named after him. The original account of the journey appeared in various versions of the weekly *Ismaili* in Bombay. An English translation of the account told by Alijah Ramzan Ali Alibhai, Pir Sabzali's personal assistant, appears online at ⟨http://www.ismaili.net/Source/pirsab zali/intro.html⟩.

13 Given the expectation that Sultan Muhammad's son Aly Khan would be designated, it came as a great surprise to some communities that Aly was passed over in favor of his son. A community in Syria, notably, was at first hesitant to accept the designation but changed its position quickly, according to a mention in Thobani (1993) among other sources. Like the splintering of various Khoja groups under Aga Khan I and III, however, the incident highlights a general historic concern on the part of the imamate with ensuring loyalty and preventing secession or schism.

14 The 1986 constitution states, "by virtue of his office and in accordance with the faith and belief of the Isma'ili Muslims, the Imam enjoys full authority of governance over and in respect of all religious and Jamati matters of the Isma'ili Muslims" (quoted in Salmaan Keshavjee 1998: 47). The concern with asserting the authority of the Aga Khan over Isma'ilis recalls the Aga Khan case from the Bombay High Court, described above.

15 The 1986 constitution asserts the primacy of its stipulations in the Isma'ili community but maintains that they should never precede the law of territorial states: "This constitution shall apply to Isma'ilis worldwide, subject only to the overriding effect of any applicable laws of the land of abode of any Isma'ili to the extent of any inconsistency" (quoted in Salmaan Keshavjee 1998: 53).

16 See Slomanson (2003) on the status of such formations in international law.

Chapter Two

1 Though he attributes it not to the institutions themselves but to external funders and forces, Salmaan Keshavjee (1998) sees in the AKDN's activity on the ground "the risk of becoming an instrument in a process of international 're-education,' where the program of 'development' is closely linked to an ideological restructuring" (91).

2 On the history of Isma'ili discourses of statehood, see my discussion of Aga Khan III in Chapter 1.

3 See Foucault 1973, 1977, 1978, 2003 on polities and bodies.

4 Recipients have included organizations working with Timurid buildings in Samarkand, Humayun's tomb in Delhi, a village constructed for orphans and abandoned children in Jordan (SOS Children's Village, Amman), the Datai Hotel in Malaysia, the Sri Lankan architect Geoffrey Bawa, the restorers of the fortress in Baltit,

Hunza, and the restorers of the (formerly Isma'ili Fatimid) Al-Azhar complex in Cairo (al-Qahira).

5 Recently both Turkey and Iran have worked on revising exhibits of their history in European museums. The Iranian exhibit in the British Museum was changed to counter the representation of the conquest of its lands found in Herodotus, reportedly because it wanted to subvert the telling of history from the victor's perspective. Despite the fact that, had the Iranians won, they certainly would have recounted the story from a victor's perspective, there is an interesting trend here in which past empires are construed as good and benevolent and are recast, in the light of modernism and nationalism, to constitute a new mode of representation of an earlier Islamic prowess. To say that AKDN is representing the Isma'ili past in this way would certainly be a distortion. However, to say that they are engaged in a loosely connected concern with the Muslim imperial past, in particular that of the Fatimids, might not be completely inaccurate.

6 In his review of the manuscript of this book, Faisal Devji points to the possibility that these designs emerge out of the adoption of an orientalist self-image and that their meanings are unknown to most users of the structures.

7 Interestingly, this information is not broadly publicized in the online materials of UCA. At the time of my research, no links led directly to information about the rector and the board; only the original document (in pdf format) makes mention of key managers.

8 Apparently within the Khoja community, critiques of the imam and the imamate were more widespread in the past. In the current situation, however, they have come to form a kind of unacceptable taboo.

Chapter Three

1 "*Jama'ati*" denotes "community," in contradistinction to "*imamati*." The *jama'ati* institutions consist of those whose primary domain is religion, ritual, and practice, rather than the provision of secular services.

2 Echoing the language of corporate capital, these newly contacted Isma'ili societies are referred to within the Khoja leadership as "emerging *jama'ats*."

3 Some Pamiris provide a contradictory report that it was Muhammad Keshavjee, not Rafique Keshavjee, who was a member of this party.

4 The first visit of the Aga Khan to Gorno-Badakhshan (May 1995), which is commemorated in a yearly holiday, "the festival of new light" (Salmaan Keshavjee 1998: 10), was notable especially because he encouraged local people to embrace the arrival of the global market. Pamiri respondents claim that they expected that "mountains might fall," and that the visit was "the thunderclap that signaled all the changes."

5 I am grateful to Faisal Devji for portions of this information.

6 An interesting parallel can be drawn between this usage of "father and mother" and one traditional usage of the Indic compound *maa-baap*," denoting political leaders and later both the British Empire and the East India Company.

7 See Thobani (1993) for an Isma'ili account of the feelings evoked by *didar*.

8 The gravity and grandeur of the imam's arrival was further impressed upon participants by the conveyance in which he arrived, a Gulfstream IV jet, with his princely
seal on the tail.

Chapter Four

1 There may have been some dissident, Qarmati-leaning Isma'ilism in the area both
before and after Nasir-i-Khusraw; most of its residents were, moreover, until relatively recently, followers of the Muhammad-Shahi (not the current and active
Qasim-Shahi) line of imams. See Daftary (1990).

2 This enumeration does not include the separate and large population of Mongol-
descended Hazaras in central Afghanistan, some distance from this central Himalayan region. Their estimated population is in the hundreds of thousands.

3 A top-level manager of MSDSP, AKDN's primary organization in the Pamir,
pointed to a local joke that everyone who is anyone in the region is from Porshnev:
"the first Komsomols, the first Ismailis, the first drug dealers."

4 Shamans in this region, in accordance with local belief, communicate with *peri*,
sprites or fairies, occupying the purest, high-altitude areas. The *peri* are believed
to drive herds of wild ibex. In order to attain a trancelike state, the shaman inhales
smoke produced by burning the branch of a certain high-mountain tree of the region. Shamans are found in Sunni, Shi'a, and Isma'ili populations of the region alike.
On my last visit to Hunza, Sultan Ali seemed hesitant to admit to me that it was a
shaman who had placed an iron talisman around the neck of his nephew, as part of
an effort to heal an infection.

5 The story of the creation of these boundaries is crucial to our discussion of the local
experience of geopolitics. Until the 1870s, the valleys of the Pamir (as well some
of those in what is now Pakistan and Afghanistan) constituted a number of small,
autonomous principalities that maintained allegiance and paid tribute only to the
Mir of Badakhshan. In 1877–78 the Emirate of Bukhara seized Darwaz in the Pamir.
Remaining adjacent areas stayed under the control of the Afghan emir through an
agreement dating from 1873 that allocated to it Wakhan, Shughnan, and Rushan.
The Afghans seized Shughnan in 1883 as a response to the Russian advance. This too
was all part of the so-called "Great Game." A number of conflicts followed, until
the Emir of Afghanistan finally settled on the river as the border in 1893 and made
it part of an accord that established the Wakhan corridor as a buffer zone between
the Russian and British empires. This was legalized in the Anglo-Russian Boundary
Commission of 1895. The Afghans gave up the eastern and northeastern portions of
Rushan, Shughnan, and Darwaz and, in turn, obtained upper Wakhan and southwestern Darwaz. Refugees from Afghan territory crossed into Russian lands in a
sort of partition in which the border first clearly demarcated two zones. It was also
the first moment that Afghanistan became a buffer state between two empires and
it represents the true birth of the border, which is still in that same spot.

6 See Shahrani (1979) for a detailed description of a similar process in the immediate
region.

7 Apparently, during the Soviet era this would not have been the case: an informant notes that back then, if an Afghan spoke to a Tajik Pamiri across the river, the latter would respond with silence.

8 And not only *to see*: an Ishkashmi Isma'ili explained that while many extended families were divided by the creation of the border, some kin connections are now being revived.

9 One Pamiri who until the civil war had resided in Dushanbe described door-to-door shootings, urban guerilla warfare, and the location of a mass grave for Pamiris in a Dushanbe children's park. "We lost our youth, we lost our innocence, we lost our love," he said. He introduced several of his (Isma'ili) friends as *mujahidin*.

10 The history detailed in this and the next several paragraphs borrows from Akiner (2001); Bliss (2006); Rubin (1998); and Roy (2000).

11 Bishkent, a village in southern Tajikistan, near Kulob, said to have been some sort of testing site, is among contemporary relocation sites for Pamiris — in this case those whose villages were destroyed by landslides. A Pamiri respondent calls it "hell on earth."

12 The history in this and the next few paragraphs borrows from Bliss (2006); Rubin (1998); Roy (2000); and Salmaan Keshavjee (1998).

13 Research on this topic was carried out largely in Gilgit and is based on a corpus of about fifty interviews, mostly conducted in Urdu. I make no claim to the truth of what I was told had happened. I was only interested in the significance of people's perceptions. During the time of my research I was the target of careful surveillance and governmental anxiety.

14 See Sökefeld (1997) for a detailed account of the identity politics of the region and its articulation with this conflict.

Chapter Five

1 I am grateful to Faisal Devji for some of this information on Panjibais. *Ginans* are Khoja religious songs usually focused on recounting legendary stories of the Isma'ili *pirs*. They feature a strong Hindu influence and are indigenous to the region of Gujarat, in western India.

2 Konunov also visited Paris to collaborate with a French opera on a joint project with Pamiri performers.

3 Salmaan Keshavjee (1998) postulates that the Aga Khan might fill the place of Lenin and Stalin in local hearts, hearths, and minds (67).

4 On "publicly accessible signs," see Spitulnik (1997); and Urban (1991).

5 As I have explained, most of those "local people" are non-Khoja Nizari Isma'ilis; a good portion of AKF's management is made up of diasporic Khojas.

6 I asked the general manager of MSDSP (at the time of my research), Yodgor Faisov, about the lack of the Aga Khan's initials in the acronym for the organization. He responded that the omission had been purposeful, and the intent was to stress MSDSP's status as a local and indigenous NGO.

7 Land tenure and distribution are critical issues in the Pamir, where cultivable land is limited. Some Pamiris believe that land was more fairly distributed under the Soviet collectives but claim that after the war ethnic favoritism and the privilege of drug-trafficking power has created new — and greater — inequalities.

8 In a commencement address at MIT in May 1994, Aga Khan IV revealed his own view on intermediate modern forms between capitalism and Communism: "The West has many strengths," he claims, "but prominent among them are science and democracy (with their public mechanisms for self-correction) and also private institutions, liberal economics, and a recognition of fundamental human rights. The Muslim world offers deep roots in a system of values, emphasizing service, charity, and a sense of common responsibility, and denying what it sees to be the false dichotomy between religious and secular lives. The ex-Communist world, although it failed economically, made important investments in social welfare, with particular emphasis on the status of women, and was able to achieve in Tajikistan impressive social goals" (quoted in Salmaan Keshavjee 1998: 56).

9 In contexts where WOs fail to exhibit the appropriate "productive" behaviors, criticism has been harsh. The World Bank report (Nelson 2002) claimed that a particular WO meeting visited by ethnographers lacked the procedural clarity of the VO meeting, in that "not a single women's group planned a presentation; no woman got to her feet to make even the shortest speech on behalf of her organization" (21).

10 The notion of the village itself as a distinct epistemic, organizational, and administrative unit in colonial and precolonial systems of knowledge, and its romanticization in orientalist discourses, deserves its own analysis. Surely the idea that every village deserves its own organization can be tied to naturalized presuppositions about what kind of unit a village is.

11 Aga Khan IV, quoted in Salmaan Keshavjee (1998): 62, from a speech given in Dushanbe, Tajikistan, May 23, 1995, originally published in "The Isma'ili: Mowlana hazir Imam's Visit to Central Asia, 22–31 May" (London: Islamic Publications Ltd., 1995).

12 An AKDN health worker, an Ishkashmi-speaker from Ryn, accompanied me on my visit to Khuf.

13 We see here again the same emphasis on constructing connections between the modern and distant, disconnected pasts. This particular set of connections mobilizes imaginaries rooted in the notion of Central Asian connections to early Indo-Europeans.

14 A reviewer suggests that the use of this term points to the arrival of the *jama'at khana* in these areas via British India, through channels developed during the colonial period and used by Khoja missionaries. For more on connections between the Bombay imamate and such remote areas, see my discussion of Pir Sabzali in Chapter 1.

15 A reviewer suggests a course of these particular events that differs — not insignificantly — from Amanullah's version. I have furthermore left out certain details in an attempt to protect his identity.

Conclusion

1 Some communities (Tajikistan and Afghanistan) have had further processes of isolation and reincorporation since the initial expansion of empire, and some (Chinese Sinkiang) remain disconnected.

2 See the "lagging behind" of the University of Central Asia promotional catalogue, or the assertion that, "Where once mountain tribes warred over control of the caravan routes between 8,000 metre peaks, they now meet regularly to plan the best use of village savings over $7.5 million" (Aga Khan Foundation 1996: 22).

3 The payment of the tithe is not always the simple act of fealty it appears to be. Monies accumulated through the tithe are funneled into a Swiss bank account that has itself been the recipient of some attention. In one scandal, Canadian Khoja community leaders had used the funds to reap profits from the narcotics trade. We see in such cases the mobilization of community status and Isma'ili structures for something more than devotion to the Aga Khan. As with any community, this one is full of agentive actors with their own goals.

4 This mobilization of an imagined utopian past, a golden age, and the imposition of collective unity on a situation of diversity brings to mind various other modern polity-building projects in which history is similarly deployed to develop an ethos of belonging, shared citizenship, and common identity.

5 See Ho (2006) for a relevant analogue in the interaction of Hadramawtis with their diasporic kin.

6 Take, for instance, the sizeable populations of Isma'ili Hunzakuts in Rawalpindi and Karachi, the clusters of Chitralis in Peshawar, the significant numbers of Badakhshanis in Dushanbe, Perm, and Moscow. In their interaction a horizontal regional or transregional solidarity forms that can circumvent not only the institutional infrastructure but also the transnational ethnic relationships that they embody.

7 An Isma'ili from Hunza, describing the deadly Sunni-Shia riots of 1988, explained that "the main reason for the tension was this bloody loudspeaker," referring to the Sunni mosque's public announcement system in Gilgit. Nazir Sabir, the famous Chapursani Isma'ili mountaineer, told me that the scene on that day between Gilgit and Hunza "was something I could never forget." He described an "exodus of people" leaving Gilgit.

8 The first Russian outpost in the Pamirs was established in Murghab in 1892 (Bliss 2006: 73), at which time the British were already moderately well-established in Gilgit, Hunza, and Chitral. Imperial presence in the area significantly predates the construction of permanent garrisons and fortresses.

Bibliography

Abelmann, Nancy. 2002. *Mobilizing Korean Family Ties: Cultural Conversations across the Border*. Paper presented at Institute of Social and Cultural Anthropology Departmental Seminar, University of Oxford.

Abu-Lughod, Janet. 1989. *Before European Hegemony: The World System, A.D. 1250–1350*. Oxford: Oxford University Press.

Aga Khan. 1954. *The Memoirs of Aga Khan: World Enough and Time*. New York: Simon and Schuster.

Aga Khan Foundation. 1996. *Annual Report*. Geneva: AKDN.

———. 2003. *Annual Report*. Geneva: AKDN.

———. 2004. *Annual Report*. Geneva: AKDN.

Aga Khan Rural Support Programme. 1994. *Twelfth Annual Review*. Gilgit, Pakistan: AKDN.

———. 1996. *Fourteenth Annual Review*. Gilgit, Pakistan: AKDN.

———. 1999. *Joining Hands in Development: Women in Northern Pakistan*. Gilgit, Pakistan: AKDN.

———. 2000. *Towards a Shared Vision: Partnerships for Development*. Annual Report. Gilgit, Pakistan: AKDN.

Aga Khan III and Khursheed Kamal Aziz. 1998. *Aga Khan III: Selected Speeches and Writings of Sir Sultan Muhammad Shah*. London and New York: Kegan Paul International.

Agha, Asif. 2006. *Language and Social Relations*. Studies in the Social and Cultural Foundations of Language. Cambridge: Cambridge University Press.

Akiner, S. 2001. *Tajikistan: Disintegration or Reconciliation?* London: Royal Institute of International Affairs.

Alibhai, Alijah Ramzan Ali. N.d. "The Voyage of Pir Sabzali." Trans. Mumtaz Ali Tajdin S. Ali. ⟨http://www.ismaili.net/Source/pirsabzali/index.html⟩.

Anderson, Benedict. 1991. *Imagined Communities: Reflections on the Origin and Spread of Nationalism*. 2nd ed. New York: Verso.

Andreev, M. S. 1953. *Tajiki doliny khuf* [The Tajik Valleys of Khuf]. Dushanbe: Trudy Akademia Nauk Tajikiskoi SSR 7.

Appadurai, Arjun. 1996. *Modernity at Large: Cultural Dimensions of Globalization*. Vol. 1. Minneapolis: University of Minnesota Press.

Austin, John L. 1962. *How to Do Things with Words.* The William James Lectures, 1955. Cambridge, Mass.: Harvard University Press.

Bakhtin, M. M. 1981. *The Dialogic Imagination: Four Essays by M. M. Bakhtin.* Edited by Michael Holquist, translated by Carl Emerson and Michael Holquist. Austin: University of Texas Press.

Barth, Fredrik. 1981a. *Process and Form in Social Life.* Vol. 1 of *Selected Essays of Fredrik Barth.* London: Routledge and Kegan Paul.

———. 1981b. *Features of Person and Society in Swat: Collected Essays on Pathans.* Vol. 2 of *Selected Essays of Fredrik Barth.* Boston: Routledge and Kegan Paul, International Library of Anthropology.

Barthes, Roland. 1973. *Mythologies.* New York: Farrar, Straus and Giroux.

Basch, Linda, Nina Glick Schiller, and Cristina Szanton-Blanc. 1994. *Nations Unbound: Transnational Projects, Postcolonial Predicaments, and Deterritorialized Nation-States.* New York: Gordon and Breach.

Baxmann, Inge. 2001. "Movement Cultures in the Transnation." Workshop presentation for *Kinetographien,* Europäische Akademie, Berlin, October 25–27.

Bennigsen, Alexandre, and S. Enders Wimbush. 1985. *Mystics and Commissars: Sufism in the Soviet Union.* Berkeley: University of California Press.

Biddulph, John. [1880] 1977. *Tribes of the Hindoo Koosh.* Karachi: Indus Publications.

Bliss, Frank. 2005. *Social and Economic Changes in the Pamirs (Gorno-Badakhshan, Tajikistan).* London: Routledge.

Boivin, Michel. 2003. *La renovation du Shiʿisme Ismaelien en Inde et au Pakistan.* London: Kegan Paul. All translations are mine.

Bosworth, Clifford Edmund. 1963. *The Ghaznavids: Their Empire in Afghanistan and Eastern Iran, 994–1040.* Edinburgh: Edinburgh University Press.

———. 1968. "The Political and Dynastic History of the Iranian World (A.D. 1000–1217)." In *The Cambridge History of Iran.* Vol. 5, *The Saljuq and Mongol Periods,* edited by J. A. Boyle, 1–202. Cambridge: Cambridge University Press.

———. 1977. *The Later Ghaznavids: Splendour and Decay; The Dynasty in Afghanistan and Northern India, 1040–1186.* Edinburgh: Edinburgh University Press.

Braudel, Fernand. 1979. *Civilization and Capitalism, Fifteenth to Eighteenth Centuries.* Translated by Siân Reynolds, 3 vols. London: Collins.

Brett, Michael. 2001. *The Rise of the Fatimids: The World of the Mediterranean and the Middle East in the Tenth Century CE.* The Medieval Mediterranean: Peoples, Economies, and Cultures, 400–1453. Leiden: Brill.

Buck Morss, Susan. 2005. "The Post-Soviet Condition." Paper presented at American Anthropological Association Annual Meeting, Washington, D.C.

Carnegie, Charles V. 1999. "Garvey and the Black Transnation." *Small Axe* 3(1): 48–71.

———. 2002. *Postnationalism Prefigured: Caribbean Borderlands.* New Brunswick: Rutgers University Press.

———. Forthcoming. "Outflanking the State, Racing the Transnation: Marcus Garvey's Politics of Transterritorial Solidarity." *Public Culture.*

Centlivres, P., and M. Centlivres-Demont. 1998. "Tajikistan and Afghanistan: The Ethnic Groups on Either Side of the Border." In *Tajikistan: The Trials of*

Independence, edited by Mohammad-Reza Djalili, Frederic Grare, and Shirin Akiner; translated by Cybele Hay. Surrey: Curzon Press.

Certeau, Michel de. 2002. *The Practice of Everyday Life*. Berkeley: University of California Press.

Chatterjee, Partha. 1986. *Nationalist Thought and the Colonial World: A Derivative Discourse?* London: Zed.

Chaudhuri, K. N. 1985. *Trade and Civilization in the Indian Ocean: An Economic History from the Rise of Islam to 1750*. Cambridge: Cambridge University Press.

————. 1990. *Asia before Europe: Economy and Civilisation of the Indian Ocean from the Rise of Islam to 1750*. Cambridge: Cambridge University Press.

Cheah, Pheng, and Bruce Robbins, eds. 1998. *Cosmopolitics: Thinking and Feeling beyond the Nation*. Vol. 14 of *Cultural Politics*. Minneapolis: University of Minnesota Press.

Christiansen, Palle. 1969. *The Melanesian Cargo Cult: Millenarianism as a Factor in Cultural Change*. Translated by John R. B. Gosney. Copenhagen: Akademisk Forlag.

Cohen, Abner. 1971. *Two-Dimensional Man: An Essay on the Anthropology of Power and Symbolism in Complex Society*. Berkeley: University of California Press.

Comaroff, Jean. 1985. *Body of Power, Spirit of Resistance: The Culture and History of a South African People*. Chicago: University of Chicago Press.

Comaroff, Jean, and John Comaroff. 2000. "Millennial Capitalism: First Thoughts on a Second Coming." *Public Culture* 12(2): 291–343.

Corbin, Henry. 1975. "Nasir-I Khusrau and Iranian Isma'ilism." In *The Cambridge History of Iran*, vol. 4 of *The Period from the Arab Invasion to the Saljuqs*, edited by R. N. Frye, 520–42. Cambridge: Cambridge University Press.

————. 1983. *Cyclical Time and Ismaili Gnosis*. 3rd ed. Boston: Kegan Paul International.

Coronil, Fernando. 1997. *The Magical State: Nature, Money, and Modernity in Venezuela*. Chicago: University of Chicago Press.

Crone, Patricia. 1980. *Slaves on Horses: The Evolution of the Islamic Polity*. Cambridge: Cambridge University Press.

Daftary, Farhad. 1990. *The Isma'ilis: Their History and Doctrines*. Cambridge: Cambridge University Press.

————. 1998. *A Short History of the Isma'ilis: Traditions of a Muslim Community*. Islamic Surveys Series. Edinburgh: Edinburgh University Press.

Dani, Ahmed Hasan. 1989. *History of the Northern Areas of Pakistan*. Islamabad: National Institute of Historical and Cultural Research.

Daniel, E. Valentine. 1996. *Charred Lullabies: Chapters in an Anthropography of Violence*. Princeton Studies in Culture/Power/History. Princeton: Princeton University Press.

Deleuze, Gilles, and Felix Guattari. 1987. *A Thousand Plateaus: Capitalism and Schizophrenia*. Minneapolis: University of Minnesota Press.

Denny, Frederick Mathewson. 2005. *An Introduction to Islam*. 3rd ed. Upper Saddle River, N.J.: Prentice Hall.

Dirks, Nicholas B. 2001. *Castes of Mind: Colonialism and the Making of Modern India.* Princeton: Princeton University Press.

Douglas, Mary. 1966. *Purity and Danger: An Analysis of the Concepts of Pollution and Taboo.* New York: Routledge and Kegan Paul.

———. 1973. *Natural Symbols: Explorations in Cosmology.* London: Barrie and Jenkins.

———. 1978. *Cultural Bias.* Occasional Paper No. 34, Royal Anthropological Institute of Great Britain and Ireland. London: Royal Anthropological Institute.

Dresch, Paul. 1989. *Tribes, Government, and History in Yemen.* New York: Oxford University Press.

Durkheim, Émile. 1926. *The Elementary Forms of the Religious Life: A Study in Religious Sociology.* Translated by Joseph Ward Swain. London: G. Allen and Unwin.

———. 1933. *The Division of Labor in Society.* Translated by George Simpson. Glencoe, Ill.: Free Press.

———. 1951. *Suicide: A Study in Sociology.* Translated by John A. Spaulding. New York: Free Press.

———. 1961. *Moral Education: A Study in the Theory and Application of the Sociology of Education.* Glencoe, Ill.: Free Press.

Emadi, Hafizullah. 2000. "Praxis of Taqiyya: Perseverance of Pashaye Isma'ili Enclave, Nangarhar, Afghanistan." *Central Asian Survey* 19, no. 2: 53–64.

Escobar, Arturo. 1994. *Encountering Development: The Making and Unmaking of the Third World.* Princeton: Princeton University Press.

Fabian, Johannes. 1983. *Time and the Other: How Anthropology Makes Its Object.* New York: Columbia University Press.

Filippani-Ronconi, Pio. 1977. "The Soteriological Cosmology of Central Asiatic Isma'ilism." In *Isma'ili Contributions to Islamic Culture*, edited by Seyyed Hossein Nasr, 109–20. Tehran: Imperial Iranian Academy of Philosophy.

Foucault, Michel. 1973. *The Order of Things: An Archaeology of the Human Sciences.* Translated by Alan Sheridan. New York: Vintage.

———. 1977. *Discipline and Punish: The Birth of the Prison.* Translated by Alan Sheridan. New York: Pantheon.

———. 1978. *The Birth of the Clinic: An Archaeology of Medical Perception.* New York: Vintage.

———. 1982. "Afterword: The Subject and Power." In *Michel Foucault: Beyond Structuralism and Hermeneutics*, edited by Hubert L. Dreyfus and Paul Rabinow, 208–26. Chicago: University of Chicago Press.

———. 1991. "Governmentality." In *The Foucault Effect: Studies in Governmentality*, edited by Graham Burchell, Colin Gordon, and Peter Miller, 87–104. Hemel Hempstead: Harvester Wheatsheaf.

———. 2003. *Abnormal: Lectures at the Collège de France, 1974–1975.* Edited by Valerio Marchetti and Antonella Salomoni; translated by Graham Burchell. New York: Picador.

Frank, Andre Gunder. 1998. *ReOrient: Global Economy in the Asian Age.* Berkeley: University of California Press.

Fussman, Gérard. 1972. *Atlas Linguistique des Parlers Dardes et Kafirs*. 2 vols. Paris: Ecole Française d'Extreme-Orient.

Gaborieau, Marc. 1999. "Transnational Islamic Movements: Tablighi Jamaʿat in Politics?" *ISIM Newsletter* 3:21.

Gellner, Ernest. 1983. *Nations and Nationalism*. Ithaca: Cornell University Press.

Gilroy, Paul. 1987. *"There Ain't No Black in the Union Jack": The Cultural Politics of Race and Nation*. London: Hutchinson.

———. 1993. *The Black Atlantic: Modernity and Double Consciousness*. Cambridge: Harvard University Press.

Glick Schiller, Nina, Linda Basch, and Cristina Blanc-Szanton, eds. 1992. *Towards a Transnational Perspective on Migration: Race, Class, Ethnicity, and Nationalism Reconsidered*. New York: New York Academy of Sciences.

Glick Schiller, Nina, and Georges Eugene Fouron. 2004. *Georges Woke Up Laughing: Long Distance Nationalism and the Apparent State*. Durham: Duke University Press.

Goffman, Erving. 1981. *Forms of Talk*. Philadelphia: University of Pennsylvania Press.

Goodwin, Morag. 2004. "The Romani Claim Non-Territorial Nation Status: Recognition from an International Legal Perspective." *Roma Rights: Quarterly Journal of the European Roma Rights Center*, no. 1: 54–56.

Graham, Laura. 1995. *Performing Dreams: Discourses of Immortality among the Xavante of Brazil*. Austin: University of Texas Press.

Gross, Jonathan L., and Steve Rayner. 1985. *Measuring Culture: A Paradigm for the Analysis of Social Organization*. New York: Columbia University Press.

Gupta, A., and J. Ferguson. 1992. "Beyond 'Culture': Space, Identity, and the Politics of Difference." *Cultural Anthropologist* 7, no. 1: 6–23.

Habermas, Jürgen. 1984. *The Theory of Communicative Action*. 2 vols. Translated by Thomas McCarthy. Boston: Beacon Press.

———. 1989. *The Structural Transformation of the Public Sphere: An Inquiry into a Category of Bourgeois Society*. Translated by Michael Burger. Cambridge, Mass.: MIT Press.

Halm, Heinz. 1997. *The Fatimids and Their Traditions of Learning*. London: I. B. Tauris/ Institute of Ismaili Studies.

Hamdani, A. H. 1956. *The Beginnings of the Ismaʿili Daʿwa in Northern India*. Cairo.

Hannerz, Ulf. 1996. *Transnational Connections: Culture, People, Places*. New York: Routledge.

Harvey, David. 1991. *The Condition of Postmodernity: An Enquiry into the Origins of Cultural Change*. Oxford: Blackwell Publishers.

Hebdige, Dick. 1979. *Subculture: The Meaning of Style*. London: Routledge.

Hedetoft, Ulf, and Mette Hjort, eds. 2002. *The Postnational Self*. Public Worlds Series, vol. 10. Minneapolis: University of Minnesota Press.

Henze, Paul B. 1998. "Dagestan in October 1997: Imam Shamil Lives!" CA & CC Press AB Publishing House (Sweden), ⟨*http://www.ca-c.org/dataeng/henze.shtml*⟩.

Hirsch, Francine. 2005. *Empire of Nations: Ethnographic Knowledge and the Making of the Soviet Union*. Ithaca: Cornell University Press.

Ho, Engseng. 2006. The *Graves of Tarim: Genealogy and Mobility across the Indian Ocean*. Berkeley: University of California Press.

Hodgson, Marshall G. S. 1955. *The Order of Assassins: The Struggle of the Early Nizârî Ismâ'îlis against the Islamic World*. The Hague: Mouton.

———. 1968. "The Isma'ili State." In *The Cambridge History of Iran*. Vol. 5, *The Saljuq and Mongol Periods*, edited by J. A. Boyle, 422–82. Cambridge: Cambridge University Press.

———. 1977. *The Venture of Islam: Conscience and History in a World Civilization*. 3 vols. Chicago: University of Chicago Press.

Hollister, John Norman. 1953. *The Shi'a of India*. London: Luzac and Co.

hooks, bell. 1992. "Eating the Other: Desire and Resistance." In *Black Looks: Race and Representation*, 21–39. Boston: South End Press.

Hopkirk, Peter. 1991. *The Great Game: On Secret Service in High Asia*. Oxford: Oxford University Press.

Humphrey, Caroline. 1983. *Karl Marx Collective: Economy, Society, and Religion in a Siberian Collective Farm*. Cambridge: Cambridge University Press.

———. 2002. *The Unmaking of Soviet Life: Everyday Economies after Socialism*. Ithaca: Cornell University Press.

Hunsberger, Alice C. 2000. *Nasir Khusraw, the Ruby of Badakhshan: A Portrait of the Persian Poet, Traveller and Philosopher*. New York: I. B. Tauris.

Institute for Ismaili Studies. 1994. *Murids of Imam az-Zaman*. Book 3 of "Primary Two" of the Ta'lim Series. London: Islamic Publications.

International Romani Union. 2000. "Declaration of a Roma Nation: We, the Roma Nation," ⟨http://www.hartford-hwp.com/archives/60/132.html⟩.

Ivanow, W. 1952. *A Brief Survey of the Evolution of Ismailism*. Leiden: Brill.

———. 1956. *Problems in Nasir-i Khusraw's Biography*. Bombay: Ismaili Society.

Jamal, Nadia Eboo. 2002. *Surviving the Mongols: Nizari Quhistani and the Continuity of Ismaili Tradition in Persia*. New York: I. B. Tauris.

Jameson, Fredric. 1991. *Postmodernism, or, the Cultural Logic of Late Capitalism*. Durham: Duke University Press.

Jameson, Fredric, and Masao Miyoshi, eds. 1998. *The Cultures of Globalization*. Durham: Duke University Press.

Jettmar, Karl. 1975. *Die Religionen des Hindukusch*. Die Religionen der Menschheit, Band 4,1. Stuttgart: Verlag W. Kohlhammer.

———, ed. 1989. *Antiquities of Northern Pakistan*. Vol. 1. Mainz: Verlag Philipp von Zabern.

———. 1993. *Antiquities of Northern Pakistan*. Vol. 2. Mainz: Verlag Philipp von Zabern.

———. 1994. *Antiquities of Northern Pakistan*. Vol. 3. Mainz: Verlag Philipp von Zabern.

Kaiser, Paul J. 1996. *Culture, Transnationalism, and Civil Society: Aga Khan Social Service Initiatives in Tanzania*. Westport, Conn.: Praeger.

Kamat, Sangeeta. 2002. *Development Hegemony: Non-Governmental Organizations and the State in India*. Oxford: Oxford University Press.

Kaplan, Martha. 1995. *Neither Cargo nor Cult: Ritual Politics and the Colonial Imagination in Fiji*. Durham: Duke University Press.

Kertzer, David I. 1988. *Ritual, Politics, and Power*. New Haven: Yale University Press.

Keshavjee, Rafique. 1981. "The Quest for Gnosis and the Call of History: Modernization among the Ismailis of Iran." Ph.D. diss., Harvard University.

Keshavjee, Salmaan. 1998. "Medicines and Transitions: The Political Economy of Health and Social Change in Post-Soviet Badakhshan, Tajikistan." Ph.D. diss., Harvard University.

Khan, Mahmood Hassan, and Shoaib Sultan Khan. 1992. *Rural Change in the Third World: Pakistan and the Aga Khan Rural Support Program*. London: Greenwood Press.

Kreutzmann, Hermann. 1996. *Ethnizität im Entwicklungsprozess: Die Wakhi in Hochasien*. Berlin: D. Reimer.

Kroeber, A. L. 1945. "The Ancient *Oikoumenê* as an Historic Culture Aggregate." *Journal of the Royal Anthropological Institute* 75: 9–20.

Lapidus, Ira. 1988. *A History of Islamic Societies*. Cambridge: Cambridge University Press.

Lewis, Bernard. 1940. *The Origins of Isma'ilism: A Study of the Historical Background of the Fatimid Caliphate*. Cambridge: W. Heffer and Sons.

———. 1967. *The Assassins: A Radical Sect in Islam*. New York: Basic Books.

Litvinskij, Boris. 1981. "Semantika Drevnix Verovanii i Obryadov Pamirtsev (1)." In *Srednyaya Azija i yeyo Sosyedi v Drevnosti Sredenevkov'e (Istorija i Kultura)*, edited by Boris Litvinskij, 90–121. Moscow: Izdatel'stvo "Nauka," Glavnaya Redaktsija Vostochnoi Literatury.

Mamdani, Mahmood. 1996. *Citizen and Subject: Contemporary Africa and the Legacy of Late Colonialism*. Princeton: Princeton University Press.

Marcus, George E. 1995. "Ethnography in/of the World System: The Emergence of Multi-Sited Ethnography." *Annual Review of Anthropology* 24: 95–117.

Marsden, Magnus. 2005. *Living Islam: Muslim Religious Experience in Pakistan's North-West Frontier*. Cambridge: Cambridge University Press.

Massey, Doreen. 1994. *Space, Place, and Gender*. Oxford: Polity Press.

Masud, Khalid, ed. 2000. *Travelers in Faith: Studies of the Tablighi Jama'at as a Transnational Islamic Movement for Faith Renewal*. Leiden: Brill.

Merleau-Ponty, Maurice. 1962. *The Phenomenology of Perception*. London: Routledge and Kegan Paul.

Metcalf, Barbara Daly. 1993. "Living Hadith in the Tablighi Jama'at." *Journal of Asian Studies* 52, no. 3: 584–608.

———. 2004. *Islamic Revival in British India: Deoband 1860–1900*. Oxford: Oxford University Press.

Mirza, Nasseh Ahmed. 1997. *Syrian Ismailism: The Ever Living Line of the Imamate, AD 1100–1260*. Surrey: Curzon Press.

Morgenstierne, Georg. 1929. *Indo-Iranian Frontier Languages*. 4 vols. Institute for Sammenlignende Kulturforskning, Series B: Skrifter 11, 35, 40, 58. Oslo: H. Aschehoug.

Morris, H. S. 1968. *The Indians in Uganda*. Chicago: University of Chicago Press.

Nanji, Azim. 1978. *The Nizari Isma'ili Tradition in the Indo-Pakistan Subcontinent*. New York: Caravan Books.

Nasr, Seyyed Hossein, ed. 1977. *Isma'ili Contributions to Islamic Culture*. Tehran: Imperial Iranian Academy of Philosophy.

Nelson, Ridley S. M. 2002. *The Next Ascent: An Evaluation of the Aga Khan Rural Support Program, Pakistan*. Washington, D.C.: World Bank.

Niyozov, Sarfaroz. 2006. "Nasir Khusraw: Yesterday, Today, Tomorrow — An Introduction." The Ismaili UK and the Institute for Ismaili Studies, ⟨*http://www.iis.ac.uk/SiteAssets/pdf/Nas_Khus_s_n.pdf*⟩.

Obeyesekere, Gananath. 1992. *The Apotheosis of Captain Cook: European Mythmaking in the Pacific*. Princeton: Princeton University Press.

O'Dea, Thomas. 1957. *The Mormons*. Chicago: University of Chicago Press.

Ong, Aihwa. 1999. *Flexible Citizenship: The Cultural Logics of Transnationality*. Durham: Duke University Press.

Ong, Aihwa, and Stephen J. Collier, eds. 2004. *Global Assemblages: Technology, Politics, and Ethics as Anthropological Problems*. Oxford: Blackwell.

Orywal, Erwin. 1986. *Die ethnischen Gruppen Afghanistans: Fallstudien zu Gruppenidentitat un Intergruppenbezienhungen*. Wiesbaden: Reichert.

Palsetia, Jesse. 2001. *The Parsis of India: Preservation of Identity in Bombay City*. Leiden: Brill.

Panagakos, Anastasia N. 1998. "Citizens of the TransNation: Political Mobilization, Nationalism and Multiculturalism in the Greek Diaspora." *Diaspora: Journal of Transnational Studies* 7, no. 1: 53–73.

Parkes, Peter S. C. 1987. "Livestock Symbolism and Pastoral Ideology among the Kafirs of the Hindu Kush." *Man* 22: 637–60.

Petryna, Adriana. 2002. *Life Exposed: Biological Citizens after Chernobyl*. Princeton: Princeton University Press.

Pietrosanti, Paolo. 2003. "The Romani Nation, or: 'Ich Bin Ein Zigeuner.'" *Roma Rights: Quarterly Journal of the European Roma Rights Center*, no. 4: 50–56.

Raffles, Hugh. 1999. "Local Theory: Nature and the Making of an Amazonian Place." *Cultural Anthropology* 14(3): 323–60.

Rahman, Fazlur. 1999. *Revival and Reform in Islam: A Study of Islamic Fundamentalism*. Oxford: Oneworld Publications.

Rieck, Andreas. 1995. "Sectarianism as a Political Problem in Pakistan: The Case of the Northern Areas." *Orient* 36, no. 3: 429–48.

Robbins, Joel. 2004. "The Globalization of Charismatic and Pentecostal Christianity." *Annual Reviews of Anthropology* 33: 117–43.

Robinson, Francis, ed. 1996. *The Cambridge Illustrated History of the Islamic World*. Cambridge: Cambridge University Press.

Rouse, Roger. 1992a. "Transnationalism among Mexican Migrants to the United States." *Annals of the New York Academy of Science*, 25–52.

———. 1992b. "Making Sense of Settlement: Class Transformation, Cultural Struggle and Transnationalism among Mexican Migrants to the United States?" *Annals of the New York Academy of Science*, 25–52.

———. 1995. "Thinking through Transnationalism: Notes on the Cultural Politics in the Contemporary United States." *Public Culture* 7, no. 2 (Winter): 353–402.

Roy, Olivier. 2000. *The New Central Asia: The Creation of Nations*. New York: New York University Press.

———. 2004. *Globalized Islam: The Search for a New Ummah*. New York: Columbia University Press.

Rubin, Barnett R. 1995. *The Fragmentation of Afghanistan: State Formation and Collapse in the International System*. New Haven: Yale University Press.

———. 1998. "Russian Hegemony and State Breakdown in the Periphery: Causes and Consequences of the Civil War in Tajikistan." In *Post-Soviet Political Order: Conflict and State Building*, edited by Barnett R. Rubin and Jack Snyder, 128–61. London: Routledge.

Sahlins, Marshall. 1987. *Islands of History*. Chicago: University of Chicago Press.

———. 1994. "Cosmologies of Capitalism: The Trans-Pacific Sector of 'The World System.'" In *Culture/Power/History*, edited by N. B. Dirks, G. Eley, and S. B. Ortner, 412–55. Princeton: Princeton University Press.

———. 1995. *How "Natives" Think: About Captain Cook, for Example*. Chicago: University of Chicago Press.

Said, Edward. 1979. *Orientalism*. New York: Vintage.

Sassen, Saskia. 2006. *Territory, Authority, Rights: From Medieval to Global Assemblages*. Princeton: Princeton University Press.

Searle, John. 1969. *Speech Acts: An Essay in the Philosophy of Language*. Cambridge: Cambridge University Press.

Shahrani, M. Nazif Mohib. 1979. *The Kirghiz and Wakhi of Afghanistan: Adaptation to Closed Frontiers*. Seattle: University of Washington Press.

Shami, Seteney. 2000. "Prehistories of Globalization: Circassian Identity in Motion." *Public Culture* 12, no. 1: 177–204.

Shodhan, Amrita. 2001. *A Question of Community: Religious Groups and Colonial Law*. Calcutta: Samya.

Silk Road Project, ⟨http://www.silkroadproject.org/about/vision.html⟩.

Sinor, Denis, ed. 1990. *The Cambridge History of Early Inner Asia*. Cambridge: Cambridge University Press.

Slomanson, William R. 2003. *Fundamental Perspectives on International Law*. Belmont, N.J.: Thomson/West.

Sökefeld, Martin. 1997. *Ein Labyrinth von Identitäten in Nordpakistan: Zwischen Landbesitz, Religion und Kaschmir-Konflikt*. Culture Area Karakorum Scientific Studies, vol. 8. Cologne: Köppe.

———. 1998. "'The People Who Really Belong to Gilgit': Perspectives on Identity and Conflict in Theory and Ethnography." In *Transformations of Social and Economic Relationships in Northern Pakistan*, edited by Irmtraud Stellrecht and Hans-Georg Bohle, 93–224. Cologne: Köppe.

Spitulnik, Debra. 1997. "The Social Circulation of Media Discourse and the Mediation of Communities." *Journal of Linguistic Anthropology* 6:161–87.

Stein, Sir Aurel. 1907/1981. *Ancient Khotan: Detailed Report of Archaeological Explorations in Chinese Turkestan.* 3 vols. New Delhi: Cosmo Publications.

———. 1921. *Serindia: Detailed Report of Explorations in Central Asia and Westernmost China.* Oxford: Clarendon Press.

———. 1928. *Innermost Asia: Detailed Report of Explorations in Central Asia, Kan-su and Eastern Iran.* 4 vols. Oxford: Clarendon Press.

———. 1929/1974. *On Alexander's Track to the Indus: Personal Narrative of Explorations on the North-West Frontier of India Carried Out under the Orders of H.M. Indian Government.* Chicago: Ares.

Stern, S. M. 1983. *Studies in Early Isma'ilism.* Jerusalem: Magnes Press, Hebrew University.

Tambiah, Stanley. 1996. *Leveling Crowds: Ethnonationalist Conflicts and Collective Violence in South Asia.* Berkeley: University of California Press.

Tapper, Richard. 1983. *The Conflict of Tribe and State in Iran and Afghanistan.* New York: St. Martin's.

Taussig, Michael. 1992. *The Nervous System.* New York: Routledge.

Taylor, Charles. 1994. *Multiculturalism: Examining the Politics of Recognition.* Princeton: Princeton University Press.

Thobani, Akbarali. 1993. *Islam's Quiet Revolutionary: The Story of Aga Khan the Fourth.* New York: Vantage.

Tölölyan, Khachig. 2001. "Elites and Institutions in the Armenian Transnation." Paper presented at Conference on Transnational Migration: Comparative Perspectives, Princeton University.

Tsing, Anna Lowenhaupt. 1993. *In the Realm of the Diamond Queen: Anthropology in an Out-of-the-Way Place.* Princeton: Princeton University Press.

———. 2000. "The Global Situation." *Cultural Anthropology* 15(3): 327–60.

———. 2004. *Friction: An Ethnography of Global Connection.* Princeton: Princeton University Press.

Tucci, Giuseppe. 1977. "On Swat: The Dards and Connected Problems." *East and West* 27, nos. 1–4: 9–104.

———. 1997. "On Swat: Historical and Archaeological Notes." Unpublished ms., Rome.

Turner, Victor. 1975. *Dramas, Fields, and Metaphors: Symbolic Action in Human Society.* Ithaca: Cornell University Press.

University of Central Asia. N.d. *The University of Central Asia* (information booklet). Geneva.

Urban, Greg. 1991. *A Discourse-Centered Approach to Culture: Native South American Myths and Rituals.* Austin: University of Texas Press.

———. 2001. *Metaculture: How Culture Moves through the World.* Minneapolis: University of Minnesota Press.

van den Berg, Gabrielle Rachel. 1997. "Minstrel Poetry from the Pamir Mountains:

A Study on the Songs and Poems of the Isma'ilis of Tajik Badakhshan." PhD diss., University of Leiden.

Vatican. "The Holy Father," ⟨http://www.vatican.va/holy_father/ index.htm⟩.

Voll, John O. 2004. *Islam: Continuity and Change in the Modern World*. Syracuse: Syracuse University Press.

Wallerstein, Immanuel. 1974a. *The Modern World-System I: Capitalist Agriculture and the Origins of the European World-Economy in the Sixteenth Century*. New York: Academic Press.

———. 1974b. *The Modern World-System II: Mercantilism and the Consolidation of the European World-Economy, 1600–1750*. New York: Academic Press.

———. 1974c. *The Modern World System III: The Second Era of Great Expansion of the Capitalist World-Economy, 1730–1840s*. New York: Academic Press.

Watt, W. Montgomery. 1988. *Islamic Fundamentalism and Modernity*. New York: Routledge.

Weber, Max. 1978. *Economy and Society: An Outline of Interpretive Sociology*. Edited by Guenther Roth and Claus Wittich. 3 vols. Berkeley: University of California Press.

———. 1991. *From Max Weber: Essays in Sociology*. Edited and translated by H. H. Gerth and C. Wright Mills. London: Routledge.

Werbner, Pnina. 2003. *Pilgrims of Love: The Anthropology of a Global Sufi Cult*. Bloomington: University of Indiana Press.

Wood, Geoffrey D., Abdul Malik, and Sumaira Sagheer. 2006. *Valleys in Transition: Twenty Years of AKRSP's Experience in Northern Pakistan*. Karachi: Oxford University Press.

Yeoh, Brenda S. A., and Katie Willis, eds. 2004. *State/Nation/Transnation: Perspectives on Transnationalism in the Asia-Pacific*. London: Routledge.

Index

Ja'far al-Sadiq (Shi'i imam), 34
Jama'ati institutions, 29, 87–88; and
  architecture, 74–75
Jama'at Khanas, 3, 10, 43, 46–47, 50, 74,
  89, 97, 99–100, 136, 145, 187, 196, 217–18
  (n. 14)
Jews, 17
Jubilee celebrations, 48–49, 51

Karimabad, Hunza (Pakistan), 3
Kashghar, China, 188
Kashmir, 131
Keshavjee, Rafique, 89
Khayrkhwah, 38
Khojas, 9, 15–16, 28, 35, 39, 42, 57, 174, 181,
  194–99, 216 (n. 5); and Himalayan
  Isma'ilis, 84, 89, 108, 117, 144, 175, 177,
  191–92, 198
Khorog, Tajikistan, 75, 120, 140, 145–46
Khorog English Program (KEP), 145–46
Khudonazarov, Davlat, 127
Khuf, Tajikistan, 182
Kolkhoz (Soviet collective farms), 140,
  169, 182
Kushans, 110

Languages, Himalayan, 114–15
Lenin, Vladimir Ilyich, 158
London, 24, 90–93

Marriott Hotel Islamabad, bombing of, 2
Missionaries, Isma'ili, 89
Modernity, 15, 16, 30, 39–42, 53, 62, 164,
  172–73
Mongols, 9, 35, 38
Mountain Societies Development and
  Support Programme, Tajikistan
  (MSDSP), 24, 165, 167–71, 181–82
Multisited ethnography, 26–27
Murghab, Tajikistan, 183, 218 (n. 8)
Murids of *Imam-az-Zaman* (children's
  book), 93–101, 159
Musta'lawiyya (Musta'lian Isma'ilis),
  34–35, 38

Nabiev, Rahmon, 127–28
Nasir-i-Khushraw, 37, 111, 148; Millennial
  Conference of, Khorog, Tajikistan,
  146–59
Nationalities policy, Soviet, 129–30,
  147–48
Neoliberalism, 153
Neoplatonism, 10
1988, Riots of (Gilgit, Pakistan), 131–34,
  218 (n. 7)
Niyozov, Sarfaroz, 152–53
Nizaris, 9, 30, 34–35; Iranian, 35–36, 97;
  Syrian, 35–36, 97
Nongovernmental Organizations
  (NGOs), 207
Nurullah (light of God), 10

Oman, 46
Oston. See Shrines

Pakistan, 2–7, 19, 22, 98, 180–81; northern
  areas of, 2–7, 131–34, 164–77, 179–80;
  and sectarian violence, 131–34
Pamir Relief and Development Pro-
  gramme (PRDP), 130, 169. *See also*
  Mountain Societies Development and
  Support Programme, Tajikistan
"Panchtani" (as term for "Isma'ili"),
  134–38
Panjebhai committees (East Africa), 50,
  52
Panjibai community, Gorno-Badakhshan,
  118, 145
Parsis, 212 (n. 9)
Pashai (people of Afghanistan), 36
Petroglyphs, 110
"Pilgrimage," 83, 92
Porshnev, Tajikistan, 113, 122, 160, 181

Qajar dynasty, 40–42
Qarmatis, 215 (n. 1)
Qasim-Shahi Nizaris, 35, 40
Québec, 6
Qur'an, 10, 20

Islamic Civilization and Muslim Networks

JONAH STEINBERG, *Ismaʿili Modern: Globalization and Identity in a Muslim Community* (2011).

IFTIKHAR DADI, *Modernism and the Art of Muslim South Asia* (2010).

GARY R. BUNT, *iMuslims: Rewiring the House of Islam* (2009).

FATEMEH KESHAVARZ, *Jasmine and Stars: Reading More than "Lolita" in Tehran* (2007).

SCOTT A. KUGLE, *Sufis and Saints' Bodies: Mysticism, Corporeality, and Sacred Power in Islam* (2007).

ROXANI ELENI MARGARITI, *Aden and the Indian Ocean Trade: 150 Years in the Life of a Medieval Arabian Port* (2007).

SUFIA M. UDDIN, *Constructing Bangladesh: Religion, Ethnicity, and Language in an Islamic Nation* (2006).

OMID SAFI, *The Politics of Knowledge in Premodern Islam: Negotiating Ideology and Religious Inquiry* (2006).

EBRAHIM MOOSA, *Ghazālī and the Poetics of Imagination* (2005).

MIRIAM COOKE AND BRUCE B. LAWRENCE, eds., *Muslim Networks from Hajj to Hip Hop* (2005).

CARL W. ERNST, *Following Muhammad: Rethinking Islam in the Contemporary World* (2003).